OUR UNIONS,
OUR SELVES

OUR UNIONS, OUR SELVES

The Rise of Feminist Labor Unions
in Japan

Anne Zacharias-Walsh

ILR PRESS

AN IMPRINT OF

CORNELL UNIVERSITY PRESS   ITHACA AND LONDON

First published 2016 by Cornell University Press
First printing, Cornell Paperbacks, 2016

Printed in the United States of America

Library of Congress Cataloging-in-Publication Data

Names: Zacharias-Walsh, Anne, author.
Title: Our unions, our selves : the rise of feminist labor unions in
Japan / Anne Zacharias-Walsh.
Description: Ithaca : ILR Press, an imprint of Cornell University Press,
    2016. | Includes bibliographical references and index.
Identifiers: LCCN 2016010774| ISBN 9781501703041 (cloth : alk. paper) |
ISBN 9781501703058 (pbk. : alk. paper)
Subjects: LCSH: Women labor union members—Japan. | Women in the labor
    movement—Japan. | Sex discrimination in employment—Japan. | Sex role in
    the work environment—Japan. | Feminism—Japan.
Classification: LCC HD6079.2.J3 Z33 2016 | DDC 331.88082/0952—dc23
LC record available at http://lccn.loc.gov/2016010774

Cornell University Press strives to use environmentally responsible suppliers and materials to the fullest extent possible in the publishing of its books. Such materials include vegetable-based, low-VOC inks and acid-free papers that are recycled, totally chlorine-free, or partly composed of nonwood fibers. For further information, visit our website at www.cornellpress.cornell.edu.

Cloth printing   10 9 8 7 6 5 4 3 2 1
Paperback printing   10 9 8 7 6 5 4 3 2 1

For my father who leads by example, and my mother who leads with her right.

And, of course, for John

"Old women who live after they have lost their reproductive function are useless and are committing a sin."

—Shintaro Ishihara, governor of Tokyo 2001

"I believe women have the potential to renew the Japanese labor movement."

—Keiko Tani, founder, WUT 2001

Contents

Preface   ix
Acknowledgments   xv

Introduction   1

Part 1 **JAPANESE WOMEN'S UNIONS**

   1. A Union of One's Own   17

   2. A Tale of Two Activists   31

   3. Women's Union Tokyo in Practice   42

Part 2 **US-JAPAN CROSSBORDER COLLABORATION**

   4. First, We Drink Tea   57

   5. Under the Microscope   84

   6. Crisis of Difference   108

   7. Made in Japan   133

   8. A Movement Transformed   151

Conclusion: Lessons for Building Crossborder
Collaborations   165

Appendix A: Characteristics of Common Nonregular
Forms of Employment   185
Appendix B: Curriculum Wish Lists   187
Appendix C: Why Japanese Women "Can't" Organize   193
Notes   197
References   207
Index   211

Preface

The first time I went to Japan, I went as a tourist. I went shopping in Ginza. I visited the ancient capital city of Kamakura. I gazed in awe at the giant Buddha and strolled meditatively through the serene peony garden where each delicate flower was ensconced in a miniature straw hut to protect it from inclement weather. I marveled at the sublime beauty of Japan's haute cuisine and the bizarre excesses of its exorbitantly priced underworld. I even started keeping a diary of the unexpected items one can buy in vending machines, from ordinary household items like sake, beer, and kilo-sized bags of rice to truly specialized items like "panties in a can"—underwear allegedly preworn and autographed by high school girls. For better or worse, I was fascinated by it all. In fact, I was so dazzled by its unrelenting exoticism that I didn't think much about the real society that was going on underneath—an odd omission considering the kind of work I do.

By trade I am a freelance labor activist. There is no established career path for my occupation. I get work by sticking my nose into the dark corners of society, where discrimination, injustice, and exploitation tend to lurk, until I find a situation where my skills might be of some help. I got in the habit when I was a graduate student at Carnegie Mellon University (CMU). As part of a class assignment, I started nosing around the university's labor management practices and found compelling evidence that the university had been engaging in a quiet campaign to bust the campus union and strip the university's most vulnerable workers—janitors, food service and physical plant workers—of decent wages, benefits, and a union contract. For more than a decade the university had been systematically whittling down the bargaining unit by hiring a subcontracted management company to take over operations in areas where the employees had unionized. In doing so, the administration could claim those unionized employees no longer worked for the university. Officially, they worked for the subcontractor and therefore their union contracts were null and void. (When I asked the university's human resources director about the people who had been working at CMU for twenty years or more, she told me, "Those people don't work for us. They work for [the facilities management company]. We have no relationship with them.") It was a favorite union-busting ploy of that era, and CMU, an institution named after two legendary "philanthropists," or robber barons, take your pick, was more than eager to jump on that bandwagon.

Beyond the duplicity of CMU's campaign, the administration's actions were disturbing because they targeted the lowest paid workers on campus, many of whom were women and minorities; they took advantage of high unemployment in the area; and by cutting blue-collar jobs, wages, and employees' access to benefits like tuition remission, they abandoned practices that had helped to strengthen communities and provide a ladder up for minority and low-income workers, adopting instead practices that increasingly resembled those of for-profit organizations.

Once I started looking in CMU's dark corners and saw what goes on there outside of the public's view and in stark contrast to the university's carefully sculpted public image, I decided that bringing to light these kinds of employer practices—and, more importantly, working people's responses to them—was what I wanted to do with my life. I started working on local labor issues in Pittsburgh in 1990 and, by the time I moved to Japan in 2000, I had worked on a wide variety of campaigns in the United States, including drives to organize home care providers, day care workers, and nursing home employees in Illinois, and public employees in Michigan. I had also written on labor issues related to steel workers in Indiana; UPS workers, janitors, truck drivers, prison employees, and college teachers in Chicago; and striking and locked-out factory workers in Decatur, IL. For ten years I was always on the lookout for burgeoning labor issues and signs of grassroots activism wherever they might be. And yet, during my first five days in Japan, the thought never even crossed my mind. Some combination of the sensory riot that is Tokyo and my own preconceived assumptions about the lack of labor activism in Japan left me temporarily blind to what was, in fact, a moment of great excitement and innovation in the Japanese labor movement.

Fortunately, I got a second chance. Two years later, upon hearing I was heading back to Tokyo, a friend with the United Electrical Workers (UE) asked me if I would be willing to work with the union to put pressure on the Japanese parent company of a US manufacturer that was stalling in contract negotiations with its newly organized workforce. I agreed, and, in the course of gathering background information I needed to do my part, I learned that the UE had long been actively cultivating organizational ties with some of the more progressive labor organizations in Japan, and that the two sides frequently engaged in activities to support each other's campaigns. As Robin Alexander, the director of the UE's international division, brought me up to speed on the support the union was getting from left-leaning labor organizations in Japan, I realized two very important things: first, there was a lot more going on in the Japanese labor movement than was dreamed of in my philosophies (There are left-leaning labor unions in Japan?); and second, that I suddenly had an entrée into a world that had been all but invisible to me until now.

With Robin's help, I was able to land interviews with some of the most influential progressive labor leaders, scholars, and grassroots organizers in Tokyo, all of whom told me that the Japanese labor movement was undergoing a period of intense reform as long-term marginalized workers had begun organizing new kinds of workers organizations outside and against traditional Japanese unions.[1] For decades, the Japanese labor landscape was dominated by company-based enterprise unions, which often include only full-time regular employees of large, private firms. But beginning in the 1980s, progressives began organizing new, network-based community unions to represent the growing pool of workers who have traditionally (and purposefully) been left out of enterprise unions. Initially, efforts to organize community unions focused on part-time workers and employees of small- and medium-sized enterprises. But, as the economy started to crumble in the early 1990s and the government loosened regulations on short-term employment, more and more Japanese workers found themselves outside the regular workforce and therefore outside of enterprise unions' sphere of influence. Suddenly, a much larger swath of the Japanese labor force was without union representation and they began looking to the community union model as an alternative. Within just a few years, a wide range of new community and "individual membership" unions had emerged throughout the country, including unions for part-time workers, non-regular workers, foreign workers, displaced workers, low-level managers, and, most surprising to me, unions for women only.

Until then, my work had never focused specifically on women's issues. I had always been interested in labor qua labor. But by the time I was conducting the interviews cited in this volume I had been in Japan long enough to see and be seriously disturbed by the relentless devaluing of women I saw at every turn. It was there in the sexist and sexualizing comments men blithely made about women in everyday conversations, in the way women at after-hours cocktail parties were expected to fix food plates and pour drinks for their male coworkers, and in the way a man blocking an aisle in a grocery store would refuse to move to the side to let a woman pass (let her be the one to walk around, damn it!). I had never experienced anything like it, even though it usually wasn't happening to me directly. As an obvious foreigner, I was somewhat outside the usual gender dynamic; Japanese men are well aware that Western women won't tolerate the kinds of Fred Flintstone-like behaviors they regularly rain down upon the heads of Japanese women. (I was frequently told I wouldn't have to worry about the notorious problem of men copping a feel on crowded subway trains because even the perverts know Western women fight back.) Still, just witnessing the pervasive subjugation was so suffocating and so infuriating that when I heard that some Japanese women were standing up and organizing their own renegade unions, I had to know more.

In particular, I wanted to know how women's unions were structured, what sources of power they sought to tap into, and how they were faring in actual practice. On a very personal level, I wanted to investigate these new organizations because I wanted to know if there was any real possibility that they could become agents of significant social change for women who worked and lived under conditions that were utterly unacceptable according to my sensibilities and, increasingly, according to their own. Finally, I wondered if Japanese experiments with new forms of organizing might have meaningful lessons for union reform efforts in the United States.

And so, in September 2000, I packed my bags, signed up for Japanese language classes, and moved to Tokyo for six months to study Japanese women's unions (JWUs) in earnest. What I learned was that the situation for women and for JWUs was far more complex, and dire, than I had imagined. Still very much in their emergent stage, JWUs were fighting for survival because of internal problems that were part and parcel of the organizational structure they adopted. "Individual membership unions," unions that organize workers as individuals regardless of company and occupation, tend to be chronically under-resourced. And JWUs not only organize women as individuals, they specifically target women who are in need of immediate help with a problem on the job. From an activist point of view that makes perfect sense. But from an organizational point of view it means that every new member increases the union's workload the instant they join. In a sense, it is reverse cherry picking, and as such it puts an almost unbearable strain on already insufficient union resources. To make matters worse, the situation only intensified as word of the unions' success at the bargaining table got out. As women's unions increasingly proved their ability to successfully resolve individual grievances, women began turning to them in greater numbers, albeit with no matching increase in staff or resources to handle their ever-growing caseload. Within just a few years, women's unions were quite literally collapsing under the weight of their own success. It was both heartbreaking and infuriating to see. Japanese women were in desperate need of union representation. That was obvious. But that very demand seemed to be what would doom them in the end, so long as they retained the individual membership structure, which union leaders believed was essential to their feminist mission.

Once I began to understand both the need for JWUs and the overwhelming obstacles they faced, it was no longer enough for me to merely study these new organizations in search of lessons to bring home. I wanted to get involved, not because I thought I had the answers; I knew very well that I didn't. But I also couldn't bear standing on the sidelines of a struggle that was this important, or where the principals were so eager for dialogue with other feminist labor activists. The JWUs welcomed me into their organizations, their discussions, and their confidence. We shared ideas and concerns, we brainstormed, we argued, sometimes we banged our heads against the wall in frustration with the seemingly insurmountable obstacles that lay before us. But in the end our conversations sparked a journey of discovery that significantly changed the shape of women's activism in Japan.

In 2004 we launched a three-year international grassroots exchange project that brought together some of the best minds and hearts in the feminist branches of the US and Japanese labor movements. The resulting exchange of ideas breathed new life into struggling women's organizations and gave birth to a national alliance of women's organizations in Japan.

Acknowledgments

I am professionally and personally indebted to a host of feminist activists and scholars in Japan who welcomed me into their organizations, their strategy deliberations, their bargaining sessions, and their lives; who had the courage to let an outsider witness their struggles, their frustrations, their failed attempts, and their victories; who taught me new ways of thinking as an activist, as a scholar, and as a feminist; who opened new worlds for me as they broke me out of my comfort zones and helped me understand the intricacies and subtleties of organizing in different contexts; and who, in the end, made the Feminist Labor Movement in Japan feel like home to me. I am deeply grateful to all of the activists, workers, union members, and scholars who gave so freely of their time and ideas and made the US-Japan Working Women's Networks Project possible. I am especially grateful to Toyomi Fujii, Midori Ito, Sachi Kotani, Makiko Matsumoto, Miyako Ōga, Naoko Takayama, Kazuko Tanaka, and Keiko Tani for educating me about women's unions and Women's Union Tokyo in particular, and for helping me to conceive, organize, and conduct the US-Japan Project. I am also grateful to presenters Kayoko Akabane, Mabel (Mei Po) Au, Kiyoko Ban, Shunko Ishiro, Takeo Kinoshita, Keiko Kondō, Emi Naruse, Kazuko Sazaki, and Fumiko Yakabi. Without their insights, generosity, hard work, good sense, and endless patience, neither the project nor this volume would have been possible. Nor could we have managed without the skill and extreme generosity of Mika Iba, her students, and Hwa-mi Park who graciously and gracefully provided translation and interpretation for the project even when we had no money to pay them. They are deeply committed feminist activists and I am thankful to them. Without question the unsung hero of the US-Japan Project was ICU Gender Center's Yuko Inoue, who worked tirelessly and with endless good humor to ensure the workshops ran smoothly. I would also like to thank Emiko Aono and Hirohiko Takasu for their support and interest in our project.

I am also grateful to the Japan Foundation Center for Global Partnership for the generous grant that funded the US-Japan Working Women's Networks Project. We also received financial and in-kind support from the International Christian University, Wayne State University, and the Japan International Christian University Fund. The AFL-CIO and the Committee for Asian Women covered expenses for Carol Edelson and Mabel Au, respectively. I also thank the Ragdale Foundation for providing me and other writers and artists with "Time and

Space" and community to enable us to do our best work. My residency at Ragdale while writing this volume was among the happiest, most productive times of my life. I am deeply grateful to each of these institutions for their support.

I am equally grateful to the many friends I made in Japan, especially my fellow book club members who helped me navigate everything from a language and culture that were new to me, to the intricacies of interpersonal communication Japanese style, to all manner of Japanese bureaucracies that a newcomer must face. Most of all they taught me about art and history and all that is beautiful in Japan. When we first met I was supposed to be their sensei, to lead the discussions of English-language books we read together. But over the many years we've known each other they have taught me far more than I could ever hope to teach them. They provided me with experiences and opportunities I would never have had on my own. And they gave me their friendship, which I treasure beyond words. They are my *senpai*, my sisters, and I love them.

I also want to thank Akira Gotō from the bottom of my heart for opening the door to Japan for my husband and me. It was because of Akira that we were first invited to Japan and our lives doubled in richness as a result. Our ideas, experiences, language skills, appreciation and enjoyment of life, number of friends, and especially the set of people who feel like family to us have grown profoundly through our years in what has become our second home. I cannot think of a better or kinder gift anyone could give to another person, and I am grateful to my dear friend Akira every single day.

On the US side, it has been my great privilege and pleasure to work with Heidi Gottfried, my coprincipal investigator on the US-Japan Project. It is no figure of speech when I say the project would never have happened without her many and varied contributions. Heidi was a true partner through every stage of the project. She brought extensive knowledge of Japanese industrial relations, institutions, and employment practices, direct experience with feminist and labor organizations and activists in both countries, and significant contacts among feminist labor scholars in the United States and Japan. She also helped to shape the project at the broadest and even the most micro levels. Her energy, support, generosity, and general joie de vivre even in the face of the most trying circumstances inspired me on countless occasions. But her true super power is in navigating with aplomb those bureaucracies and bureaucratic absurdities that would have most people pulling out their hair. Her boundless sangfroid is such a stark contrast to my own fiery personality that I often think we would make as good a comedy team as we do colleagues in research and activism. I also want to thank Heidi for the support, patience, guidance, and generosity she has shown me throughout the writing of this book.

I am also indebted to the US union leaders, activists, and scholars who gave so generously of their time and expertise throughout the project, including Dorothy Sue Cobble, Louise Fitzgerald, Leah Freid, Gloria Johnson, Cynthia Negrey, Laura Smith, Ronnie Steinberg, Karla Swift, and Beverly Vail. I am especially grateful to Carol Edelson, Tess Ewing, Linda Meric, and Emily Rosenberg who also made invaluable contributions to the US-Japan Project through the customized "training the trainer" workshops they created and conducted for the Japanese participants, and for their continued support as the Japanese women went on to create their own versions. I think that they, more than anyone, were responsible for the lasting trust and goodwill the project generated, not to mention the "cascade of learning" that continues to ripple through activist communities in Japan.

Beyond the direct players in the US-Japan Project, numerous friends, colleagues, and family members were crucial supporters through the writing of this book. I am grateful to Benjamin Forest, Juliet Johnson, Robin Leidner, and Catie Zacharias for, among so many other things, their comments on drafts, grant proposals, and other daunting communications. I am also grateful for the support of Carlos Aguilar, who fills my life with laughter and love, and to: Lisa Coburn, for her friendship, for telling me about Ragdale, and for helping me get to Bordeaux, France, when I really needed to; Mary Frank Fox and Dan Fox for, in addition to their support, wisdom, friendship, and good humor, the idea for the title of this volume; Suzanne and Frank Mullen, who kindly provided space and sanctuary for writing on so many occasions; Alyson Fryer and Kathryn Suzman-Schwartz for support and encouragement above and beyond; and the late and much loved Nancy Pinzke, whom I will never stop missing. I am also and always grateful to my family, especially my parents and siblings, and to a few supporters who have meant the world to me but are too modest to have their full names appear in print: KP, EG, MB, PA, and LE.

My thanks also go to ILR/Cornell University Press; my editor Frances Benson for her wisdom, her patience, and her support; acquisitions assistant Emily Powers; production editor Michael Bohrer-Clancy; and copy editor Elliot Bratton.

So many people have been instrumental in bringing the volume to fruition, but without question the Oscar for Best Supporting Author goes to Pam Popielarz. What Heidi Gottfried was to the US-Japan Project, Pam has been to the writing of *Our Unions, Our Selves*. The support she has given me as a friend, scholar, sounding board, close reader, constructive critic, and fellow writer with perfectionist tendencies is beyond expression. Her wisdom, knowledge, unfailing logic, and superior ability to construct rigorous arguments have made this a far better book than I could have produced on my own. Also, on many occasions when things got difficult, she talked me out of running away to join the circus. On most days I am grateful for that as well.

Finally, this book belongs as much to my husband and fellow activist John Walsh as it does to me. His contributions and sacrifices—as mentor, scholar, colleague, first reader, chief critic, head cheerleader, travel partner, best friend, and person I cherish most in this world—have been boundless. I have, throughout the years of writing this book, wonder how I could ever express in words what he has meant to me, to this project, and to my ability and opportunity to pursue my dreams. Eventually, I realized that any attempt to enumerate the many ways he has made this book and my life the best possible versions of themselves would only embarrass him. And so I will confine myself to saying, "In this, as in all things, puzzle pieces."

OUR UNIONS,
OUR SELVES

Introduction

Our Unions, Our Selves is the story of the emergence of women-only unions in Japan and their extraordinary efforts to transform their workplaces, their lives, and the national labor movement as a whole. It is also the story of the three-year grassroots exchange project that brought together struggling Japanese activists and US activists and scholars who, like their Japanese counterparts, were searching for new ways to organize workers whose circumstances did not quite square with traditional models of organizing. That long-term collaboration led to important discoveries about the complex and often conflicting nature of women's unions' mission and organizational structures and practices. The project also produced crucial lessons about the difficulties of and necessity for cross-border (where borders are not limited to national boundaries) collaborative social justice efforts in the face of the increasingly dehumanizing demands of global capital.

In the late 1980s Japanese women began creating their own labor unions to confront long-standing gender inequality in the workplace as well as newer "American-style" lean and mean management practices that degrade employment conditions for all workers and hurt women workers most of all (Liddle and Nakajima 2000; Broadbent 2005a, 2005b, 2007; interviews with union members and leaders 2000).[1] The first women's union, Kansai Women's Union (KWU), was founded in Osaka in 1987 after corporate Japan's palpable shift to the right led a small group of activists to conclude that "establishing women workers' rights as basic human rights will require women to organize their own labor movement" (KWU 2004).[2] Soon after, women's unions opened in Sapporo,

Fukuoka, Tokyo, and Sendai. By 2003, twelve women-only unions were operating in Japan (Broadbent 2007).

Women's unions are autonomous grassroots workers' organizations that organize by gender rather than by company, industry, or occupation. Based on the community-union model, women's unions connect working women within a geographical area to collectively address workplace issues such as gender-based wage inequality, sexual harassment, lack of childcare, and forced retirement. They also provide representation to the growing number of women working on part-time and temporary contracts, who are ineligible for membership in traditional enterprise-based unions. Although they are similar in some ways to other alternative unions that emerged around the same time (e.g., community unions, part-time and temporary workers unions), women's unions are unique in that they play the dual role of advocating for women's human and workers' rights. As workers' organizations, women's unions seek to wield the collective power of women as workers whose issues have long been neglected by mainstream unions. As women's organizations, they seek to empower women to recognize and claim their status as independent selves, with the same rights to self-determination, self-actualization, and full participation in society as their male counterparts. In other words, women's unions are in the business of pursuing the often contradictory goals of helping members to develop collective consciousness as workers and individual consciousness of their rights to full and equal personhood. And it is within that conflict that both the promise and pitfalls of this new form of organization lie. As organizations that, by their very nature, combine labor concerns with at least one other marginalized constituency, women's unions could provide a bridge to the broader kind of social movement unionism that progressive activists and scholars in Japan are currently seeking (Suzuki 2010; Weathers 2010).

Gender Inequality in the Japanese Workplace

Despite the passage of equal employment legislation in the mid-1980s, Japan's workplaces remain mired in anachronistic gender relations and discriminatory practices. According to the Japan Institute for Labour Policy and Training (JILPT), Japanese women are no less likely to be employed than women in other developed countries. Approximately twenty-four million women were employed in 2013, making up about 43 percent of the total workforce (JILPT 2014). And in 2012, the employment rate of Japanese women was at 60.7 percent, slightly exceeding the average rate across Organisation for Economic Co-operation and

Development (OECD) countries (OECD 2013). Yet, according to the World Economic Forum's Global Gender Report 2014, Japan ranked 102nd out of 142 nations for economic participation and opportunity (Kawaguchi 2015). Comparing female-to-male ratios of Japan with other countries, Japan ranked 112th in women as legislators, senior officials, and managers; 83rd for labor force participation; 78th for women in professional and technical positions; 74th for estimated earned income; and 53rd for equal pay for similar work.

Working women's advocates point to two institutional factors they say are primarily responsible for the continuing gap between men's and women's workplace experiences: the persistence of traditional gender roles in society (reinforced by lack of institutions that could enable women to work full-time, such as child and elder care), and discriminatory labor management practices that are designed to ensure that Japanese companies always have access to a pool of cheap, disposable labor (Brinton 1993; Gottfried and O'Reilly 2002; Broadbent 2003; Osawa 2007; Kawaguchi 2015).

Japan's postwar employment system was ostensibly based on the promise of well-paid, lifetime employment in exchange for total dedication to the firm (Kanai 1996; Osawa 2007; Gottfried 2008). But that promise was never extended to all segments of the workforce (Brinton 1993; Lam 1993; Kanai 1996). In order to guarantee lifetime employment, family wages, and regular raises to regular full-time workers, firms needed access to a pool of workers they could more easily hire and fire in response to fluctuations in the business cycle (Shinotsuka 1994; Kumazawa 1996; Gottfried 2008). Employers also needed people to fill low-skilled, support positions, but did not relish the idea of offering the same level of compensation or guarantees for merely supplemental work (Cook and Hayashi 1980; Ogasawara 1998). For much of the twentieth century, Japanese firms achieved these goals largely by making job assignments on the basis of gender (Kumazawa 1996). Male employees, assumed to be family breadwinners, were hired as full-time regular employees with all the rights and privileges (and responsibilities) pertaining thereto. Women, whose wage and job security needs were assumed to be lower than men's, were typically slotted into low-wage, short-term support jobs as a matter of course (Cook and Hayashi 1980; Liddle and Nakajima 2000; Gottfried 2008).

In the mid-1970s women's groups intensified their efforts to force Japanese companies to end discriminatory workplace practices. In 1985, after a decade of intense activism and international pressure, Japan adopted equal employment legislation that, at least on paper, outlawed some but by no means all management practices that discriminate on the basis of gender (Gelb 2003).[3] But, at the same time, Japanese firms and the state were under increasing pressure from global capital to modernize their employment practices (JILPT 2014). In order to compete in the global economy, Japanese firms needed more not less access to workers who could be employed outside the corporate embrace of the lifetime employment system. Firms responded by shifting to new labor management practices, particularly the increased use of nonregular/nonpermanent employment patterns and the two career-track system, which allowed them to continue and even intensify practices that segment the labor force without explicitly invoking gender as the dividing line (Gottfried 2008, interviews with union leaders 2000–2009).[4] Far from being gender-neutral, both systems disproportionately disadvantage women, according to the labor ministry's analyses (JILPT 2014).

Regular Versus Nonregular Employment

Hiring workers under nonregular and/or nonpermanent employment contracts has become increasingly common in recent decades, largely as a result of increased pressure from global competition (JILPT 2007).[5] Nonregular, nonpermanent positions typically provide lower wages, fewer benefits, little or no opportunity for promotion, and less job security than full-time regular positions do—even when the work is identical. In addition, nonregular, nonpermanent employees are typically ineligible for membership in in-house unions, some social welfare benefits, and pension schemes (Osawa 2007; Gottfried 2008; Weathers 2010).[6] By virtually all measures, nonregular and nonpermanent employment patterns are inferior forms of employment from the employee's perspective and, not surprisingly, women are overrepresented in all forms of precarious employment (Liddle and Nakajima 2000; Gottfried 2008; JILPT 2014). Also, while it is true that nonregular employment has been increasing across the board in Japan, from 20 percent in 1995 to 35 percent in 2014, only about 20 percent of men are categorized as nonregular employees, compared to 50 percent of women (JILPT 2014). The severity and long-term consequences of the gender gap are even more apparent when we look at the figures by age group. According to the JILPT (2014), the gap between men and women is smaller at the extremities: very young (15 to 24 years old) and post-retirement age men and women have relatively high rates of nonregular employment. The rate for young men was 43.9 percent compared to 50.6 percent for young women. And for over 65, the rate for men was 66.9 percent to women's 71.4. But looking at the rates for employees during their prime earning years, ages 25 to 55, we can see that the gap widens dramatically. Nearly 41 percent of women ages 25 to 34 are classified as nonregular, while only 15.5 percent of men in that age group are nonregular. In the 35 to 44 age group, 8.2 percent of men are nonregular compared to women's 53.8. And in the 45 to 54 age group, the rates are 8.6 percent for men and 58.4 percent for women.

Between ages 55 and 64 the gap narrows somewhat to 31.4 percent for men and 65.4 percent for women, but that still means women are twice as likely to be working in nonregular positions than their male counterparts. Considering that nonregular workers' wages are about half that of regular employees (Weathers 2010), the effect of being concentrated in nonregular employment for the bulk of their careers on women's total lifetime earnings and pensions is catastrophic, and its effect on Japanese society at large is scarcely less so: "The non-regular work pattern has come to be regarded as a factor obstructing measures to combat the declining birth rate and aging population [problem]—identified by the Japanese government as its most important policy target" (JILPT 2014, chap. 2, sec. 2, 3).

Two Career-Track System

The two career-track system is another labor management practice that disadvantages women in the workforce. Feminists and other labor scholars argue that the two career-track system was developed specifically to enable employers to sidestep equal opportunity legislation (Gelb 2003; Weathers 2012).[7] The two-track system creates two distinct career paths: the management track (*sōgō shoku*) and the general clerical track (*ippan shoku*). The overwhelmingly male management track provides high wages, including regular bonuses, premier benefits, access to training and exams necessary for promotion, and increased responsibility and decision making over time. The overwhelmingly female clerical track, on the other hand, offers lower pay, fewer benefits, and little, if any, opportunity for advancement. Clerical track employees are assigned to routine tasks with few or no decision-making opportunities, and are typically denied access to company training programs and the chance to sit for the exams required for promotion.

Although the management track is overwhelmingly male and the clerical track overwhelmingly female, employees are not assigned to these categories explicitly on the basis of gender; that would be illegal. Instead, they are assigned on the basis of their willingness to accept the transfers, relocations, and extreme work hours Japanese companies require. But, in a society where women are responsible for virtually all outside-the-workplace obligations, that "willingness" in practice constitutes a reliable proxy for gender (Gottfried 2008; Kawaguchi 2015).[8]

As with the nonregular employment system, the two-track system is extremely damaging to women's economic position. Even holding the differences in wages, benefits, and job security aside, the JILPT describes the lack of access to training, which is a central feature of both the nonregular and the two-track systems, as having "such negative consequences as to be life-defining" (JILPT 2014). That is especially alarming considering that nearly half of all major Japanese firms use a two-track system (Kawaguchi 2015).

Nevertheless, Japanese courts have upheld the legality of the two-track system, saying that the law allows for comparison only within categories, not across. Employers must provide the same opportunities (including access to training) for everyone in the management track, and the same opportunities for everyone in the clerical track, but it has no obligation to offer people in the clerical track (women) the same opportunities it offers people in the management track (men).[9]

Enterprise Unions

Japan's mainstream labor institutions have been slow to respond to the decades-long decline in wages and employment conditions. The Japanese labor movement is dominated by enterprise unions, which differ significantly from industrial unions in several ways. Enterprise unions organize the employees within a given company rather than by occupation or industry. As in-house organizations with no independent existence outside of the firm, most enterprise unions operate on a cooperationist model (Kume 1998; Weathers 2010). Their philosophy is that the best way to protect their members is to work in cooperation with management to ensure the success and profitability of the company (Kumazawa 1996; Gordon 1998; Broadbent 2007; Suzuki 2010; interviews with labor leaders in Japan 1999–2009). Most enterprise unions limit their membership to full-time regular employees, the majority of whom are male (JILPT 2014).

Historically, enterprise unions have done little to address women's work issues (Cook and Hayashi 1980; Simpson 1985; Kumazawa 1996; Broadbent 2003, 2007, 2008; Mackie 2003).[10] As company-specific organizations whose fortunes depend on the company's survival, enterprise unions accept the premise that management must have access to cheap, disposable labor as a buffer against the vicissitudes of the business cycle (Kumazawa 1996; interviews 1999, 2000, 2009). As representatives of full-time regular employees, enterprise unions tend to agree with employers that those jobs should be higher paying, more secure, and offer greater possibilities for promotion than nonregular positions do (Simpson 1985; Broadbent 2007). And, as majority male organizations, enterprise unions tend to be more responsive to male issues, have more expertise in addressing issues that are common to male employees, and be willing to accept compromises that preserve members' (i.e., men's) jobs and working conditions at non-members' (i.e., women's) expense (Brinton 1993; Kotani 1999; Broadbent 2003,

2007, 2008; Gelb 2003; Mackie 2003; interviews with union leaders and members 1999–2004). That is not to say that enterprise unions are monolithically indifferent to women's issues, but even when more progressive enterprise unions seek to address issues that primarily affect women, such as sexual harassment, their efforts are often hampered by their lack of experience and expertise (Broadbent 2003, 2008; interviews with union leaders 2000).

Community Unions

The women-only unions of today grew out of the broader community union movement that began in the 1980s. At the same time that Japanese women activists were reaching the apex of their frustration with conventional labor institutions, left-wing labor leaders were introducing new kinds of unions whose purpose was to organize workers who were outside the enterprise union bubble. Leftist labor federation *Sohyo* (now defunct) began organizing regional unions for employees of small- and medium-sized enterprises (SMEs) as well as public sector employees who lost their full-time, union-eligible jobs in that decade's frenzy of privatization (Suzuki 2010). Typically called community unions or attribution-based unions, these network-based unions organize individual workers by nontraditional criteria such as geographical area and terms of employment instead of occupation, industry, or enterprise.[11] Most also operate on the individual affiliation model, meaning workers can join as individuals rather than as part of a larger bargaining unit.[12] By the 1990s, as pressure from global competition and labor market deregulation steadily eroded working conditions and job security for workers across the board, a broader swath of the Japanese workforce found themselves unemployed or underemployed and ineligible for membership in traditional unions. As a result, community unions grew in number and kind throughout the nineties, when newly disenfranchised workers joined the search for union representation (Weathers 2010).[13] By the mid-1990s, Japanese workers had founded an impressive array of attribution-based unions, including unions for part-time and nonregular workers, foreign workers, temp agency employees, displaced and unemployed workers, low-level managers, and unions for women only.

Women's Unions, in Theory and Practice

Japanese women's unions (JWUs) are similar to other community unions in that they are network-based organizations that connect members across enterprises and industries. But they differ in that they focus on women's work issues, and they are structured and attempt to operate along feminist principles and practices. Like other attribution-based unions, women's unions seek to close the gap between highly paid "lifetime employees" and those hired as lower paid, expendable "extras" to whom the company makes no long-term commitment. But JWUs go further by explicitly rejecting the idea that it is natural and just for women, by virtue of being women, to be automatically funneled into inferior jobs or employed under inferior conditions. Women's unions also differ from other alternative unions in their willingness and ability to address workplace issues that primarily affect women, such as sexual harassment, hostile work environment, work-life balance, and gender discrimination. Although some alternative unions and even some mainstream enterprise unions are genuinely concerned about violations of women's work rights, JWU members say that even the best intentioned mixed-gender unions tend to be male-centered and to lack the experience and membership support to pursue women's grievances (Broadbent 2008; interviews with workers and union members 1999, 2000, 2004, 2007).

Women's unions constitute a significant development in Japanese women's and workers' activism. With their innovative outlook and practices, women's unions have the potential to play an important role in reshaping existing labor laws, institutions, and practices; political and legal discourse around women's and workers' issues; and the inter- and intraworkings of advocacy organizations and social movements writ large. Although JWUs organize women only, many of the founders hope that ultimately women's unions will serve as a model for creating social justice organizations whose internal operations more fully embody the principles they advocate (Broadbent 2005a, 2005b, 2007, and 2008; interviews with union leaders and members 2000, 2002, 2004, 2007).[14]

Yet, for all their potential, JWUs have not evolved in the way their founders had envisioned. The founders believed that union membership would "snowball" organically as more and more women became empowered by the experience of collective bargaining. By standing up for themselves and each other, women would automatically develop feminist and union consciousness, which would in turn motivate them to remain active in the union long after their own issues were resolved. That didn't happen. Instead of snowballing, JWU membership patterns look more like a revolving door. Women join the union when they have an active grievance at work and need immediate help, but once their grievance is resolved, most women become inactive members or they quit the union entirely. This has led to critical shortages in human and other resources among JWUs. Continuing deterioration of working conditions coupled with JWUs' high rate of success in resolving women's grievances (relative to enterprise unions and government labor agencies) meant that the number of women seeking union services increased over time. But revolving door membership left JWUs unable to develop new cohorts of trained, active members to keep pace with that demand.

The US-Japan Working Women's Networks Project

From my first meeting with members of the Women's Union Tokyo (WUT) in November 2000, it was clear that Japanese women activists were grappling with many of the same questions labor feminists in the United States were asking: How do we build effective workers' organizations that operate on feminist principles? What does a feminist labor union look like? How can we reach, organize, and empower workers who are employed in small or dispersed work settings, or who are not represented or underrepresented by existing labor unions? Our circumstances were, in some ways, very different. The conditions Japanese women worked under sounded a lot closer to the problems of my mother's or even my grandmother's generation, but their questions about how to move forward had a decidedly familiar ring. It didn't take us long to realize that both sides would benefit from intense, crossborder dialogue. Japanese women's organizations clearly stood to benefit from opportunities to engage in dialogue with each other and with feminist individuals and organizations from other countries, including the United States. And reform-minded US activists like me had a lot to learn from Japanese women who were turning their nation's profoundly male-centered labor movement on its head.

That was the start of the US-Japan Working Women's Networks Project. With a grant from the Japan Foundation Center for Global Partnership, we developed a multi-year grassroots exchange program that brought American and Japanese women activists together to educate each other about their organizations, brainstorm solutions to critical ongoing problems, and create new Japan-specific resources to foster feminist consciousness and union solidarity within JWUs. The project was unique because we met several times over the course of three years, and because we designed the project in a way that would allow it to organically grow and change over time in response to the insights and innovations that emerged in the course of sharing new ideas.

The project had several interlocking goals. We sought to help JWUs to develop Japan-specific training materials to encourage solidarity and long-term participation among members, and to enable each generation of activists to pass their knowledge and skills on to the next. We also hoped that working together on educational materials would organically stimulate deep organizational discussions, and that this cross-pollination of ideas and perspectives would enhance organization- and movement-building efforts in both countries. Finally, we sought to establish solidarity ties between and among US and Japanese women's groups as a step toward building a larger international network of working women's organizations.

At first I worried that our goals had a whiff of hubris about them, but from the moment the project started, the Japanese women pushed our aims and efforts to a level beyond what Heidi and I imagined possible. In addition to the three international meetings the project called for, the Japanese groups convened a variety of additional gatherings—national, regional, and local meetings to process and build on what they were learning and creating through the US-Japan Project; conferences, workshops, lectures, and retreats to refine and disseminate the new practices and materials they were creating. They brought new activists and women's groups into the project. They reached out to women in other Asian countries to extend the knowledge exchange beyond the original scope of the project.

In the end, the Japanese women used what they learned through the US-Japan Project to revolutionize the way Japanese feminists do business. The project changed the way Japanese women's groups operate, individually and as a movement. It changed the way they interact with women's groups in other countries and with other types of unions and social justice organizations. And it changed the way JWUs approach developing new generations of activists. The project also led to the creation of a new national organization that seeks to link Japanese women's groups, facilitate resource and information sharing, and coordinate national campaigns.

On the American side, the US-Japan Project was an eye-opening experience for scholars and activists alike. We learned about Japanese workers' increasing dissatisfaction with traditional company unions and their ongoing efforts to create new kinds of unions outside the company structure. We learned of the existence of an array of emerging alternative unions, including women's unions, part-time workers' unions, community unions, and other kinds of network-based workers' organizations. We became particularly well acquainted with the internal operations of JWUs and the kinds of organizational problems they face. We gained significant knowledge about the range of on-the-job problems Japanese women encounter, as well as the many ways Japanese women have tried to combat those problems. We also came away with a far more nuanced understanding of the similarities and differences between Japanese and American employment systems and labor-related laws and institutions, and how these factors shaped (and continue to shape) women's activities in each country.

Our Unions, Our Selves

Our Unions, Our Selves tells the story of the development of these innovative, dual-advocacy organizations and their evolving efforts to radically reshape the Japanese labor movement and society at large. Focusing on the case of Women's Union Tokyo, Part I looks at the evolution of JWUs; their origins, goals, philosophies, and daily practices; and the internal and external obstacles they face in practice. Chapter 1 centers on my first meeting with Keiko Tani and Midori Ito, the founders of the WUT, in which they described in detail the inner workings of their union and offered their take (echoed by other feminist labor activists and scholars) on how various phases and practices of the postwar employment system contributed to the eventual creation of unions for women only. Chapter 2 traces Midori's and Tani's personal histories as workers and as activists. Their stories reveal common workplace experiences for women of their generation and provide insights into how and why JWUs developed the way they did. Chapter 3 covers the six-month period from December 2000 to May 2001 when I was a participant-observer with the WUT. The chapter includes my observations and analysis of significant internal pressures the union was experiencing at that time as well as an account of the running dialogue among WUT leaders, members, and me, which led to the US-Japan Working Women's Networks Project.

Part II focuses on the insights and innovations that grew out of our unique grassroots exchange project. Chapters 4 and 5 detail the lessons and insights from the first phase of the project, in which participants from both sides laid the intellectual groundwork necessary for engaging in meaningful problem solving. Chapter 4 focuses on our first face-to-face meeting in Detroit, when each of the participating women's groups introduced themselves at a fairly broad level: who they are, how their organizations came about, what they hope to accomplish and by what means; and an array of scholars provided overviews of the social, economic, and legal contexts in which these organizations operate. Following these wide-lens reports, chapter 5 discusses the highly telescoped "self-analysis" the WUT presented at this first meeting, in which the union laid out in detail all of its organizational warts and challenges, as well as the problem-solving discussions that followed. The chapter summarizes activists' and educators' presentations on how participatory labor education has been used to foster greater union democracy and membership participation in the United States.

Chapter 6 looks at our second meeting, when US educators came to Tokyo to model participatory education techniques as a first step toward enabling Japanese women's groups to create their own educational programs. While ultimately productive, that phase of the project generated significant conflict among some of the participants. Although they made us terribly uncomfortable in the moment, the controversies yielded important lessons about differences in how US and Japanese labor-feminists think about organizing, empowerment, and individualism. In trying to work through the tensions, we gained valuable knowledge about what it takes to create and maintain successful crossborder collaboration.

In chapter 7 we see the first concrete fruits of the project as the Japanese participants pilot their own newly created educational programs. In addition to showcasing some of the most innovative ideas the Japanese women came up with, chapter 7 documents various processes of creation the women established to enable the groups to work together across time and space to develop their new educational programs. Beyond facilitating that immediate goal, those processes also constituted the beginnings of an infrastructure for a national network of Japanese women's organizations.

The final two chapters offer my conclusions on the two intertwined narratives that make up this volume. Chapter 8 reflects on the lasting impacts of the US-Japan Project some ten years after its completion, particularly on its effect on the women's movement as a whole, and on its role in promoting democracy within unions—but also across a variety of social movements and organizations—through participatory membership education programs. The chapter also includes my reflections on JWUs as far as: their viability over time; their ability to fulfill the essential role of a labor union, which is to confront capital; and what role they might ultimately play in reshaping the Japanese labor movement even if they are unable to develop to the level the founders initially envisioned.

The final chapter explores the lessons we learned—sometimes the hard way—about the necessity, but also the difficulties, of crossborder collaborations. In designing the US-Japan Project, we made a number of fortuitous decisions about how to construct the project to increase our ability to work effectively together despite significant differences in language, culture, and industrial relations laws and institutions. On the other hand, there are a staggering number of ways well-meaning American and Japanese colleagues can, culturally speaking, knock heads, step on toes, offend, confuse, and generally piss each other off, and I think we managed to find each and every one of them in the course of the project. In this volume I catalogue both, in part for your enjoyment but also in the hope that our gaffes as well as our insights will prove instructive to future crossborder projects, which are urgently needed today. The issues facing US progressives today—the disappearance of middle-class jobs and wages, the intensification of poverty in the face of rising profits and productivity, the resurgence of hate crimes and police violence, and the persistence of economic activities that are causing catastrophic damage to our environment—by their very nature cut across a variety of constituencies that don't necessarily have a lot of experience engaging with each other, particularly as equal players in a collective effort. "Fight for $15" rallies, for example, routinely bring together such strange bedfellows as fast-food workers, adjunct professors, home care workers, and Black Lives Matter activists. At some very basic level, these groups are united by their fight against poverty. But there are also significant borders that separate these constituent groups, and their success as a movement rests in part on their ability to recognize, plan for, and "translate" across organizational, historical, and experiential divides. By providing an account of the obvious and not so obvious borders the US-Japan Project encountered, and our successes and failures in negotiating those crossings, *Our Unions, Our Selves* will, I hope, serve as both invitation and guide to future crossborder projects that seek to unite workers and other marginalized people in the face of ever encroaching global capital.

Part 1

JAPANESE WOMEN'S UNIONS

A UNION OF ONE'S OWN

My first introduction to Japanese Women's Unions (JWUs) came in 2000 when a fellow activist arranged for me to interview the founders of Women's Union Tokyo (WUT), Midori Ito and Keiko Tani.[1] We agreed to meet at the WUT office in a part of town called Yoyogi.[2] Finding a random address in Tokyo is tricky business. Many streets have no names. Addresses have no discernible sequence or pattern. Even among native Tokyoites it is common for a host to provide a hand-drawn map or to meet guests at the nearest train station and escort them to the venue in question. In my case I had written instructions to the union office but was not feeling particularly confident about finding it in the maze that I knew awaited me outside the train station. Nothing can prepare you for the visual cacophony that is most of Tokyo, and Yoyogi is no exception. Outside the station I made my way past the usual chaotic bricolage of fast-food restaurants, pachinko parlors, noodle shops, western-style cafes, trade schools, hair salons, office buildings, massage spots, designer boutiques, convenience stores, and the cram schools for which this neighborhood is particularly known.

Following my directions, I cut through the parking lot behind the music school, walked down what I thought was an alley but turned out to be the street I was looking for, and stopped when I came to a nondescript two-story building that I thought stood some chance of being the union office for the sole reason that it wasn't definitively anything else. Not that it looked like an office building. It did not. And it certainly didn't feel like a place that was interested in welcoming newcomers. Walking up what felt like a fire escape, I was afraid I had gotten the directions wrong and was about to burst into someone's private apartment.

On the other hand, I had lived in Japan long enough to know that I was still too culturally ignorant to read the architectural markers. In the absence of the most glaring commercial identifiers—neon golden arches, for example—I routinely had trouble distinguishing between a private home and an expensive restaurant, or a community bath house and a government agency, based on outward appearances alone. I held my breath, knocked on the sliding door, and entered.

Once inside, there was no mistaking the scene in front of me: I was in the office of yet another underfunded, overburdened, grassroots organization trying to scratch out a few victories for those on the lower rungs. The entire operation consisted of one small room with a tiny sink off to one side. Every inch of horizontal space was pressed into service. Utilitarian bookshelves hugging the walls sagged from the weight of books, binders, government reports, and court judgments. Soulless metal work desks were piled high with current case notes, newsletters, meeting notes, and materials of all kinds, as was the large, rectangular common table in the center of the room. I would later learn that meetings and celebrations took place at that table despite the fact that it was habitually spilling over with the documents of their trade.

Several women were on hand answering phones, working the computers, and bustling about in preparation for upcoming negotiations. With the exception of the two I had come to interview, the women greeted me briefly then got right back to their tasks. Despite the flurry of activity, a cloud of exhaustion hung over the scene. When we sat down at the table for the interview, I couldn't pull my chair in because the area under the table was chock-full of file boxes. As my eyes trailed around the room, I tried to imagine keeping my spirits up working in this grim environment without a splash of color anywhere, except for the dollar-store slippers one dons at the front door.

Midori and Tani were easy to spot, each looking the part of long-time activist. A year or two on either side of fifty, they are sturdy, practical-looking women. No mincing or giggling into their hands as Japanese women are often taught to do. No cloyingly cute apparel or talking in high-pitched falsetto voices. They are serious women with serious work to do. Yet, for all they have in common, they are as different in personality as they are alike in purpose. Tani is all warmth, a motherly figure whose manner inspires women to find the strength to push on even when the fight has worn them down. Midori, on the other hand, has the flinty aspect of someone who cut her teeth on hardship. She exudes strength in a way that is by turns inspiring and intimidating. While not without her critics, Midori commands tremendous respect among labor activists, in part because of the sacrifices she has made for the movement, and in part because the sheer force of her personality belies the myth of women being inherently weak and subservient. Where Tani is a warm, fortifying bowl of noodles, Midori is a bracing shot of whiskey.

I sat at the center table as Tani and Midori cleared a small space to serve hot green tea and Japanese crackers. Just making tea in that cramped space seemed tricky enough, but a few weeks later I saw members cook a full dinner on a hot plate perched on one of the work desks. We ate the dinner at the center table amidst piles of papers so high I could barely see the people on the other side when I was sitting down. I quickly learned this was standard practice. No matter how busy the members were, the sharing of tea and at least a small snack was never dispensed with. Most of the time it struck me as a delightful ritual that made the grim and crowded office feel cozier. On my grumpier days, it struck me as an impediment to getting down to business when we had so much work to do—an attitude that would get me in trouble many times in the coming years. But at that moment, it put me very much at ease as the two local legends walked me through the specifics of their union.[3]

Characteristics of Japanese Women's Unions
Mission

At the broadest level, the WUT's mission includes such ambitious goals as: eliminating sexual harassment, power harassment, and other violations of women's human rights; closing the wage gap and establishing the principle of equal pay for equal work; achieving work-life balance "with a greater degree of humanity" by eliminating the gendered division of labor; and creating an environment in which women can exercise their rights as a matter of course in the workplace and in society at large. On a more day-to-day basis, the union provides individual-level assistance for women who contact the union either in person or through its "job counseling" hotline. By "job counseling" they mean anything from providing strategic support to women who are having on-the-job problems but are not yet ready to join a union, to helping women prepare for court or arbitration cases, to helping women who do join the union to enter into negotiations with their employer. Japanese women's unions use the English term "collective bargaining" to refer to the type of negotiations that in the United States we call grievance resolution.[4]

The WUT also engages in legislative and political advocacy, often in cooperation with other national and international women's organizations, such as the Committee for Asian Women (CAW), Equality Action 21, the Society for the

Study of Working Women (SSWW), and the League of Lawyers for Working Women. Together, these organizations work to promote working women-friendly legislation at national and local levels and encourage the Japanese government to adopt and enforce international labor and anti-discrimination standards. The League of Lawyers for Working Women also provides legal support in cases that go to trial. Like other women's organizations, the WUT also provides support services such as English language lessons, computer skills training, and a "safe space" for survivors of sexual harassment.

Daily Operations

Tani likes to describe the WUT as a union "of women, by women, and for women" because it relies on active participation of the members to carry out its daily operations. With the exception of two paid staff (Midori and Tani held those posts at the time of the interview), the union is run by member-volunteers, who do everything from answering phones and handling clerical tasks to providing job consultations, signing up and training new members, serving on bargaining committees, lobbying, and assisting fellow members whose cases have gone to mediation or court. To maintain its independence from the government and other organizations, the WUT primarily relies on membership dues for funding.

Although many of the most active members would prefer to spend more time on movement-building activities, the volume of calls to the job hotline means their day-to-day efforts focus instead on immediate conflict resolution. According to union records, the WUT received 3,391 requests for job counseling from 1995 to 2004, of which 506 resulted in direct negotiations with the company (WUT 2004b). Between 1995 and 2000, the union engaged in direct negotiations in 265 cases, and reached a settlement in 90 percent of those cases (interview with union leaders 2000).

Membership

A survey conducted just prior to my first meeting with the WUT found that the women who joined the union came from a variety of companies and occupations (Kotani 1999). Clerical workers make up the biggest category at 48.1 percent. Twenty-two percent are specialists or engineers, 7.4 percent are in sales, and 3.7 percent are service workers. Approximately 35 percent of WUT members have children under the age of six. Most WUT members (63 percent) are regular permanent employees (*sei-shain*).[5] The remaining 37 percent are non-permanent employees (*hisei-shain*), including part-time, temporary, and contract employees.

The same survey found that the most common reasons women gave for joining the WUT were:

- Because there is no union in my company (64.2%);
- Because the WUT is run by women (49.4%);
- To solve issues in the workplace (43.2%);
- Because the WUT lent a sympathetic ear (42.0%);
- Because of anxiety over the future (39.5%);
- Because it was impossible to solve issues with help from public institutions (30.9%).[6]

Most women find the union by searching the Internet. Others learn of it through government agencies that deal with labor issues, newspaper articles, word of mouth, or by searching phone listings for women's groups.

Joining the WUT

The path to membership usually begins when a potential new member calls the union's hotline about a work-related problem she has been unable to resolve through more traditional means. The hotline is staffed with member-volunteers who are trained to talk with the callers about their grievances and advise them on their rights and options. In some cases, all the caller wants is an outlet for her frustration or a little support and encouragement before she goes back to her company to tackle the problem on her own. In other cases, the caller might decide she wants to join the WUT to pursue a solution with the union's help. In that case, union members will meet with her in person and provide information to help the woman choose a course of action. Most women in this category are seeking to return to work on better conditions, or, if that proves impossible, to negotiate a financial settlement.

The WUT offers women who are already represented by their company's union two options for membership.[7] One is to work with the WUT—as Midori put it, "clandestinely"—while keeping her current enterprise-union affiliation. In this case, the woman consults with the WUT to develop strategies that she can use on her own in dealing either with her employer or the enterprise union. A woman might choose this pattern for several reasons, for example, if she fears retaliation from the enterprise union for going "outside." Ironically, a woman might also choose this path if she has a relatively good relationship with the enterprise union in general and doesn't want to jeopardize it. Even if the enterprise union is unwilling or unable to help her in her current situation, the woman might want to remain a member in good standing for future considerations, not the least of which is that serving as an officer in the company union is often a pathway to landing a promotion to management.

The second course is for the woman to formally resign from the enterprise union and join the WUT as a full member. In this case, the woman would pursue her grievance with the WUT as her sole bargaining representative. This is a more radical course of action because it takes the issue outside the enterprise unit, and that raises company as well as company-union hackles.

The next step for new members is to decide how they want to pursue their grievances. That could mean anything from requesting a meeting with the company to discuss the case, to taking their complaint to government mediation or the courts.[8] Once new members decide on a course, the union helps them assemble a committee of more experienced members to provide advice and support through all the stages of their case. Whichever course a new member chooses— negotiations, mediation, or filing a lawsuit—she is expected to play a leading role in pursuing her case, with her union sisters providing guidance and assistance based on the lessons they learned from their own experiences.

Issues

Many of the complaints that bring women to the WUT will be familiar to US workers: sexual harassment, wrongful discharges, forced early retirement, unreasonable changes in working conditions, and violations of laws governing part-time, temporary, and contract work. But, while many of the underlying issues are similar, local laws and customs significantly affect the ways they play out.

Sexual Harassment

Sexual harassment is an epidemic in Japanese workplaces, which is hardly surprising considering how institutionally disempowered and vulnerable working women are. Most women who experience sexual harassment on the job have no realistic options for resolving the problem. Except in the rare case of a responsive supervisor, complaining to management usually amounts to throwing gasoline on the fire. As we have already seen, traditional in-house unions are typically ill-equipped for handling sexual harassment issues, and, more to the point, often don't consider it a matter for the union. Moreover, many women are not eligible to join their company unions because they are not full-time employees. Some women take their complaints to the various government agencies that are supposed to help resolve sexual harassment and gender discrimination cases. But many of the remedial avenues created by the govern-

ment have proven largely ineffective because they rely on voluntary compliance, lack investigative and enforcement authority, and/or allow for mediation
only if both sides agree to the process (Gelb 2003). All too often, women who
muster the courage to stand up to sexual harassment end up losing their jobs,
losing their health from stress and humiliation, and losing the support and
friendship of coworkers who are afraid to associate with the office pariah. According to Midori and Tani, it is not uncommon for women who have left a job
due to sexual harassment to become virtual shut-ins. Shame and loss of confidence make it hard for them to venture into society, and finding new employment is especially difficult because no one wants to hire someone who was a
troublemaker in her last job.

Gender Harassment

Closely related to sexual harassment, gender harassment refers to comments and
actions that are aimed at preserving traditional gender roles and keeping women
in what some still feel is their proper place. Women are routinely subjected to
comments that make it abundantly clear that the workplace is by rights a male
domain and that women are interlopers who are better suited for doing other
things, such as having children and keeping house. When I talked with women
about their daily working experiences, I was always astounded by the kinds of
Fred Flintstone-like comments they reported hearing on a regular basis. "Isn't it
time you got married and had children?" "Don't become too strong or no man
will want to marry you." "You are just here until you find a husband." These kinds
of remarks are as common as air; an ordinary part of Japanese women's daily
lives. They are often said without a second thought, largely because there is little
fear of reprimand.

Making job assignments on the basis of gender role stereotypes is another
form of gender harassment, but the problem is not perpetuated by management
alone. The culture at large plays a role in shaping the gendered division of labor
inside the company. One bank employee told me that all the front line employees were men while the data entry people behind them were all women. "There
is a feeling that clients want to be greeted by a female voice when they call, but
they do not want to talk to a woman when it comes to actually doing business,"
she explained. Another young woman who worked for a trading company said
her boss promoted her from her clerical position to a position with more responsibility and direct involvement with the clients. But she was soon demoted
because customers refused to entrust their business to a mere woman. It was fine
for her to answer the phones, so long as she passed the call to a male employee
immediately after chirping a cheery "Hello."

Japanese women also have to combat discriminatory practices that are rooted in long-standing customs that much of society still defends as being part of Japan's "unique" culture. One example is the custom of after-hours drinking parties, which often mingle sexual and gender harassment. A common part of modern corporate life in Japan, drinking parties are neither voluntary nor for the purpose of simple pleasure (Mehri 2005). They are company-mandated bonding exercises that play an important role in socializing employees in proper corporate behavior and ideology. Such parties typically involve heavy drinking and various types of "male bonding" behaviors, including sexual jokes and innuendo. For women, drinking parties are a no-win situation. If they do not attend, they lose bonding and networking opportunities, anger their bosses, and alienate their coworkers. If they do attend, they often become the target of embarrassing sexual banter. Moreover, they will be expected to play along with traditional gender roles, such as pouring drinks and artfully serving food to the male employees. Serving their male colleagues in this way is especially demeaning because it recalls highly sexualized images of the geisha or other types of hostesses whose job it was to pamper and titillate male customers by engaging them in witty repartee and pouring their drinks. While the women forced to enact this role for their bosses, male coworkers, and clients often feel angry and humiliated, many Japanese people regard it as a distinct and beautiful feature of Japanese culture that should be preserved.

Japanese companies also frequently require women office workers to pour tea for male employees, even if they outrank them. Many women bitterly resent this custom and say that it is a clear violation of gender equality laws. But such cases are hard to win because, as one WUT member said, "The firm and the [company] union said, 'It's not discrimination. It is just a social custom.'" Activists have made some progress in freeing relatively high-ranking women from tea duty, but getting people to consider the gender implications of traditional practices more generally is tough when even the government agencies that are tasked with overseeing implementation of the Equal Employment Opportunity Law (EEOL) are unwilling to take a firm stand against customary forms of discrimination. A 2007 report from the Japan Institute for Labour Policy and Training invoked the long-standing tradition of gender discrimination to justify its kid-glove approach to dealing with the problem, for example, offering "corporate awards" to companies for merely *complying* with existing law (JILPT 2007).

Gender and sexual harassment cases such as these make it clear that not all problems can be solved at the bargaining table. To make serious inroads into the kinds of harassment women face at work, women's unions and other organizations also need to raise awareness and change cultural perceptions about the place of women in society, their abilities, and their rights to self-fulfillment. Neither enterprise unions nor even the most progressive alternative unions face the challenge of remaking society at such a fundamental level. But women have no choice. They have to fight discriminatory employers while at the same time building a movement to overturn long-standing beliefs that help to perpetuate gender and sexual harassment.

Nonpermanent Employment

As mentioned earlier, the very existence of the nonpermanent employment system is itself an issue that women's unions are taking on. But the WUT also sees complaints from employees who are even being denied the already dismal working conditions nonpermanent employment offers. Such cases include companies illegally terminating employees before their contracts have expired; falsely categorizing employees as subcontractors to avoid paying social insurance premiums; keeping employees on temporary contracts for many years; and signing employees to increasingly short-term contracts, or illegally forcing them to accept unwanted changes from full-time to part-time or temporary status. Some of these actions directly violate Japanese labor law. Others are technically legal but arguably constitute a breach of socially accepted business practices. Employees on temporary contracts, for example, might request negotiations as their termination dates approach. The union would not argue such cases on legal grounds. Rather, it would seek to persuade management that it is in the company's best interest to retain trained and loyal employees or that the company is being a bad corporate citizen by violating accepted norms of the paternalistic relationship between employers and employees. Although breaking that bond is the whole point of nonpermanent employment, Japanese companies are still vulnerable to criticism and public censure if they are considered to be too brazenly embracing "American-style practices" (interviews with union leaders 2000, 2004).

Forced Retirement and Wrongful Discharge

Although early retirement as official company policy was largely eliminated by anti-discrimination legislation, the practice is still alive and well when companies want to cut payroll or eliminate a "problem" employee. When I first started interviewing WUT members about the experiences that brought them to the union, the most common reply was, "My company tried to fire me but I refused." The first few times I heard that I was totally confused. Refuse to be fired? You can do that here? Or does it mean you just keep showing up for work? You sit on the doorstep with a picket sign? Eventually, one of the members explained that firing someone is legally and socially frowned upon in Japan, so when a company wants to get rid of someone they try to get that person to resign "voluntarily." If a woman became pregnant, for example, management would start by gently suggesting she take early retirement. If she resists gentle hints, the company keeps upping the pressure until it becomes so unbearable that she either leaves or does something drastic like join a women's union. Companies use forced early retirement to get rid of workers who become pregnant, miss work because of illness, or talk back to or in some other way fall out of favor with management. Forced retirements also help companies avoid layoffs when business is slow.

Bullying and Power Harassment

Japanese management keeps almost unimaginably tight control of the workplace using a potent combination of power harassment and bullying to squash even a glimmer of dissent. Feminists in Japan use the term "power harassment" to refer to misuse of one's superior position to force employees into complying with illegal or inappropriate orders. "Bullying" refers to a *group* of people ganging up on a single individual to browbeat (or physically beat) him or her into line. Used together, they make for a formidable and coercive system for guaranteeing employee acquiescence to even the most extreme demands (Mehri 2005).

Bullying is a form of social control kids learn very early. It is used liberally in schoolyards and playgrounds throughout Japan to enforce conformity and maintain the various hierarchies that exist among school children. We see such behaviors in other cultures, but in Japan it's been raised almost to an art form. Even among adults it's the go-to method for enforcing codes of behavior, and that works out great for Japanese managers who want to punish anyone who has stepped out of line. It's a ready-made weapon that managers can wield to (in most cases metaphorically) beat employees into submission. All they have to do is get the message out to the other employees, and they'll know what to do. Sometimes the call to bully comes as a direct order to ostracize a particular person because she is being "disloyal" to the company or is in some other way putting people's jobs and the company in jeopardy. In other cases, the boss will take some action that signals to the group that an employee has become persona non grata. That could be anything from not giving the employee any work to do or moving her desk to some isolated position, to spreading sexual gossip about her or ridiculing her in front of her peers.

One part-time office worker I interviewed became the target of bullying after she complained about an unreasonable increase in her work hours. Her hours ballooned after the company dismissed three employees in the same division. "After the layoffs, the company made it clear that the workload would not be scaled back just because the department was now down three people. I was working from 9 a.m. to 10 p.m. (with no overtime bonus) five days a week, even though I am still classified as a part-timer," she told me. Since she had a family to take care of, the company generously allowed her an hour off in the evening to dash home, cook dinner for her family, then return to work for several more hours until her work was done. Within a few weeks, she was exhausted. Knowing she could not keep up this pace for long, she went to her manager, "hoping to find some way to humanize my workload," she said. Instead, her supervisor declared war. "The supervisor gathered all other workers and told them I was involved in a sexual affair," she said. "Even if the other workers don't believe the rumors, they know that the presence of such rumors is usually a sign that the employee has been marked as a target and those wishing to keep their own jobs should steer clear." Her coworkers took the hint and diligently started harassing her and making her a pariah. Each morning when she arrived, the boss would call her into his office and allege that a coworker (a different one each day) had complained that she was harassing him or her. The boss would order her to write a letter of apology. "Every day there was an apology letter to be written in the morning. The whole office was in on it, pressure and bullying."

Even her husband, who worked for a different company, started to feel the heat. "The company wrote a letter to him making a scandal of me and one of the men who supported my case." Her husband had to give her "silent support" she said, in part out of fear for his own job but also out of concern that their children would face reprisals at school. "The school is in the same district as the company dormitory, so a lot of the children of my coworkers go to the same school as our children. I worried about them being harassed by the kids at school.

"I just tried to speak up when something seemed wrong," she said. "It was a small act to start with, but then it snowballed because of the company's reaction."

Another woman, a part-time bank worker, described being bullied when she resisted the company's attempts to fire her after she suffered a work-related injury. Management was furious because she insisted on taking disability leave, and even angrier when they found out she had joined a union and started a petition drive to force the government to recognize work-related injuries among part-time employees.[9] All management had to do was let it be known that she was in disfavor, and suddenly her once friendly workplace became the site of daily humiliation and shaming.

"All of my coworkers had the same purpose: to bully me to force me to leave," she said. "When I greeted my coworkers in the morning, no one would respond to me. I became invisible. They wouldn't give me any work. When someone passed out cake, there was none for me. I was isolated." The effect is overwhelming.

"Suddenly I felt strange—hot, and itchy. I went to the restroom and found I had broken out in a rash all over and my eyes were beginning to swell up. I left work early and went to a doctor who diagnosed me as suffering from acute stress."

Besides being a very effective way to discipline employees who step out of line, the public nature of this type of bullying has the added benefit of sending a message to the rest of the employees that nothing but unflinching obedience will be tolerated.

Even coworkers who don't want to participate usually go along with the treatment for fear of the evil eye being turned on them. "One of my colleagues, a person who had a physical disability, came to my desk and made a scene to embarrass me," the bank employee said. "The disabled person was hired because of the disability law. But that person always fears for his job so he shows his loyalty to the company by bullying me."

Bullying is also a favorite way to force out unwanted employees when the company wants to cut labor costs. Under Japanese law, employers have to show just cause to fire an employee. Employers seeking to cut staff often get around the law by harassing employees until they quit. An account specialist from an information technology firm came to the WUT for help in fighting her company's campaign to bully a group of longtime employees into quitting. Her company had merged with another firm, and management at the newly formed company wanted to shed high seniority employees, including people who had been managers before the merger. The new company instituted several organizational changes that targeted the older workers and sent a not-so-subtle message that the company wanted them to quit. Job grades were compressed and many of the targeted employees were squeezed into the lower grade, stripping them of their management status. They also suffered pay and benefits cuts, and were no longer eligible for training necessary for promotion.

She complained, and on cue the harassment began: "I was targeted, teased, harassed by nasty comments from managers. On the day I signed out to go on holiday, the boss put up celebratory decorations."

In this case, management was misusing its power to force the employee to quit. "They put me in a new position and didn't train me. They never told me what was expected of me, and they never told me when problems came about. They gave me a low score on my performance review, but they wouldn't direct me or help me or even answer my questions about why my score was so low."

It took me a long time to really appreciate just how powerful bullying can be, largely because I could not fathom management being able to control employees enough to make it work. The goal of bullying is total isolation, and total isolation requires absolute compliance from the rest of the workforce. The wall around the target has to be rock solid, which means everyone in the workplace has to go along with the plan. Until I saw it with my own eyes, I would never have believed management could command nearly unanimous compliance. In my experience, it's tough to get US workers to march in lockstep under any circumstances, but in response to an imperious command from on high—especially one that bids the employees to badger a coworker into submitting to management? Not likely. While kicking up a fuss will get you ostracized in a Japanese workplace, in the United States it's the guy who kisses up to the boss that sits alone at the lunch table. Also, most of the workers I know would be deeply offended if management tried to dictate something as personal as who you can be friends with at work. By American standards that would constitute a gross overreach of authority and would likely end in some form of pushback. In the early 1990s I worked for a chain of newspapers in suburban Chicago, where I also served as union steward and the "bad cop" in our contract negotiations. For weeks I had been a pain in the company's neck, so management decided to make an example of me. My supervisor brought in the top brass from the main office and made a big show of hauling me into a closed-door disciplinary hearing that was meant to strike fear in the hearts of my coworkers and intimidate them into backing off of their support for me and the bargaining committee. But their heavy-handedness backfired. When the bosses and I walked out of the hearing room, my coworkers were already gathered around my desk, waiting to thump me on the back and shake my hand in full view of the brass to make it very clear that they still stood behind me.

In that case, solidarity was especially high because we were in the midst of contract negotiations. But even under normal circumstances, US workers don't take kindly to imperious directives, especially ones that bid them to do management's dirty work. Even when employees aren't in a position to flagrantly defy their bosses, in my experience there are always a few who will find some way to quietly exercise their middle-finger rights, and they're often heroes to the others for doing it. Labor history is rife with stories of creative ways employees have found to tweak the boss's nose. One of my favorites comes from a former steel worker who told me that he and his coworkers had a technique called "cupping" for knocking out-of-control bosses down a peg. One of the materials the guys worked with was a highly viscous oil that made a perfect glue for sticking an empty Styrofoam coffee cup on top of the boss's hard hat. On days when the boss was being particularly insufferable, one of the workers would surreptitiously place the prepared sticky cup on the boss's hat and let him walk around like that for as long as they could get away with it. Their supervisor was notorious for flying off the handle and verbally abusing employees, but the cupping trick neutralized him because, no matter how riled up he got, no one could take him seriously with a cup bobbing up and down on his head as he frothed and blathered in their faces.

In the United States, humor and ridicule can be very effective for chipping away at management's authority, and for that reason it can be a good strategy for fighting bullying in the workplace. But if that type of collective shop floor resistance exists in Japan, I didn't see it. Management's grip is so strong that when someone is targeted for bullying, most people will, at the very least, turn their back on that person, leaving them completely isolated in the workplace.[10] Women's unions are one of the very few sources of support for female employees who are facing the overwhelming experience of having one's entire company turn against them.

Individual Affiliation

To me the WUT's most surprising, even puzzling, characteristic is its individual-membership structure, which allows women to join the union as individuals, with no expectation on either side of bringing their coworkers into the union. Most Japanese women's unions embrace the principle of individual affiliation because it makes it easier for women to join unions. But, in exchange for ease of membership, JWUs give up the ability to leverage the kind of collective action that is the primary source of union power. Midori and Tani recognize many of the problems inherent with the individual-membership model, but they argue that, for all its drawbacks, the individual structure is the solution that best fits Japanese working women's current needs and circumstances. The individual structure is not, as I first feared, a fundamental misunderstanding of the concept of unionizing. Rather, it is a reasoned response to the lived experiences of women workers and activists of Midori and Tani's generation. While Midori's and Tani's personal biographies are obviously their own, their stories, which follow in the next chapter, echo common experiences of the working women of their generation and help to illustrate how and why Japanese women's unions took the forms we see today.

A TALE OF TWO ACTIVISTS

Born in 1947 into a politically progressive family, Keiko Tani made a conscious choice to devote her life to working for social justice. A student at Tokyo Women's University during the Vietnam War, Tani joined the student movement to protest the war and to work toward fundamental social change. During Tani's senior year, when she was one step away from completing her degree in education, the students voted to go on strike. That left her with a serious dilemma. She was due to start a mandatory internship that was the last stage of her training. If she missed her internship, she'd be kicked out of the program and her aspiration to become a teacher would be gone for good. On the other hand, if she accepted her internship, she would have to cross the picket line and betray the student movement. Tani honored the strike, knowing that decision would change the course of her life.

Unlike Tani, Midori Ito was an accidental activist. Her thoughts were not on social movements when she was young. The daughter of two working-class parents, Midori longed to go to university to study art, but her mother's early death ended that dream. After graduating high school, she moved to Tokyo in search of a job. Following a series of low-paying service jobs—some of which required her to work "service overtime," a.k.a. working overtime off-the-clock—she eventually landed a factory job making telephone parts. It was a good job in the sense that she was a regular full-time employee, but it was a rude awakening to the realities of factory work. "For me that was the first step toward serious involvement [in the labor movement]," Midori said. "I saw that there were many workers there who were just out of junior high school. They had come to Tokyo as a group to work at the company. They were just young girls. All of them worked and lived in the company dorms and went to school at night. That's what I saw. It was just like the assembly line in the Charlie Chaplin movie *Modern Times*. They would increase the speed. One by one the girls collapsed and got sick. It was culture shock for me."

The labor movement was still relatively strong in Japan at that time.

> The union I belonged to was ready to fight. But then the oil shock happened [in 1973] and the labor movement started to break down as the economy faltered. The working conditions for these junior high girls were so poor. The baths in the girls' dorm in particular were in very bad condition. But because most of the union members were men, the union compromised with the administration. They agreed to accept the company merely changing the water temperature. The women at that time fought fiercely to change some of the terrible conditions but, in the end, I felt like the core [male] members of the union betrayed us.

Soon after, the union agreed to another speedup. The plant was a union shop, so in theory all full-time employees were members of the union. In practice, however, the predominantly male executive committee routinely cut deals that protected male jobs at the expense of the women workers. "Most of the workers on the line were women, but the men were making the decisions about what the working conditions on the line would be. Most of the men were 'pencil pushers' who would not be affected by the speedup. But it hurt the women," she said. Only twenty years old at the time, Midori launched a fight against the speedup. She organized a group of about fifty women in her section. "The core members [of the company union] were shocked to see our section's movement," she noted. The Women's Group fought hard but ultimately lost, largely because the company union undercut their efforts.

Midori's faith in the union was shattered for good when the leadership stood idly by as the company announced the firing of all part-time workers, the vast majority of whom were women. "This was happening as the labor movement was weakening and becoming company-oriented. The Women's Group objected [to the firings] but again the male committee members went along with it. The union started to lose the trust of the women workers." And yet, while the women ultimately lost the fight to save the part-timers jobs, the Women's Group had grown from 50 to about 600 members, and Midori had emerged as a symbol of resistance to her female coworkers, a challenge to the union leadership, and a thorn in the side of management.

At the same time, a separate fight was brewing over the opening of Narita Airport. Community advocates, many of whom were members of the New Left movement, argued that building the airport in that area unfairly burdened local farmers whose land was being gobbled up by the government project. Midori joined hundreds of other activists in a protest that culminated in occupying the airport's air traffic control center. Three hundred people were arrested—including Midori and several of her coworkers—and had to stay in jail until their individual cases came before the court. "So many people were arrested that the court was overwhelmed. It took a year and three months for my case to get to court and I had to stay in jail the whole time." By the time the court dismissed Midori's case, her job was gone.

For Midori, still in her early twenties, the disappointments were piling up. Like so many women activists of her generation, Midori was deeply disillusioned when she saw her male colleagues in the New Left engaging in the same discriminatory and harassing behaviors as men "on the outside." "Women who were in the Narita battle, women activists, were sexually harassed by male activists. We didn't have the word for it then. The first woman who complained just said what happened to her. Then, so many women started to declare: 'It happened to me. It happened to me.' Core leaders of the New Left were harassing women activists."

Eventually, all the losses and betrayals caught up with her.

> I mentally collapsed. We finished all the court procedures and failed after three years. I became sick from psychological depression. I left the New Left movement and the union movement. I was deeply disappointed in the activities. Life had become so difficult for me. My name was in the newspapers. I was a target. Police visited me at home. They watched every movement. I got a job with a small company but was fired. Then I found a job with a very small factory. The working conditions were horrible but I needed a job desperately. I just wanted a normal, quiet life.

At first Midori tried to keep a low profile at her new job, but the conditions in the factory were hard to ignore. "The job involved handling hazardous chemicals used in the silk printing process. I often came home from work bleeding but I said nothing. I just wanted to stay and be quiet. For one year I was not an activist. I just kept working in that terrible place." But she couldn't keep the blinders on for long. "My coworkers—my friends—were quitting one by one. We had to work from 9 a.m. until 9 p.m. Then we would just go home, exhausted. I started thinking: Is this going to go on forever? This is how I thought about my life. I became so desperate." Midori wanted to build an organization that would give her coworkers a collective voice, but her past disappointments made her reluctant to put her faith in yet another union based on the model that repeatedly had failed women. Instead, she began searching for a different kind of union that would respond to women's concerns as well.

Meanwhile, Tani was continuing her life as an activist. Determined to stay active in social movements, Tani chose not to accept a protected, full-time job after she finished university. Instead, she worked a series of second-tier jobs, seesawing between full-time and part-time work, as she struggled to balance her desire to work for social justice and her growing family's economic needs. Some years she was able to get by working part-time or doing paid work at home while she took care of her two young children. But other years the financial pressure was too great and she had to put the kids in day care so she could work full time. Either way, she continued to devote her evenings to social causes.

Early in her career Tani was involved with a wide variety of causes, but by the 1980s she began to focus on organizing small community unions in Iidabashi, an industrial neighborhood in Tokyo.[1] Although Tani saw independent community unions as a step forward from traditional company unions, her experiences had taught her that even these more progressive unions were limited in their ability to understand the concerns of women workers. "I began to see more clearly that women have so much burden at work. Women at different working places had the same experiences: wages far below men's; men who are less competent become the bosses of more competent women and are paid more to boot. Also, [there was] age discrimination for women. The Iidabashi local labor union was controlled by men, so they didn't really understand women's issues."

Paths Converge

Midori and Tani met when their search for alternatives brought them to the National Union of General Workers-Tokyo (NUGWT). A network union that is open to individuals as well as organizations, the NUGWT organizes workers from a variety of occupations and companies who are not being served by traditional unions. Midori joined the NUGWT in 1984 and quickly got involved in a campaign to organize a new branch in another part of Tokyo. "There were union activities, court proceedings, union meetings, bargaining. I learned all those skills and procedures while I was working at the bad company by day and at the union at night. For me it was such a great experience, establishing a union from scratch. I learned everything."

But, as forward thinking as the NUGWT was in some regards, when it came to working women's issues, even it had its blind spots. "At that time the EEOL contained no provisions relating to sexual harassment," Tani said. "It was a big problem but not recognized by labor unions, so we sent a survey to women members of the NUGWT." The survey revealed that members were routinely subjected to sexual harassment, including incidents within the union. But instead of seeking to correct the problem, the male members tried to stop the women from publicizing the results to spare the union embarrassment.

Other issues languished because of lack of interest on the leadership's part. In one such case, a group of nursery school teachers were trying to organize a union but were meeting severe resistance from the school administration. "Everyone thought the school was democratic but, once the teachers formed a union, management began to harass them," Tani said. When Tani brought it to the NUGWT's attention, she found there was virtually no interest among the male leadership in pursuing the case, and that nothing would be done unless she made it happen. "The nursery school union was still fighting with the school leaders. So when I got to the NUGWT, I could not ignore that issue. I had to get involved." Tani convinced a few male members to give their full support to the teachers, who eventually went on strike and won. Without Tani's insistence, the case would never have registered on the NUGWT's radar screen.

In another case, the director of the union's day care center, who was also a core union member, fired existing workers and replaced them with his family members. "He was trying to kick out the other union members who worked at the day care center," Tani said. "Most of them were women. And he had all the power. Anyone who was against him, he could dismiss. The day care center was subsidized by union members' contributions, so I felt he was using union members' money for his own interests."

Once again faced with the lack of attention to women's issues, Midori and Tani began working together to reform the NUGWT. The first step was to elect women to the then all-male executive committee. Midori, Tani, and one other woman won seats and together they helped to usher in a new era of openness in the NUGWT. It was during this time that the NUGWT came up with the plan to launch the first women's union in Tokyo. Ironically, the idea did not come from the women members. Instead, it came from the male leadership, which saw launching a women's union as a way to build on recent successes. In 1993, in response to a wave of management layoffs, the NUGWT set up a union for displaced managers, the first of its kind in Japan. The move was so successful (and netted the union so much publicity) that the leadership wanted to launch another innovative idea, this time a union for women only.

"I wasn't so sure," Midori said. "I was working during the day, and I was so busy unionizing at night, so I was fully occupied. Can I really start yet another union?" But Tani lobbied hard. "I had seen women workers coming to the union for consultation but getting men, who had no understanding of their issues, as advisors. I felt there really needed to be a union by women and for women," Tani said.

In the end, Midori agreed.

> What triggered me to go on was the sexual harassment within the union movement. We did a questionnaire regarding sexual harassment. When we saw the results we found there were so many cases in the union by core members. We warned them, but even the director of the NUGWT couldn't understand why it was such a big deal. They also couldn't understand the problem of part-time work for women. They had no understanding. Even the professional union activists couldn't understand why it was wrong to say, "Part-time women can just be supplemented by their husbands."

If there were any doubts about whether a women's union was needed, they were dispelled when the union's phone began ringing off the hook even before it had officially opened. The plan was to open the union in March in time for *Shunto*,[2] in the hope of drawing maximum media attention. Tani convened a preparatory meeting in January, which five or six other women attended.

> One of them was Midori, who was the only other person who had any organizing experience. The rest were workers who had come for consultation in the past. We did not have sufficient experience or financial backing but we had to push on. In the beginning of March, the *Asahi Shinbun* did a story on the union, and from that time on the phone didn't stop ringing. At that time I was still working a regular job at the marketing research firm, but I had to take time off to answer phones. But even that wasn't enough because, in Japan, the fiscal year ends on March 31 and, according to law, if an employee wants to challenge an action by their company, they must file their complaint by the end of the fiscal year in which the alleged offense took place. So, we were inundated with calls and almost all of them had to be acted on immediately.

The overwhelming response from women who needed help presented an immediate organizational challenge because most traditional unions are based on a model that includes full-time staff to handle all the incoming business. "We couldn't do that at that time," Tani said. "We had to step out of that model and make the model where each member can take part as an organizer, where all are equal. The big question was how do we organize a union of that form, a form that did not exist?"

It was that question that prompted Midori and Tani to take inventory of their experiences as activists and as workers, to identify organizational structures and practices that they believe necessarily perpetuate inequality, and those that have historically promoted women's participation. The result was the WUT.

Imagining a New Kind of Union

Tani and Midori identified certain common organizational factors that they believe *by their very nature* perpetuate gender inequality and fundamentally compromise organizations' ability to respond to and empower women—regardless of the organizations' intentions. Time and again they had seen that top-down, hierarchical organizational structures (which tend to reproduce existing power relations) promote material and ideological barriers to women's participation and limit their ability to enter leadership positions. Such structures privilege traditionally male behavioral patterns, and thereby discriminate against women who have been socialized to avoid behaviors that appear confrontational or self-serving.

Midori and Tani also argue that unions that are organizationally tied to a particular company are vulnerable to management cooptation through company bribes or promotions in exchange for cooperating with the company's agenda. Moreover, company unions often put the company's interest above the members', because they are organizationally dependent on the company's success. Such unions tend to overlook or discount women's problems because the majority of members are men. Yet, while company unions often fail to represent women's voices within the union, they also tend to resist attempts by effectively disenfranchised members to form secondary in-house unions or special divisions within the existing union, thereby leaving women employees with no voice.

But the failure to represent women's interests does not apply only to company unions, Tani said. "Labor unions in Japan are androcentric. Most union executives are men, even in unions where most of the members are women. These unions will fight to raise the wage scale in general, but they don't fight about the wage gap between men and women—or sexual harassment cases. Women who had these problems had to fight them without support from labor unions."

According to Midori and Tani, unions that have the following characteristics inevitably will under-serve women members:

- All-male leadership and lack of affirmative action mechanisms or commitment to bring women into leadership positions;
- Lack of mechanisms to foreground minority voices and issues;
- Membership limited to full-time regular employees; and
- An internal culture that accepts and perpetuates gender stereotypes and engages in practices that reproduce the gendered division of labor.

Organizations that retain these characteristics are constitutionally incapable of understanding working women's problems and giving them the same priority they give problems common to working men.

The WUT was constructed along wholly different organizational lines to encourage rather than limit women's participation, and to address issues that were invisible or unimportant to traditional unions. "We thought, all the negative aspects of the unions, we'll just eradicate them," Tani said. "We knew from experience what those [negative aspects] were and decided to set up a union that didn't have those elements." In place of the single-enterprise, top-down, do-as-you're-told model of union, they sought to create its organizational opposite by constructing a network-style, individual-membership union based on feminist practices.

Feminist Structure and Practices

Midori and Tani argue that, in order to achieve equality in their workplaces, women must first discover their own power and ability to effect change. Few women have that experience in the male-oriented environment of traditional unions where hierarchy, domination, and competition rule the day. Instead, women are better off creating their own organizations based on the kinds of human interactions that Midori and Tani consider more ethical and more comfortable for women, such as cooperation, power-sharing, and consensus-building. Accordingly, the WUT's structure and practices are based on feminist ideals such as democracy, egalitarianism, cooperation, and respect for individual and human rights. For example, the WUT tries to create egalitarian relationships inside the union by observing certain operating practices: asking members to call each other by their names without regard to title or position; asking members to be mindful of the power differential between consultants and consultees; empowering members to recruit and assemble their own bargaining team; soliciting and respecting input from new as well as experienced members; and requiring all members to take part in the scut work of running the union, including cleaning and making tea (WUT 2004a).

To promote democratic power-sharing, the WUT holds a regular convention, which must be approved by a two-thirds majority of the participants (including proxy votes). The convention provides opportunities for members to discuss activities of the past year, future policy, and accounts, and to approve new board members, who are elected by a majority vote. Every union member can participate in the convention and has the right to vote.

The WUT also has an executive board, which included fifteen people in 2004. Executive board members are responsible for: carrying out decisions approved at the convention; attending all meetings (tardiness and absence are recorded); reporting on all actions carried out in the name of the union; and listening to others' opinions, respecting differences, and creating an atmosphere in which members can express their thoughts. The executive board holds monthly meetings, which must have a quorum and be approved by a majority of board members. A unanimous vote is required to make decisions as a union; in other cases, a two-thirds vote by the board members is necessary. All union members can participate in monthly meetings; however, only executive board members have the right to vote in those meetings.

The WUT also holds monthly case-study meetings in which members who are currently involved in bargaining, lawsuits, or some other form of dispute resolution can report on their cases. Members can also recruit other members to join their bargaining team or support group at this meeting.[3] Although all members can participate in case-study meetings, generally only executive board members and the individuals pursuing grievances attend.

Network-Style Organization

Network-style unions provide an organizational option for people who are employed by companies that have no existing union, employees who are ineligible for membership in their company's union, and minorities who are underserved by their unions. Previously, if an existing union was unresponsive to women's issues, women employees essentially had two choices. They could either organize a minority block inside the union or form a secondary union that would be inside the company but outside the original union. In both cases, their organizations would constitute a minority voice with very little leverage. Moreover, real minority unions (those that aren't started by the company to undermine an existing union) frequently face opposition from both the employer and the primary union. And, as Midori discovered, the company and an existing company union will sometimes team up to squelch upstart minority groups.

Midori and Tani decided on a network structure as a way to address these issues. By organizing across companies and across industries, the network structure enables women to organize both nonorganized and under-organized women and to form unions in which women are not the minority. Also, since network unions exist outside the single-enterprise environment, they are less vulnerable to underhanded machinations by the company or the company union. And they encourage members to develop strategies beyond a single organizational logic (in this case, strategies for promoting the interests of women workers rather than for employees of a particular company), which might be a better base for future movement building.

Principle of Individual Affiliation

According to Tani and Midori, the individual-membership structure is necessary for a variety of reasons. First, it enables women to create unions in which they are not minorities. Women have had limited success in getting traditional unions to expend resources on women's issues because both their organizational logic and ideology impel enterprise unions to put the male majority first. Even when women organize an internal women's departments or some other form of minority caucus to amplify their voices, the union leadership will side with the dominant majority if the women's demands conflict with male employees' interests.

Second, joining an individual-membership union is much easier than trying to organize a new union. The prospect of organizing a union is daunting for anyone, even more so for someone who is already in the midst of a crisis at work. With individual-membership unions, an embattled employee can seek immediate help—even if no one else in the workplace is willing to stick out their necks. Individual-membership unions also can be a life raft for women who are being bullied. That is no small thing. In all the years I've been interviewing Japanese women's union members, I have not met a single woman who *did not* become the target of bullying as soon as she started to resist. Individual-membership unions give these otherwise isolated women a place to go for advice, resources, and emotional support.

The principle of individual membership also allows workers from a variety of occupations and industries to unite, which, from the perspective of building a broad-based women's movement, is a big advantage. Not only does it offer the possibility of organizing a broader range and (potentially) a larger number of women, it also allows the members to better analyze the gender dimension of their workplace problems by enabling them to see how gender plays out in an array of work settings.

Finally, individual unions are important because options for handling individual grievances are disappearing, especially for the growing number of employees who are not eligible for membership in an enterprise union. Part of that is the result of political machinations. Conservative forces such as the Ishihara administration in Tokyo, put the squeeze on government agencies that handle grievances. Labor administration offices, which have the highest rate among governmental agencies for settling cases, are being eliminated and replaced with "information centers" (WUT 2004a).

By the time I first interviewed Midori and Tani, they had put into practice many of the ideas that grew out of their experiences as workers and as activists. Their union based on feminist principles was up and running, and it was effective in helping women resolve individual grievances. Within five years of its founding, the WUT had successfully overturned wrongful dismissals, blocked forced retirements, corrected wage disputes, and negotiated settlements in harassment cases. These victories made important differences in real women's lives, albeit usually one person at a time. But I was curious about the status of the WUT's larger goals, such as taking on issues at a global rather than individual level, generating an ever-growing, self-sustaining membership whose momentum would lead to the development of a larger women's movement, and creating conditions that organically foster solidarity and a person-to-person flow of knowledge and skills that would inspire and enable women to be long-term activists. I wondered whether the union had made any progress on those kinds of goals. More to the point, I wondered whether any individual union could generate the level of activity and leverage the kind of power necessary to achieve those goals. In the end, my first encounter with the WUT raised more questions than it answered, and I wanted nothing more than to further my inquiries. Apparently Midori and Tani could see that in my face because, when I mentioned that I would be in Japan for the next six months, they invited me to come back as often as I wanted to meet the members and observe the union in action.

WOMEN'S UNION TOKYO IN PRACTICE

Over the next five months I met with dozens of WUT members, including caregivers, educators, account managers, sales representatives, cooks, factory workers, and clerical employees, often referred to as "office ladies." I attended union-membership meetings and case-study meetings in which the progress of active grievances was reviewed and future strategies were outlined. I participated in lectures and workshops, and got to know members on a more personal level by attending parties and other social events that would attract WUT members and other feminist activists. I was allowed to sit in on inner sanctum activities, including bargaining sessions and meetings to discuss problems within the union. I even got to go on the WUT's annual retreat, where the vibe was decidedly laid-back, and anything and everything related to the union was up for discussion.

At first, the union's openness surprised me. Few organizations are keen to let outsiders riffle through their metaphorical underwear drawer, and yet the WUT welcomed not just me but several other researchers, journalists, and activists who were interested in women's organizations. One reason for their transparency was that the members saw the WUT as a potential model for other women who work in circumstances that aren't conducive to traditional organizing. They wanted as many women as possible to hear about their union, and in enough detail that they could consider its possibilities for their own circumstances.

A second reason for the union's openness was that the leaders freely admitted the WUT was a work-in-progress and openly sought input from other activists and scholars. For me as a journalist, this was a very new experience. Established organizations—unions, companies, schools, whatever—are usually at great pains to manage what we see and hear about them. It's all about controlling the message and creating the right image. But the WUT was completely devoid of that spirit of ass-covering, perhaps because the union was new enough that controlling its image was not the leadership's first concern, and because the leadership wasn't interested in concealing the union's problems—they were interested in resolving them. The WUT invited people like me to shine our spotlights into their darkest corners because they wanted to flesh out those problems, examine them in detail, and collect a variety of ideas about how to resolve them. They believed in the power of collective analysis and collective creativity and they sought collective solutions. The upshot, as far as I was concerned, was that I was going to get to see a Japanese women's union in action, warts and all, and report on it to my reform-minded colleagues at home.

If the women I'd met in my everyday life in Tokyo challenged stereotypes about Japanese women, the women I met through the WUT tore those stereotypes to shreds. The women I met in those first few weeks were experienced, hard-core activists. At the bargaining table they were skilled negotiators, unfazed by intimidation tactics, corporate trickery, and lawyerly sleights of hand. They were well versed in Japanese labor and anti-discrimination laws, and their knowledge of international labor laws eclipsed my own by a long shot. (I was frequently called out for the US government's failure to endorse or enforce international workplace and gender-equity standards, many of which I had never heard of, as if I had any say in the matter.)[1] Many had attended national and international feminist and labor forums, which was reflected in their sophisticated analysis of the workings of gender discrimination in the Japanese economy, and the ways Japanese companies perpetuated gender inequality at home and abroad. At the same time, they articulated a social vision that went beyond gender and labor equity. They were also concerned with environmental issues, the treatment of foreign nationals living in Japan, Japan's increasing use of its self-defense forces in international conflicts, and so on. In other words, these women had the skills and knowledge of full-time professional activists, even though most of them had outside jobs and family responsibilities as well. Their intensity, their dedication, their absolute defiance in the face of overwhelming odds made them exhilarating to be around.

And yet, there was one glaring problem. The women I saw answering phones on Monday were the same ones I saw at the bargaining table on Thursday and working the fund-raiser on Saturday, which seemed a far cry from the task-sharing collective the founders intended to create. I soon learned that, although on paper the union's membership hovered around 250 women (which is itself a vanishingly small number in a city the size of Tokyo), the union had actually developed as a de facto two-tier union: with one tier being the small group of experienced activists who were doing virtually all of the work; and the other a much larger rotating cast of women who were active members while their cases were pending, but who tended to fade away and eventually drop out once their individual problems had been solved.

The unintended division within the membership undermined the union in several ways. To begin with, it perpetuated and exacerbated the union's internal labor shortage. The founding members knew they would have to do most of the work in the beginning, but they expected that period to be temporary because the pool of skilled activists would grow as new members gained skills and experience by working on their own cases. Yet, five years after its founding, that expectation was not panning out. In fact, the situation was getting worse. The early members were still doing almost all of the work, while the number of women asking for help increased over time. As dedicated as those core activists were, even they couldn't keep up that pace forever.

The two-tier problem also radically constrained the union's ability to fulfill its mission. It was all the core members could do just to keep up with the growing number of requests for job counseling and bargaining. There was virtually no time or energy left for functions that were necessary for the union's ability to fulfill its larger mission. Fund-raising, membership education, community outreach, all the activities that unions must engage in to grow in membership and influence were getting short shrift. With so few active members, there was no time for fund-raising; with no fund-raising there was no money for developing educational materials; and with no educational materials there was no way to foster consciousness and solidarity. With no consciousness and solidarity, members drop out, leaving fewer members to carry the load, fewer members to contribute to union coffers, and the cycle begins again. Despite its grander social vision, the WUT was becoming increasingly limited to resolving individual grievances, rather than creating an environment in which such grievances would be less likely to occur.

Equally heartbreaking, the split was undermining the union's intention of operating along feminist principles of decentralized power and shared decision making. The founders had developed a committee structure and regular meetings to give members a say in all aspects of decision making, from electing executive board members to allocating resources, to setting political and legislative priorities. But peripheral members rarely joined committees and rarely attended meetings where votes would be taken, meaning they rarely availed themselves of decision-making opportunities. In effect, and against the union's most heartfelt wishes and organizational design, power and decision making were pooling in the hands of an elite leadership, leaving peripheral members disconnected and disengaged while the core members were frustrated because their union, in spite of itself, was reproducing the exact sort of hierarchy it sought to break down.

Finally, the division within the membership, and related to that, the union's failure to grow, were sapping morale because they contradicted one of the central tenets of the WUT's philosophy. The union's viability and potential for sparking a broader women's movement were premised on the idea that the act of participating in the union would organically organize the members.[2] The founders believed that participating in the union would be a transformative experience. Women who came to the union for help with their individual problems would, by virtue of experiencing collective action, undergo a shift in consciousness. They would, organically, start thinking and acting collectively. They would, organically, choose to stay on with the union, choose to do for newcomers what the founding members did for them, and choose to reach out to other women and women's groups to build a larger women's movement. It was all supposed to happen naturally, automatically, as an outgrowth of their own experience with the union. But it did not, even (and, as we would later learn, especially not) for women whose cases had been bargained successfully (WUT 2004b).

The core members were well aware of these problems. In interviews, new members with active grievances generally talked in great detail about their problems at work and the union's efforts to help them resolve their issues with their employers. But the veteran members rarely talked about their own histories. Instead, they talked about how exhausted they were from trying to keep up with the steady stream of bargaining requests, and how frustrated they were that so few of the women who got help from the union would stick around to help the women who came after them. Most of all, though, they talked about their fears for the union's future. At some point, the cohort that was doing all the heavy lifting would be gone and what would happen to the union then?

Origin of the US-Japan Project

Over the course of getting to know the WUT and its members, my purpose changed. Initially, my goal was to study this new form of organizing in the hopes of finding insights I could take back with me to share with my reform-minded colleagues in the United States. But as I got to know the core members, saw their predicament, and watched them become increasingly exhausted with every success, I stopped being just an observer and joined the conversation. Seeing firsthand the indignities Japanese women are subjected to at work, the undeniable need for organizations that would address women's issues, and yet the precarious situation such organizations were in, it was no longer enough to simply understand how this new union functioned. In spite of the fact that I was an outsider, in spite of the reality that I had to leave Japan in just a few months, I became committed to finding some way to contribute to helping the WUT break through the tangle of barriers that was holding the union back. I don't think I ever formally announced my change in purpose to Midori and Tani; I didn't need to. Our conversations had naturally shifted into problem-solving mode before I was even aware of it. Although Midori and Tani were skeptical that there was any solution beyond everyone simply working harder, they and other WUT members were always willing to sit down and hash over ideas with me as I cast about for an alternate way forward.

The first step was a period of intense analysis and discussion. Although the union of course had to go on with all of its regular tasks, whenever and wherever we were together—at union meetings, at social gatherings, in seminars with other activists—our discussions always came back to the central question that was on all of our minds: Why didn't women who had received help from the WUT become permanent members, and what could the union do about it? Many of the members blamed the negative image of unions in general, and the WUT's inability to create a more positive image and experience of union membership. They particularly stressed the need to reach out to young women who would have the energy and new ideas to make the union more vital. But young people, especially those who had not yet encountered significant problems on the job, generally saw unions as dry, dusty institutions from another era—repositories for commies, losers, and whiners, definitely not people they wanted to be associated with as they sought to climb the corporate ladder. To bring young women into the union, and to encourage them to stay, the union would not only need the resources to present their new type of union in a more positive and engaging light, it would also need the resources to rework its internal operations to make the reality of union membership fit that image. The WUT needed to offer experiences that were more positive and less confrontational than the steady diet of bargaining sessions, crisis intervention, and endless meetings that characterized much of WUT membership.

Other members, especially Tani and Midori, thought that the high drop-out rate was evidence that the WUT was not doing enough to empower women individually. They argued that the union needed to do more to empower women while they were in the process of bargaining their own cases so that, by the time their cases were resolved, they would be so energized they would want to stay on as part of the movement. The problem for so many Japanese women, Midori told me, is that they don't believe they can make a difference in the world. But once they start to see themselves and other women doing things they thought were impossible—facing down the boss, talking to elected officials, giving testimony on pending legislation—they would see the union in a whole new way and want to be part of the movement that was changing their society. In other words, the members who advocated this position had not changed their assumptions about participation organically leading to consciousness; they just thought the union needed to work harder and do more to make that happen.

Coming from a significantly different context, I had a different take on the source of their problems. To my mind, the WUT's difficulty in overcoming negative stereotypes about unions and its inability to more fully empower its members were symptoms of a much more fundamental problem. My opinion was that the WUT was structured in a way that was fundamentally at odds with the kinds of outcomes the union's founders were hoping to achieve. Specifically, the WUT would never have the human and financial resources necessary for accomplishing its goals so long as it remained structured as an individual-membership, service-style union.

Service Unions

Service unions are notorious for producing high dropout rates and low levels of participation among members. To solve problems on the job, service unions tend to emphasize what the union (positioned as an entity outside the membership) can do for the members, rather than what the members can do for themselves through collective action. They typically employ professional staff to represent members at the bargaining table, in grievance hearings, and in other legal forums. They also tend to focus on bread-and-butter issues, to be bureaucratic in structure, and to use direct action sparingly and often in merely symbolic ways.

Service unions were popular in the United States in the 1970s and '80s because they relieved working people of the burden of trying to run a union after a full day's work. But, over time, the service structure weakened US unions by taking the members and their collective power out of the equation. As members got used to their issues being settled by lawyers and boardroom negotiations, they lost the experience of standing up for themselves, of feeling their collective power coursing through their veins, and of seeing the results of their actions. Instead of seeing the union as an expression of their own power, members began thinking of the union as an outside agency—like a law firm or insurance company—whose job it was to fix their problems. Concepts such as solidarity and active participation lost their meaning because, in the members' minds, they've "hired" the union to do it for them.

From my perspective, the WUT had inadvertently structured itself in a way that inevitably recreated service-union dynamics. These conversations were taking place in early 2001, when the so-called Sweeney Revolution—a reform movement that rejected the service model and advocated restructuring unions to rely on direct action and membership participation—was big news among labor folk. I was frequently invited by labor and other social movement organizations, including the WUT, to give talks on the subject, so WUT members frequently heard me talk about the inherent weaknesses of service unions. Initially, I hoped that those talks would prompt WUT members to start asking themselves questions about their own service-oriented operations and how they might be contributing to the union's problems. But, while the women agreed in theory that service-style unionism undermines workers' power, the WUT never saw itself as a service union. Its goals, so global in scope, were commensurate with the broader social movement orientation of activist unions. Above all else, their purpose was to unleash the inner-activist in each of their members. With this being the union's most dearly held intention, the members couldn't see that in both structure and practice the WUT was a classic service union. Nothing made that more clear than the language they used to reach out to potential members. On their website, in their ads, and in their conversations with other women, the WUT promoted itself as a place for women to come to *get help*. As *individuals*. *When* they had a problem on the job. While that is a very accurate description of what the WUT does, it is not at all the talk of an activist union.

At bottom, the central conundrum for the WUT was that the leaders wanted the grand outcomes of the big industrial unions in their heyday, but they had fashioned an organization whose structure bypasses the very weapon that made those outcomes possible: the workers' ability to shut down the company's operations by collectively withholding their labor. Since individual-union members are scattered across companies and industries, the chance of the union having enough members in any one enterprise or industry to make a work stoppage a viable threat is extremely low, and management knows that.[3]

Individual Unionism in Practice

Midori and Tani chose the individual-membership structure to make it easier for women to join the union, but the union they were joining was necessarily less powerful than other forms of unions. I saw that very clearly when I attended union bargaining sessions. The first bargaining session I attended concerned a woman named Hasegawa who had become the target of harassment when the company she worked for merged with a newer company whose first goal was to shed staff. Hasegawa had worked for her company for eleven years as an account specialist in the sales division. Soon after the merger, the new company restructured in ways that were designed to elbow out the employees from the older company. The new company eliminated several job categories, forcing those employees into lower-level jobs with less responsibility and lower pay. The unwanted employees also received not-so-subtle hints, such as being transferred to a new position but denied training or even an explanation of what that new job entails. Most of the employees bowed to the pressure and resigned, but Hasegawa said that as a woman she didn't have that luxury. If she left this job, not only would she have to start over at the very bottom of her new company, as a midcareer woman she would almost certainly have to accept a part-time or temporary job.[4]

The session I attended was not their first meeting. I could tell as soon as we walked in the room that a feeling of acrimony had already accrued between the two sides. There were no opening niceties. As we took our seats, each side muttered a curt hello then segued almost immediately to shouting. I recognized the company negotiators' tactic. They were deliberately trying to pick a fight with Hasegawa. The lead negotiator insulted her, talked over her, and treated her as dismissively as he could without actually reaching across the table and patting her on the head. It's a typical stalling tactic negotiators use when they are meeting strictly out of legal obligation and have no intention of actually bargaining. The idea is to chew up time with pointless squabbling until the grievant runs out of money or patience and gives up.

On the union side, I was impressed by how Hasegawa handled herself in the face of open hostility. She spoke for herself forcefully and with confidence. She made a compelling case, calling on the company to do the right thing and treat long-term loyal employees honorably and with respect. But there was absolutely no movement from the other side of the table because the union had no bargaining chip and the company knew it. Short of taking the case to court or arbitration, the union's only hope was to play the endurance game: to keep pestering the company until it either offered Hasegawa a settlement to rid themselves of the nuisance or fired her, which would be actionable in court. But that tends to be a high-cost, low-impact strategy for the union. It eats up enormous amounts of time and energy, two resources that are already in short supply. And it typically only works for relatively low-stakes, one-off grievances. For small, single grievances, a company might well decide that it's cheaper to give in than to continue sending a negotiator to meet with a union that is proving to be irksomely tenacious. But not so for the kinds of sweeping work-rules changes the WUT ultimately hopes to usher in. No company is going to give in on using low-wage temp workers if using them is increasing its bottom line. To win those kinds of victories, the union has to be able to make the cost of pursuing the offending practices higher than the cost of eliminating them. And that takes a united workforce, not an individual grievant. Finally, bargaining on behalf of an individual leaves the door open to retaliation. We saw a lot of that in WUT cases. Women who returned to work after settling a grievance often found themselves permanently marked as disloyal troublemakers, and permanently marginalized within the company.

Another problem with the individual-membership structure is that it keeps the WUT's focus firmly trained on individual grievances, undermining the union's ability to foster solidarity and union consciousness among its members and to articulate a compelling reason for women to stay on with the union after their individual grievances are resolved. When core members talk to new members about the need for them to stay on after their grievances are resolved, they tend to frame their arguments in terms of members' duty, either to pay back the union for the help they received or to pay their debt forward by sticking around to help future members. Another common argument was that members should stay on in case they run into another problem in the future. But neither of these arguments was effective. To begin with, instilling a sense of duty is not the same as fostering solidarity. Japanese women are already drowning in duty and obligation: to their children, to their husbands, to their families, to their jobs. I can't imagine anywhere in the world that unions could hope to compete for women's time on the grounds of some abstract notion of duty to unknown others; not when they have their own families to care for. The only way most women can justify giving time to their unions is if their continued participation will continue to benefit them and their families directly. Unions that seek to build a strong, lasting workplace presence can provide continuous benefit to workers, but individual-membership unions, with their emphasis on resolving grievances rather than organizing workplaces, do not.

Moreover, an individual union's inability to retain members exacerbates the workload crisis that the WUT and other Japanese women's unions face. Women rarely come to the union unless they have an existing problem. And in most cases their problem has reached the crisis stage and they need immediate help. That means each new member represents an increase in the union's workload and additional strain on the union's resources, but without simultaneously adding to the union's strength. Also, by keeping the union tethered to a constant stream of incoming grievances, the individual structure reinforces the image of the union as a service organization, a place for individuals to get help, rather than a way for them to help themselves.

But perhaps the biggest cost is that members never experience the full potential of what it means to be in a union. Individual unions give their members a way to redress grievances, but they can't give members an ongoing voice in workplace practices or protection against management abuses and misdeeds before they happen. An ongoing union presence is especially important in Japanese workplaces, where intimidation and bullying are routine management practices. Earlier, I talked about the part-time employee who became the target of bullying after she asked management to scale back her excessive workload. Her supervisor took to calling her into the office every morning and ordering her to write a letter of apology for the fabricated infraction du jour. As an individual-membership union, there was little the WUT could do for her except to demand after-the-fact remedies. On the other hand, if that woman had been a member of a union with a strong workplace presence, she and her fellow union members could have taken matters into their own hands on the spot. For example, they could march into the supervisor's office en masse and inform him that, from now on, if he wanted to meet with the employee, it would be in the presence of her fellow union members or not at all. Whatever other benefits individual-membership unions have, they cannot offer the kind of power that comes from direct, on-the-spot collective action.

The WUT activists understood the disadvantages of the individual model but said that women's position in the labor force is too precarious and their workplaces are often too small (or distributed) for traditional workplace organizing to be a viable option. Since the WUT's raison d'être was to provide options for women who fall through the cracks of traditional organizing, the union has to give those women the option to join as individuals or the WUT would be abandoning its core constituency. Tani told me, emphatically, that while fully recognizing the social origins of the discriminatory practices working women face and the limitations of individual-membership unions, Japanese women's unions must, of necessity, treat women's problems on an individual basis (interview 2004).

Much like undocumented workers in the United States, women workers in Japan say they need a new approach that better fits their specific circumstances (see Fine 2006). Instead of building workers' power, the WUT leaders argued that Japanese women need to look toward building alliances with other working women's groups across the country. Instead of collectively confronting capital as workers, the WUT activists seek to create a powerful network of women's groups with diverse skill sets that can exert pressure from multiple angles—legal, political, social, discursive, and economic—to force changes in Japanese business practices.

Fair enough, this was their movement and certainly they understood what would and would not work for Japanese women far better than I did. Since the individual-membership structure was nonnegotiable, our next step was to explore possibilities for counteracting the inherent weakness of that model, particularly its lack of ability to foster consciousness and participation among the membership. It seemed to me that the WUT needed to develop internal organizing practices, beginning with an educational program to help members develop basic activist's skills (to give them the ability and confidence to play a more active role in the union) and to introduce them to feminist and union principles and perspectives. Tani in particular recognized the value of a program that would help disseminate the skills and knowledge of each generation of members to the next. We talked often about internal organizing and membership education programs in the United States, such as the Service Employees International Union's worker-to-worker organizing program. But when I explained that programs designed for US workers wouldn't necessarily work in a Japanese context and that Japanese activists would need to use content and teaching methods that fit Japanese women's circumstances, all the air seemed to go out of the room. While some of the union leaders recognized the benefits of membership education in theory, they had no concept of what such a program would look like in practice, much less how to create one of their own. And even if they did, where would they get the time, money, and energy to take on yet another project? I had, in effect, just offered a bucket of water to a drowning man.

Just as my time in Japan was coming to an end, it seemed we had reached an impasse. A number of ideas were on the table for possible paths forward but all of them required an expenditure of resources we didn't have. The Japanese women were firmly convinced that there were no new resources to be had from inside Japan. They said that if they were going to find some way to keep the union going, it would have to come from reaching even more deeply into themselves and "powering through" the union's struggles. Noble, no doubt, but not a sustainable plan in my opinion. I didn't and still don't know enough about Japanese civil society to know whether there were other sources of funding and support for emerging unions and women's groups, but even if there were no new home-grown resources for us to tap into, I was certain that we could find sharable resources and new allies if we looked beyond national borders. I firmly believed that if we could develop some kind of exchange project to bring Japanese and US activists together, and give them the tools they would need to engage in meaningful problem solving, their combined knowledge, experiences, and creativity would help the Japanese women find ways to break through their current impasse. At the same time, such an exchange would introduce US activists to the fresh new ideas that were coming out of Japan's alternative union movement, which was largely unknown outside that corner of Asia.

I returned to the United States in the spring of 2001, determined to find a way to get Japanese and US activists in the same room to tackle these thorny issues. It took two years to pull all the pieces together. I moved back to Tokyo in the spring of 2002 with the beginnings of an idea (but no funding) for an international solidarity project to foster sustained knowledge and resource exchange between US and Japanese activists and scholars who were interested in working women's issues. The project would have many branches but would likely center on helping emerging organizations develop the resources they need to train their members to become effective, engaged activists. Midori and Tani supported the idea, and with their help I was able to reach out to other feminist labor activists in the Tokyo area to get their input on what such a project should look like.[5] The WUT held various internal union meetings as well as open discussions with other women's groups through which the plan for a US-Japan exchange project continued to grow and evolve. As word of our efforts spread, we gained several important allies, including feminist scholars Kazuko Tanaka, professor of sociology and founder of the International Christian University's Gender Center in Tokyo, and Heidi Gottfried, professor of sociology at Wayne State University, whose research area includes employment policies and women's movements in Japan, Europe, and North America. Their participation was crucial, not only for the wealth of knowledge and added "manpower" they brought to the table but also because their academic affiliations gave the project a legitimacy that is rarely bestowed on small, grassroots organizations on their own—a legitimacy that was necessary to capture the kinds of grant dollars we needed to proceed.

Once Heidi and Kazuko joined the project, all of the elements were in place. We secured funding to hold three international workshops over the course of two years to educate each other about working women's organizations and their activities in each country, to explore ideas for creating workers' organizations that would be more democratic and responsive to women and other minorities, and to help the Japanese groups develop their own labor education programs as a crucial first step in facilitating member retention. The international meetings were intended to provide a forum for women to share their ideas, experiences, and the practical knowledge they had gained through their union activities, in the hope that such cross-pollination would produce new insights that might not be visible from a single vantage point. Because we wanted the international meetings to act as a petri dish, as a place where previously unforeseeable ideas would have space to grow, we didn't want to impose too many preconceived parameters on the project at this beginning stage. Nevertheless, we did have a few specific, long-term goals we expected the project to achieve.

At the international level, our goal was to build lasting relationships among Japanese and US women's organizations. We hoped that the project would lay the foundation for an international solidarity network through which US and Japanese working women could continue to share information and resources, develop coordinated campaigns, and provide support for each other's efforts to increase gender equality in the workplace. At the national level, the project was aimed at fostering similar solidarity ties among women's organizations within Japan. Ultimately, we hoped the project would be the catalyst for a national network of women's organizations which, like the international network, would enable under-resourced women's groups to pool information and resources, leverage greater power with employers as well as public policymakers, and provide support for each other's cases and campaigns. The third goal of the project was to give grassroots Japanese groups access to educational methods and materials developed by their US counterparts to serve as a basis for creating their own peer-to-peer membership education program appropriate for the Japanese context. The fourth goal was to provide opportunities for both sides to explore the promises and the challenges of network-style unions in post-industrial economies, where traditional models of unionism (big industrial unions in the United States and company unions in Japan) have proved to be irrelevant or unworkable for broad swathes of the workforce. Finally, we hoped that the process of collaboration would stimulate discussions on some of the broader theoretical issues that reformers must address but that often get sidelined by more immediate, hot-button concerns that arise on a daily basis. In particular, we hoped the project would provide a concrete basis for asking questions about the relationship between the ways Japanese organizations were structured and the particular chronic problems these organizations faced.

Part 2

US-JAPAN CROSSBORDER COLLABORATION

FIRST, WE DRINK TEA

The planning phase for the first international workshop was, by turns, eye opening, funny, tedious, frustrating, and creatively demanding. And doing it through the stifling heat of a Tokyo summer in the cramped, under-air-conditioned office of the Women's Union Tokyo did not ease the task. But the sheer excitement of what we hoped to accomplish got us through the rough spots. We had assembled a unique team of women who had already done so much to improve the lives of working women through their activism, scholarship, and teaching; women with vision, who knew the circumstances in their respective countries cold and knew how to put ideas into action. Simply by bringing these women together, we could help to produce a breakthrough for this nascent Japanese women's movement and perhaps even spark a new wave of innovation in US women's organizations based on the example and enthusiasm of the Japanese activists.

Thinking of it that way, I felt that this was the most important thing I would ever do in my career. And that thought was very motivating while the workshops were in the planning phase and the concrete reality well off in the distance. But, as I stepped onto the plane heading to Detroit for the first of the three workshops, the flip side of that statement hit me: What if it doesn't work? What if this project is a giant fizzle? A phhhht? What if the women greet each other's stories with a deep and resounding primal shrug? I took a few deep breaths and told myself, realistically, that wasn't going to happen. We had succeeded in outlining the problems the Japanese women's organizations faced, secured enough funding to give us time and opportunity to go in-depth into the problems, and attracted an impressive array of US and Japanese activists who were extremely dedicated to improving working conditions for women. There was no chance the project would fall flat from lack of interest. But there was still one very real concern: What if we are not able to bridge the language and cultural barriers? What if the women aren't able to communicate the particularities of their situations well enough to enable the group to engage in meaningful problem solving? More than anything, I did not want this project to end up being just another feel-good, motivational encounter. I wanted something permanent and real to come out of it. In my heart of hearts, I hoped the Japanese women might even retool their organizations to make them less service-based and more focused on organizing women across the board, not just those with active grievances. But, even if they didn't go that route, I wanted our project to both spark and facilitate deep, meaningful change that would enable the Japanese women's unions to move beyond their current plateaus and grow into the kind of organizations their founders envisioned. If we couldn't communicate with each other beyond the level of what we have in common as targets of discrimination, however, that wasn't going to happen. The project would go the way of the other US-Japan encounters I had seen. We would all feel happy and energized at the end, but when the Japanese women got home, they'd still have the same problems to contend with and no new tools or strategies for fighting back. It was that much more realistic fear that kept me company on the thirteen-hour flight back to the United States.

First Impressions

We met for the first time at Wayne State University in Detroit on September 24–25, 2004. I arrived a few days early to get a head start on combating jet lag and to help Heidi and her staff handle last minute details on the ground. We took turns going to the airport to greet our incoming guests. This was my first chance to meet several of the Japanese participants from organizations other than the WUT. I was struck by the energy and hopefulness they exuded, even as they stepped off their long flights. I was especially impressed by Kiyoko Ban, an activist about ten years my senior who looked as fresh and energetic as someone who had just stepped out of a spa. She immediately went to work networking with me and the other activists who shared the airport limo back to our hotel. She talked very fast in Japanese and, since I was still a little brain-dead from jet lag, I was having some trouble following what she was telling me about herself. It sounded as though she said she is currently working "part-time" at a bank, running the family farm, working as a full-time homemaker, volunteering at the part-time workers' union, and trying to launch a new women's union. I thought I had gotten the tenses wrong; surely those were things she had done over the course of her life. But no, turns out I'd heard her right the first time. These were all things she was doing right now, *and* she was thinking of converting part of her farmhouse into a bed-and-breakfast (or B&B). I couldn't bear to ask what she'd done in her younger years.

The US contingent arrived with equal enthusiasm. Some were old friends of mine, people I had had the privilege of working with in Chicago. Others were women I knew only from reading their books or from their achievements as activists. Most of them had never heard of the Japanese women's movement until we contacted them for this project, yet it was clear from their energy that they were happy to be here and eager to learn more about these fledgling women's organizations. My first rush of the project came when I walked into the lobby and saw a number of the women trying their best to mingle as they slogged through the interminable check-in procedure. Shrieks of laughter filled the air as they tried to pantomime their way through self-introductions and words of welcome. Despite the language barrier and before anything official had gotten under way, the room was already filled with so much excitement and goodwill that I knew we had cleared the first hurdle.

I remember very little else about that day, except that several of the Japanese women commented with concern on the apparent "fanciness" of our accommodations. They were concerned that we had spent too much money on a place we would only use to sleep and grab quick breakfasts. I tried to assure them that, despite its outward appearance, the B&B was no more costly than staying at one of the budget motels in downtown, particularly when you took into account the cost of transportation. From the B&B we could walk to the conference center on campus, whereas we would need to take cabs from any of the available budget motels. Meanwhile, the B&B seemed to be trying its utmost to assure the guests that it was indeed a low-budget establishment by providing spectacularly bad service, faulty rooms, and a seemingly endless supply of spoiled milk for our morning coffee. And yet, the image of Grand Old Manor held steadfast in the Japanese participants' minds and marked the beginning of one of the cultural misperceptions that would come back to haunt us again and again throughout the project. But we didn't know that at the time. It was early in the project and I was naïve enough to think that the specter of possible food poisoning was a problem worth worrying about. Little did I know that in the scheme of what was to come over the next few years, those curdled lumps in my coffee were small potatoes compared to the dramas that lay before us.

Formally, We Begin

The next morning we made our way to the conference center. The first thing that struck me as I walked into the conference room was that the positive energy I had felt in the lobby the day before seemed temporarily replaced by a hint of shyness in the face of formality and class markers. The conference room was large and elegant compared to the meeting rooms available to most of the Japanese women's groups. A fully equipped simultaneous translation booth manned by two translators and a sound engineer sat in one corner of the room. In another corner was an elaborate spread of fruits, pastries, and a giant silver coffee urn—luxuries that seemed starkly anomalous to most of the activists in the room. My mind flashed back to the cramped conditions in which the WUT women make tea to honor their guests and I felt a pang of embarrassment. There were a few tense moments as the participants walked in and inadvertently divided themselves along national lines. In this more formal setting, the Japanese participants suddenly seemed uncomfortable and became alarmingly reserved. One by one they each went to the same side of the room and sat quietly together. At the same time, several of the US participants were rushing with boisterous enthusiasm to the other side of the room to greet each other. There was nothing nefarious in their actions. Feminism is a small world, and the world of Labor Feminism is smaller still. Many of the US women had long histories together as friends and as colleagues, and for them this was a rare and happy reunion. The problem was that it was happening at the same instant the Japanese were experiencing an especially alienating moment, where everything was uncomfortably unfamiliar to them, except for the uncomfortably familiar markers of class and national privilege that highlighted the inequalities between the two sides.

Mercifully, that dynamic was short lived. A few of the US organizers were quick to spot a dividing line forming and immediately went to sit with the Japanese women and pantomime their "good mornings." As people settled into their seats and the welcoming speeches got under way, the feeling of cohesiveness from the night before began to reemerge and I felt like the workshop was officially on its way.

Purpose

The purpose of this first meeting was to get to know each other, personally and organizationally, in as much detail as possible in preparation for the collaborative work we hoped to do in Workshops II and III. We needed this first in-person meeting to put a human face on the organizations and issues we would spend the next three years talking about. We also hoped that we would all begin forming personal attachments with each other, which would help sustain the project over the long haul and help us to gel as a committed, collaborative group. At the organizational level, we needed to learn everything we could about each other's operations, and about the labor laws and institutions we have to deal with, before we could engage in realistic problem solving and program development. We especially needed to understand the constraints the Japanese women's groups face in order for our discussions to yield meaningful innovations that could be put into practice. In short, we wanted to walk away from Workshop I with a deep enough commitment and a solid enough knowledge base that we could spend the next three years working together—in concrete and practical ways—to make women's organizations on both sides stronger.

Format

Since the first meeting was about laying an informational foundation, we structured it like a conference, with a series of talks followed by Q&A. Most of the talks focused on introducing the various women's groups. Representatives from each women's group provided written and oral reports describing their organization's goals, origins, structure, strategies, current projects, major operating problems, and problem-solving efforts to date. We also heard from a variety of labor analysts about the state of long-standing hot-button issues including sexual harassment, part-time employment, and comparable worth. These presentations, coupled with historical and economic perspectives provided by US and Japanese scholars, gave us a concrete basis for specific strategy and materials-development discussions in the subsequent workshops.

Participants

The US speakers included several academics who specialize in gender and labor studies, including: Dorothy Sue Cobble from Rutgers University; Louise Fitzgerald from the University of Illinois at Urbana; Ronnie Steinberg from Vanderbilt University; and Cynthia Negrey from the University of Louisville. On the Japanese side, the academic participants included: Shunko Ishiro from Tokoha Gakuen University; Takeo Kinoshita from Showa Women's University; and Kazuko Tanaka from the International Christian University, who, along with Heidi and I, cohosted the workshop. The three Japanese professors also represented the Society for the Study of Working Women.

The participants from Japanese women's organizations included: Kiyoko Ban from *Fureai* Part-time Workers' Union in Nagoya; Kayoko Akabane and Fumiko Yakabi from Kansai Women's Union (KWU) and *ICORU* Human Rights Center, both in the Osaka area; Keiko Kondō from Sapporo Women's Union; Toyomi Fujii, Midori Ito, Makiko Takagi, and Keiko Tani from Women's Union Tokyo; and Emi Naruse and Kazuko Sazaki from Working Women's Voices in Fukuoka.[1]

From US labor organizations were: Gloria Johnson from the Coalition of Labor Union Women (CLUW); Linda Meric from 9to5; Karla Swift of the United Automobile Workers (UAW) Women's Department; UNITE HERE Local 34 President Laura Smith and worker/organizer Beverly Vail; United Electrical Workers (UE) organizer Leah Fried; Emily Rosenberg, director of the DePaul University Labor Education Center; and Tess Ewing from the University of Massachusetts Boston Labor Extension Program and the Women in Leadership Development (WILD) program.

The Cobble Effect

We had asked Dorothy Sue Cobble to open the conference with a talk on the history of US Labor Feminism to provide the historical context to help the Japanese audience understand how the US organizations they were about to hear from fit into the larger picture of women's and workers' social movements; when, how, and why they arose; and why they took the particular shapes they did. She did that handily. But in the end, her presentation also accomplished something far more important by enabling the Japanese women to see that they have a lot more in common with their sisters from the United States than they imagined.

Beginning with the mobilization of women's groups in response to the Triangle Shirtwaist Factory tragedy, Cobble recounted signature moments in US women's movements, and the way women's organizations have reinvented themselves over time to fit the historical and economic circumstances of the era. She described women's participation in strikes to demand safer factory working conditions in the 1910s and '20s, the sit-down strikes of the '30s, and women's efforts to organize garment and textile workers and telephone operators in the early days of industrialization, and later flight attendants, hotel and restaurant employees, and other pink-collar workers who had been largely overlooked by traditional unions. Cobble also pointed out the pivotal role women and women's organizations played in mid-century political battles to win legislation that established a federal minimum wage, banned most forms of child labor, created anti-poverty programs such as Social Security and Unemployment Insurance, and, in the latter half of the century, their efforts to establish pay equity, outlaw sexual harassment and gender discrimination, and ensure the availability of affordable health, child, and elder care.

Cobble argued that US women achieved much in the first three quarters of the twentieth century, in part because of the power they gained by organizing as workers within the labor movement. In fact, the mass movements of the 1970s had their roots in the labor movements of the first half of the century. And yet, by the Baby Boomer era, women were becoming disillusioned with their labor unions, perhaps because those unions were beginning to look radically different from the organs of social change that they had once aspired to be. Women workers such as the flight attendants withdrew from established unions and began to form their own. They also began to rely on different methods. Instead of strikes and direct actions, they began to use publicity campaigns, lawsuits, and other forms of pressure.

"At the beginning of the twenty-first century, US feminists are once again entering a new phase," Cobble said. Women are again experimenting with new forms of organizing in response to the changing circumstances of women and of workers. With the increase in informal forms of employment (contracting, subcontracting, and other work arrangements), the increase in immigrant and undocumented workers, the intensification of global capitalism and the domination of global markets, workers are once again facing a new set of challenges and need to look beyond contract unions to alternative forms of organization, such as community unions, professional associations, and workers' centers.

Cobble's talk was an eye-opener for the Japanese activists, most of whom were familiar with US and European women's lib and other feminist movements of the 1970s and '80s, but had little awareness of the working women's movements that—as Cobble put it—were going on long before Betty Friedan's *The Feminine Mystique* burst on the scene in 1963. This was extremely important because it broadened the lens through which the Japanese women saw US feminism and feminists. Much of the world thinks of US feminism as being the province of elite, professional women, and largely a phenomenon of the 1970s (with some space reserved for the suffrage movement), because that is the story that most often gets told. But Cobble focused on the lesser-known history of working-class women, which clearly shows that not all US women's movements were middle-class movements, and that nonelite women have been the driving force behind many of our greatest advancements.

By its very nature, Cobble's talk helped to bridge a subtle but important gap that existed between US and Japanese activists. Despite the fact that they eagerly sought interaction with US women activists, many of the Japanese activists were deeply ambivalent about working with us, largely because they have an exaggerated concept of how good women in the United States have it. Women's groups in Japan regularly asked me to tell them how US women had "gained equality with men," as if gender inequality was over and done with in the United States, just a bad memory that lives on as a cautionary tale. With that image in mind, some of the Japanese activists wondered whether relatively privileged US women could truly appreciate the hardships Japanese women experience and the obstacles they face. Some even seemed to harbor a sneaking suspicion that—with all due respect to how far US women have come—we probably didn't have to fight *quite as hard* as other women for the gains we've won; after all, equality was one of the founding principles of US society, right?

Believing that there was a significant difference in their experiences of gender discrimination, the Japanese activists had a tendency to court our input while at the same time maintaining a certain social distance, as if they thought of Americans as sort of second-tier allies (compared to, for example, the more robust solidarity they developed with various Asian women's groups). It wasn't that they dismissed the hard-won achievements of US women. In fact, that's what made it so interesting. They seemed to simultaneously look at US working women as role models and evidence of what women can achieve, while maintaining the belief that our fight took place—past tense—under far more favorable conditions than the ones they face. No one ever said it this bluntly, but their attitude seemed to be that US and Japanese working women are cousins more than sisters. We can work together, certainly, but we are not the same, just as sympathetic intellectuals are never quite as "authentic" as actual workers.

The problem is that this concept of US women's experiences is based on unrealistic media images of what our lives are like. Most Japanese people have little exposure to what life in the United States is really like, especially for those who fall outside of the white, middle-class demographic. By providing a long view of US women's struggles, as well as glimpses of the kinds of discrimination that nonwhite, nonelite women have faced and continue to face, Cobble's talk helped to break down those false images and dispel some of the Japanese women's reservations about the possibility for true solidarity with US women. The Japanese women had come into the meeting that morning feeling a strong sense of difference, but as Cobble made these points I could feel the energy in the room subtly shifting. Tensions eased, guards dropped, and in their place came the palpable feeling that we were coming together as a group, as if the room had suddenly gotten smaller and cozier as the commonality of our current situation was revealed.

Cobble's presentation also gave us a new way to think about an issue that weighed heavily on the minds of some of the Japanese activists I'd talked with. Enterprise unions have criticized the founders of women's unions, saying they weaken the labor movement as a whole by taking activists away from existing unions. Hard to imagine them having the nerve to make such a statement considering that so many of the women left their original unions precisely because those unions were ignoring their concerns. In any case, traditional unions have had some success in casting the creation of alternative unions as a betrayal of the cause, and while that has not stopped these women from doing what they had to do, it did cause them a certain amount of psychic pain. But Cobble's review of the many different ways US labor feminists have fought their battles over the years reminded us that there are many ways to organize workers, and some work better than others depending on the historical circumstances. While large-scale, industrial-style unions were the way to go for people employed in automobile factories in the 1930s, that model is not especially helpful for clerical employees in small firms or day laborers who work for a different boss every day. These workers have different circumstances and workplace issues. They need to develop new tactics and organizations as new work configurations develop, as new constituencies enter the labor market, and as new types of needs arise (such as the increased need for day and elder care as women entered the labor market). This willingness to consider alternatives does not constitute being a traitor to the labor movement. Instead, it shows that creating new organizations and new theories of organization is not only necessary, it is exactly what every generation of activists must do to confront the challenges of its particular moment.

Finally, Cobble's talk was important because the central theme of the talk gave us heart over the next three years as we pursued what felt at times like an unattainable goal. Cobble emphasized that social movements—and the institutions that make up those movements—are not and cannot be static entities. Social movements live and die on their ability to respond and adapt to changing economic, political, and social circumstances. Over time, social movements change—indeed, must change—because the social conditions around them change. As Cobble walked us through the various phases of US women's movements, she pointed to the changes in issues over time, and to the accompanying changes in strategies, tactics, and types of organizations and alliances that formed in each period. This point was extremely relevant to our project because it reminded us that what we were trying to do—to create new kinds of organizations and strategies to fit our current moment—was eminently doable. At times the prospect of creating a whole new movement and completely new organizations felt so huge, so overwhelming, that it seemed impossible, even hubristic, to imagine such a project. But when we'd reflect on the developments, adaptations, and innovations of women's organizations in both countries over the course of time, our task would once again seem within the realm of human possibility.

US Women's Organizations

Following Cobble's talk, we heard presentations from three US women's organizations that the Japanese women asked us to include: the Coalition of Labor

Union Women; 9to5; and the United Automobile Workers Women's Department. Each of these groups represents a different way of structuring women's organizations. Our goal in including them was to give the Japanese women a variety of organizational models to analyze and to consider whether they held any merit for their own context. For the Japanese participants, these speakers also added legitimacy to the workshops because these organizations are "famous." I was surprised that even among these radical outsiders, "brand recognition" carried such a positive valence, more so than I was used to in similar circles in the United States. Yet there was no question it did: the fact that they recognized some of the names gave the Japanese women confidence that they were participating in something important.

Coalition of Labor Union Women

The first speaker was former CLUW president and founding member Gloria Johnson, who spoke of her fifty years in the US labor movement, and of how the civil rights movement helped bring about a new wave of working women's organizations, including her own. The Coalition of Labor Union Women was founded in 1974, at a time when women were entering the workforce in greater numbers but were still very much on the periphery of most unions' radar screens. Organizing female-gendered occupations and workplaces was not a priority for most unions, nor did most unions consider problems such as gender discrimination and sexual harassment to be the sort of problems that labor unions should get involved in. Like their Japanese counterparts, US women unionists were becoming increasingly frustrated with doing their part to support the union as a whole, only to find their own issues immediately put on the back burner whenever "real issues"—issues that could affect male members—flared up. But after seeing what civil rights activists accomplished through organizing, a small group of women unionists decided that the answer was to organize *as women*.

The Coalition for Labor Union Women is not a labor union; it is an advocacy group that seeks to organize women who are already members of a union to further amplify women's political clout as well as their collective power within the labor movement. Comprised of women from a wide variety of unions, CLUW works alongside existing unions to promote awareness of and action around women's issues, from pay equity to affordable health, child, and elder care, to cervical cancer prevention. By organizing as women, CLUW also seeks to unite women across racial and ethnic lines, and to expand the reach and vision of existing unions by creating a space for minority members to enter the dialogue in a meaningful way. A free-standing organization in its own right, CLUW is also one of the seven constituency groups within the AFL-CIO that work to bring minority voices to the fore. The other constituency groups include: the A. Philip Randolph Institute, Asian Pacific American Labor Alliance, Coalition of Black Trade Unionists, Labor Council for Latin American Advancement, Pride At Work, and Union Veterans Council.

United Auto Workers Women's Department

Karla Swift from the UAW Women's Department presented a different approach to organizing women, an approach that is both familiar to and controversial among Japanese activists. The UAW Women's Department is an internal division within the nationwide union. Created in 1955, the Women's Department's primary function is to educate UAW members, male and female, about issues of concern to women workers, and to mobilize members around these issues. The Women's Department is active in lobbying efforts around such issues as pay equity, sexual harassment, and domestic violence prevention. The Women's Department also helps local UAW chapters set up standing women's committees within the locals, as mandated by the union's constitution. Like the national Women's Department, local women's committees educate women, foster personal growth, build self-esteem, provide leadership training, and promote participation in union activities. The Women's Department also helps to ensure that UAW policies on equality, sex discrimination, and sexual harassment are maintained at local and regional levels.

One of the advantages of forming an internal women's department is that it would typically have access to union resources, including financial and staff support as well as start-up and educational materials. But such women's divisions have a long and complicated history in Japan (Simpson 1985; Molony 1991; Mackie 2002, 2003). What's more, several of the Japanese participants had already tried the women's division route and been sold out by the male majority when difficult decisions had to be made (see chapter 2). So I was surprised during the planning phase for this workshop when the Japanese contingent asked us to include a representative from a women's division in a US union in the program. But once Swift opened the floor for Q&A, I understood why. The Japanese participants peppered her with questions that all revolved around the central theme: how do US women get men to work with them and to take women's workplace issues and grievances as seriously as they take their own? This was another one of those moments when what happened among the participants exceeded what the organizers of the workshop foresaw or hoped for. The US participants quickly jumped in with a spontaneous, collaborative lesson on how internal organizing, especially through good, participatory education programs, can and has helped to overcome these sorts of internal divides within unions. That was the lesson I hoped the Detroit meeting as a whole would build toward, but just a few hours into the first day, the US unionists were putting it right out there: sacrificing any constituency within the union is a crime against solidarity pure and simple, and if any part of the union doesn't see that, you have a consciousness problem, which we solve with education and organizing.

9to5

Linda Meric, executive director of 9to5, introduced her organization, which in many ways is the closest in structure and activities to the Japanese women's unions. I was surprised when I first came to Japan at how often women asked me about 9to5; it seemed to have much more name recognition in Japan than it did in the United States. I soon learned that it was because of the 1980 film *Nine to Five*. To me, that film had been just another dopey Hollywood comedy. I was dumbfounded when I discovered that Japanese women resonated with that film the way women at the turn of the twentieth century did with the play *Mrs. Warren's Profession*. Whenever the film came up, the women would start talking animatedly about their favorite scenes, doubling over with laughter at the beloved scene at the end where the ridiculously evil boss gets his, reminding me that repressed anger is the bread and butter of comedy writers. What was sheer shtick to me was joyously cathartic for them.

The real 9to5 was founded in 1973 by a small group of clerical workers in the Boston area. After attending a conference for women office workers, eight women started a newsletter to discuss the types of problems they had on the job, such as low pay and the demeaning treatment they were subjected to by bosses and male workers. Meric said unions, feminists, and anti-poverty programs ignored the fledgling organization, but it got the attention of working women themselves. The founders decided to hold their first meeting, hoping to attract maybe a couple dozen potential new members. But when three hundred women showed up, they knew they had tapped into a serious and widespread problem that needed immediate attention.

As an organization, 9to5 sits at the intersection of the labor and women's movements. It is not a labor union, nor is it an internal division within a union. It is an organization of women who lacked access to union representation but recognized the need for collective action to achieve gender equality in their workplaces. Like CLUW and the UAW Women's Department, 9to5 lobbies for legislation and public policies that support workplace equality and low-income families. Its legislative priorities include living wage and family-supporting wage standards, affordable health and family care programs, and measures to establish rights and fair working conditions for people in nonstandard employment.

Moreover, 9to5 provides educational programs to ensure that women know their rights on the job, and advisory services to help women access resources and develop strategies for pursuing their disputes. On the other hand, 9to5 differs from CLUW and the UAW Women's Department in two important ways. First, it is not part of the formal union structure. Second, its primary constituency is women who are not already members of a union, which means women who lack the protections of a union contract and who have significantly less access to the resources for fighting back.

At the same time, 9to5 has much in common with the Japanese women's unions: their legislative goals and strategies are similar; both strive to educate women about their rights, and to provide support to women who are not currently in union positions; and, like most of the Japanese women's unions, 9to5 maintains a helpline to provide advisory services for women who are having problems at work. Unlike the Japanese women's unions, however, 9to5 has no legal standing as bargaining agent for its members. While 9to5 can provide valuable advice to help women wage their fights, it cannot force employers to the bargaining table to discuss grievances. In this sense, Japanese women's unions would seem to be in a more powerful position for effecting change than 9to5 is. But, as we would soon learn from the Japanese presentations, other factors keep their potential power very much in check.

Although we had hired Cadillac simultaneous interpretation services, the quality of the translation was borderline disastrous. Even so, I could see from their faces that the Japanese women were resonating with what Meric had to say. As she described the organization's beginnings, its hybrid structure, and the barriers it faces, the Japanese women were nodding as they recognized the natural affinity between 9to5 and their own organizations. It was a labor organization that was willing to acknowledge that some problems cannot be adequately addressed through traditional union structures. It was even willing to take the next step and try to create whole new structures despite disapproval from labor's establishment. And yet, for all its similarities to women's unions, 9to5 was not collapsing in on itself the way JWUs were. At the first break after her talk, several of the Japanese women pulled me aside and said they definitely wanted to pursue a deeper dialogue with 9to5 as our project moved forward.

Japanese Women's Organizations

During the afternoon session, the learning arrow was reversed as the Japanese participants introduced their organizations. Takeo Kinoshita, the lone male participant at the Detroit workshop, set the stage by explaining the differences between the US and Japanese industrial relations systems to help the US audience understand the circumstances out of which the women's unions emerged. Following his presentation, three women's unions, a part-time workers' union, and two working women's support organizations told us the story of their beginnings, giving us background on their goals, structure, activities, and how, when, and why they came into being. These organizations included: Kansai Women's Union, Sapporo Women's Union, the Japan Institute of Workers' Evolution Union, Women's Union Tokyo, *ICORU*, and Working Women's Voices.

Kansai Women's Union

Kayoko Akabane and Fumiko Yakabi introduced Kansai Women's Union. Based in Osaka, the KWU was founded in 1987 in response to a series of shifts in the employment system that were particularly detrimental to women. Akabane explained that during the 1980s the Japanese labor movement was weakened by the collapse of several labor organizations, including the National Railway Workers Union and *Sohyo*, the General Council of Labor Unions, which was a relatively progressive labor federation associated with the Japan Socialist Party.[2] The collapse hastened the labor movement's already discernible drift to the right, with more and more unions embracing the corporate principles of lifetime employment and labor-management cooperation. Not coincidentally, this same period brought on a number of changes in the overall employment system, including an increase in the number of nonunion temporary and part-time jobs, and an intensification of the gender-based division of labor, spurred on by new government policies aimed at "strengthening the foundations of the family," which, according to Akabane, is political code for ensuring that women remain in the home and economically dependent on their husbands.

"It was normal to think of women as receiving low salaries because they only worked to supplement household budgets and only to assist men. Women were excluded from opportunities for economic independence," Akabane said. Around this time, major corporations began to introduce the two-track employment system in response to the 1985 passage of the Equal Employment Opportunity Law. "As unions embraced the principle of lifetime employment, the demands of female workers were discarded," she reported.

The continuing decline of working conditions for women convinced a group of activists that women needed a labor movement of their own. "The women's labor problem is one with which women themselves must grapple," Akabane argued. "Women workers must themselves directly confront capital. To establish women's right to make decisions for themselves, our activities would become a means for women to establish independent 'selves.'" The founding members of

KWU included members of the Kansai Women's Dispute Collective (an organization comprising plaintiffs in labor-related lawsuits and their supporters), public and private sector temporary employees who were protesting a rash of improper dismissals, and women who were interested in gender issues generally.

The KWU's membership includes: private sector, regular employees; nonregular employees (temporary, part-time, contract, and occasional workers); public sector workers; women who have been fired; and the self-employed. Virtually all KWU members join the union as individuals; the union has no locals at this point.

The union's primary role is to help women address problems at work through direct negotiations with companies, appeals to local labor committees and the courts, and public demonstrations to raise awareness and support. Through its counseling hotline, the union also provides support and advice to women who are not members of a company union. Typical complaints include improper dismissals and transfers, failure to pay wages, sexual harassment, broken contracts, and wage discrimination.

KWU also engages in political activity. Its legislative priorities include outlawing the use of temp workers in the public sector, reforming the Part-time Workers Employment Law to prohibit indirect discrimination, passing meaningful pay equity legislation, and reforming the tax and pension systems so that married women are not penalized for working full-time jobs. Its broader goals include mobilizing workers to oppose performance-based pay systems, deregulation, and globalization. At the same time, KWU seeks to reform the existing labor movement so that it recognizes gender-based discrimination as a legitimate issue for unions to address and makes fighting all forms of gender discrimination a priority.

To achieve its goals, the union holds public lectures and training programs to empower women, publishes a newsletter, and hosts workplace exchanges.[3] Its allies include the Kansai Dispute Collective and other dispute collectives nationwide, *ICORU*, Equality Action 21, Working Women's Network, Committee for Asian Women (CAW) and CAW Japan, and local labor federations. Kansai Women's Union is also a member of the Community Union Kansai Network, which engages in joint struggles with other unions throughout the country.

According to Akabane's report, KWU's most persistent organizational problems include low participation rates among rank and file members, low interest among the general population in joining a union because of the economic risks of standing up at work, little turnover in leadership positions because of the demands of serving as a full-time union official, and lack of support from company unions for jointly staged workplace actions. Its organizational goals include: developing activities that promote member participation; increasing membership and the union's power to win disputes; developing more effective communication strategies; learning new techniques for building positive relationships with other organizations; creating a rapid response network; and expanding joint activities, above all with other Asian women both inside and outside of Japan.

Sapporo Women's Union

Next, Keiko Kondō, secretary-general of Sapporo Women's Union, described how her organization came into being. In 1993 feminists in the Sapporo region opened a new resource and support organization called Women's Space ON. The plan was that the organization would provide resources and support for confronting a broad array of women's issues including domestic violence, sexual violence, divorce, and issues of inheritance. But, from the moment the center opened its counseling hotline, an unexpected pattern emerged. The majority of requests for counseling centered on women's workplace issues, such as unfair dismissals, unpaid wages, and sexual harassment.

"[T]he office was deluged with so many requests that staff members could not even have time to blink. It was a tremendous shock for staff members to acknowledge how deep and wide distress was among women who had no idea where they could bring a case," Kondō said. Even public administration offices, police departments, and labor unions began calling the women's center for help with cases involving sexual violence and sexual harassment. "It is very obvious that [the] institutions involved and labor unions were not prepared for issues regarding gender discrimination, sexual violence, and women's rights."

The types and frequency of complaints shocked even seasoned activists like Kondō:

> Reviewing each case, our rage flared up again. Why do women have to be treated in such unfair and unreasonable ways in the workplace? It seems that employers call their bluff by saying and doing anything illegal to women workers, especially women part-timers. On the one hand, employers have repeated illegal actions for the last several years because of recession. On the other hand, it seems expected for women workers to accept unjustified rights violations based on the idea that it is because they are part-timers, because they cannot find another job after quitting the current job, or because every woman worker endures the same kind of issues.

Women Space ON members began to see that working women needed labor organizations of their own that would recognize and have the expertise to address the kinds of problems women face at work; a union that would unite them *as women* regardless of company, occupation, or social status; a union that would be able to engage in direct negotiations with companies and provide legal guidance when necessary. Later that same year, Women's Space ON launched the Sapporo Women's Union.

Sapporo Women's Union is similar to Kansai Women's Union and Women's Union Tokyo in structure and function. Membership is open to all women regardless of company, occupation, or social status. Women can call the union hotline for information and advice. Like other women's unions, Sapporo Women's Union helps women pursue their own grievances, either through bargaining with the company, or by filing complaints with the government labor offices or lawsuits with the courts. Each woman is in charge of her own case but will usually put together a support team of more experienced union members who will attend bargaining sessions or court hearings with her and assist her along the way.

Kondō spoke passionately about the need for Japanese women to create their own unions, calling existing unions "dysfunctional" and private sector workplaces "a lawless area for women workers" and "a lair for people who commit sexual harassment":

> Japanese women must form their own unions because existing androcentric enterprise unions have proven time and again that they are willing to sacrifice the needs of women workers to protect the male regular employees they consider their core membership. Women must begin building their own organizations, first, because of the number of women workers who lack access to the means and information to stand up to outrageous misconduct by employers and second, because traditional male-centered unions are either unwilling or unable to fight gender discrimination in the workplace.

Although women make up nearly half the labor force, 80 percent remain unorganized or stuck in the netherworld of nonstandard employment, she explained. Not only have traditional unions failed to address such inequities, many go so far as to retaliate against women for speaking up. "It is a well-known fact that many women workers who took action for unfair dismissal, wage discrimination, or sexual harassment have been excluded from the body of labor unions and were forced to create a support network outside of the union on their own to keep fighting in judicial trials," she said. No longer willing to cast their lot with male-centered unions that themselves "play a role in suppression and discrimination," working women in Sapporo decided it was time to take matters into their own hands.

"Historically, the phrase 'one for all, all for one' sustained international labor movements," she said. "However, women's struggles have not been respected as part of the 'one' by these movements."

Kondō said that educating women about their rights is one of the most important functions of women's unions. The lack of labor education—inside and outside of the labor movement—has left women unsure of what their on-the-job rights are, much less how to protect them. One of the primary roles of women's unions is to fill in that knowledge gap and raise awareness among women that they do not have to sit back and accept the kinds of human rights violations they are routinely subjected to in the course of the working day.

"Women are [trying] to create their own style of labor movement by groping their way and settling very rare cases through their own resources, and by learning about each other through their shared struggles."

Japan Institute of Workers' Evolution Union

How the Japan Institute of Workers' Evolution Union came into being was an especially bitter—if all too familiar—tale. Presented by Kazuko Sazaki, the birth narrative of this union is the story of yet another social justice organization that would not extend to its own employees the very rights the organization was supposed to protect.

The Japan Institute of Workers' Evolution, an agency attached to the Ministry of Health, Labour, and Welfare, was founded in 1986 following the enactment of the EEOL. Its mission includes "promoting full use of women's abilities, balancing work and family life, and promoting equal treatment of part-timers and full-time employees." The agency operates programs that are designed to promote compliance with the EEOL, the Child Care and Family Care Leave Law, and the Part-time Workers Employment Law, and to encourage companies to take positive action toward utilizing women's abilities. For example, the agency offers educational programs to help supervisors learn how to prevent sexual harassment in the workplace, to encourage better management of part-time workers, and to enhance employees' awareness of laws and government policies that affect them.

The institute also has a variety of support programs to help individuals and companies develop methods for balancing work and family life. For example, it provides a hotline for working women who are faced with providing childcare or home nursing care, and support for women who are seeking to reenter the labor market after their children are grown. The institute also has a program to help defray the company's costs when employees takes family leave so that management will have less incentive to discourage employees from exercising their rights.

Yet, despite its mission statement, the agency didn't practice what it preached when it came to its own part-time employees. According to Sazaki, a part-time employee in the Fukuoka office, most of the work in her office, including planning and conducting seminars, telephone counseling, and making funding decisions, is handled by part-time counselors and advisors.

"What led to our organizing a union was that, as employees of a Ministry of Health, Labour, and Welfare auxiliary organization, we were thoroughly familiar with labor law, including the Labor Standards Act, and our work consisted of working to improve the management of employment for part-time workers. Nonetheless, the Labor Standards Act and Part-time Workers Employment Law were not being upheld in our workplace," said Sazaki. "Although we were part-timers who were in the office from 9 a.m. to 5 p.m., working under the direction of the manager and section head, we were treated as independent contractors, not part-time workers." The institute also denied part-time employees benefits that were standard for full-time employees, including semi-annual bonuses, retirement allowances, reimbursements for transportation expenses, vacation time, and leave for weddings, funerals, and other family events. "The full-time employees receive salaries, other benefits, and terms of employment equivalent to those of civil servants, while we worked under conditions that were barely within the law, and were not even covered by the social insurance program, which includes the Employees' Health Insurance System and the Employees' Pension Insurance System," Sazaki reported. Even here, at this public agency charged with advocating for workers' rights and worker self-development, women workers faced the familiar list of grievances.

In October 2000 the Japan Institute of Workers' Evolution Union was founded in Fukuoka, a city in the southern part of Japan. The organization is not a women-only union, but most of its members are women, and the majority of its issues are related to women's working conditions. According to Sazaki, "Our union's basic policy is to demand improvements in employment management that are appropriate in terms of the guiding concepts of the Japan Institute of Workers' Evolution: 'Promoting full use of women's abilities, balancing work and family life, and promoting equal treatment of part-timers and full-time employees.' We seek to achieve a working environment in which our human rights are respected as a matter of course and in which our abilities can be utilized more fully."

In the beginning, the union had only nine members. The original organizers were part-time workers. By August 2001 they had organized the National Council of the Japan Institute of Workers' Evolution Union, which serves as a negotiating body for bargaining with the Japan Institute of Workers' Evolution headquarters. Membership is open to full-time and part-time workers at the Japan Institute of Workers' Evolution, although the vast majority of members are part-timers.

At the time of our first workshop, the most pressing issue for the union was the threat of dismissals in response to federal budget cuts. Sazaki explains: "In March 2003 thirty-six of our members nationwide were told that they were being terminated. At that time, the institute's headquarters said, 'Part-time employees are under one-year renewable contracts; we offer them new terms each year and renew the contracts of those who agree. The terms of employment for the next fiscal year do not therefore constitute a change in working conditions and are not an issue subject to negotiation but only explanation.' We demanded that they retract that statement, but the institute went ahead with terminating part-timers' employment."

In disputes such as this, the union's strongest strategy is to try the case in the court of public opinion. Instead of arguing that the agency acted illegally, the union highlights the way the agency's actions violate community standards for reasonable treatment of employees.[4] Japanese companies would love to shift to what they call US-style management, where "redundant" workers can be kicked to the curb with Dickensian ease. That is the whole point of contract labor. But, even in the case where employees are on short-term contracts, the Japanese public tends to see employers as bearing some responsibility to their employees because, in the course of working together, a relationship is formed and certain obligations on both sides accrue. The Japanese public tends to criticize companies that readily dispose of employees, either through layoffs or by terminating contracts, as being unnecessarily brutal and not acting in the public good. In the case of the Japan Institute of Workers' Evolution, the blatant hypocrisy of management's position left the agency even more vulnerable to public disapproval.

In the face of the union's continued pressure, management eventually relented. "The institute later changed its attitude completely, responded to our demand for presentation of materials in writing, and also arranged new places of employment for those who had been terminated. In addition, contract renewal for the next fiscal year will be subject to negotiation by our union. We have also exchanged written confirmations that the institute will not engage in speech or actions associated with unfair labor practices," Sazaki said.

This victory marked a turning point for the union. "We think that, in the fourth year after organizing, we have at last reached the starting line and are ready to go to work as a union." The case highlighted many of the issues that Japanese women workers face, and showed the US women that these small, alternative unions have had some success beyond resolving individual grievances.

Taken together, the stories of Kansai Women's Union, Sapporo Women's Union and Japan Institute of Workers' Evolution Union helped lay a foundation for understanding the need for women's unions and the problems they faced. The presentations also helped start the conversation on how these organizations might develop through mutual cooperation during the workshops and beyond.

ICORU Human Rights Center for Working Women

We also heard from two new organizations that promote women's rights on the job, but as support/resource centers rather than as labor unions. *ICORU* Human Rights Center for Working Women is an Osaka-based nongovernmental organization (NGO) dedicated to promoting a gender-equal society in which the dignity and human rights of both sexes are respected. According to its mission statement: *ICORU* seeks "to solve labor issues, such as the improvement of working conditions and the elimination of discrimination in the workplace, with support, counseling, and coordination with government, labor unions, nonprofit organizations, and professionals. We aim to raise and broaden consciousness toward women's labor issues through creative activities, for example, holding workshops and symposiums, conducting surveys, advocating, and offering information."

ICORU grew out of the long-term collaboration among a variety of workers' and social justice organizations in the Kansai region (the area in western Japan that includes Osaka, Kyoto, and Kobe). A small, community-based union called Senshu Union was established in 1988 to address the issues of part-time and other nonregular workers. The group had strong ties to the peace and environmental movements, and the movements to combat discrimination against people with disabilities, women and foreign workers, and *Burakumin*, a cultural (some claim ethnic) minority group in Japan whose members have historically been treated as outcasts by mainstream Japanese. Initially, Senshu Union had a small but important role to play in the community, but in 1995 everything changed for the people living in the area. On January 17, 1995, the Great Hanshin Earthquake struck the Kansai region, killing more than 6,000 people and devastating much of the local economy. "Enterprises in the area began laying off women workers whose lives had already been turned upside down by the earthquake," said founding member Fumiko Yakabi (who is also a founding member of Kansai Women's Union). "Women who had recently lost family members, friends, their homes were now suddenly out of work on top of it all."

The special plight of women following the earthquake served as a wake-up call for women in the coalition. Workers of every stripe were affected by the earthquake (and by the shifts in the national economy that were happening at the same time). But women workers were hit especially hard, in part because they made up the majority of nonregular workers, in part because it was hard for their male coworkers to even see the problem, and in part because they were locked out of the mainstream unions or at the very least out of mainstream unions' concerns. These difficulties led women to seek a new form of organization that could address needs that the coalition of community unions could not. Senshu Union was the first to suggest creating a human rights center focused on the problems of working women, Yakabi said. "The *ICORU* Women Workers' Human Rights Center began with overnight trips for women. These trips became an opportunity to discuss problems impossible to solve in a framework involving multiple unions. This is where the idea for a Women Workers' Human Rights Center was born."

On January 11, 2004, *ICORU* held its first official meeting. Lawyers, academics, and activists from the labor and women's liberation movements flocked to the hall. "Attendance at the meeting was far larger than the organizers had anticipated, with participants from a broad range of different social strata caught up together in the excitement of the moment," Yakabi said. "We need to recall this excitement."

As with women's unions, *ICORU* provides phone or in-person counseling on issues such as sexual harassment, wrongful dismissals, and lack of benefits that are standard for regular full-time employees. Working closely with the Community Union Kansai Network, *ICORU* is active in developing and promoting women-friendly legislative and policy initiatives. The group works with other women's organizations to present legislative proposals to the government, to educate the public, and to build support for issues such as proposed revisions to the Part-time Workers Law and the EEOL.

ICORU members also work to develop innovative community outreach programs. The group has been able to win scarce government funds to help launch groups such as the "Single Mothers Cheerleading Squad," a resource and support group for single mothers, and the "Care Worker Cheerleading Squad," which visits and conducts exchanges among unions for nursing care facilities.[5] In December 2004 *ICORU* held "Labor Fest," a film festival focused on labor themes. The group also offers classes to help women become more independent and work more actively, and engages in research activities such as a 2004 questionnaire on work and child-rearing issues. It publishes a quarterly magazine which, Yakabi proudly told us, they hope will become the next *Seitō* (*Bluestocking*), an influential women's journal (published by the Bluestocking Society from 1911 until 1916) that is credited with stimulating much of the labor and feminist activism that arose in the early twentieth century (Mackie 2002).

Working Women's Voices

Kazuko Sazaki, who presented earlier on the Japan Institute of Workers' Evolution Union, and Emi Naruse introduced us to their women's support organization called Working Women's Voices.

Working Women's Voices (WWV) evolved out of an earlier organization called "Changing the Equal Employment Opportunity Law in Fukuoka," part of a nationwide network to bring women's voices to the process of revising the

1985 Equal Employment Opportunity Law. The law was scheduled for revision on the 10th anniversary of its implementation. After the revised version passed in 1999, the group changed its name to Working Women's Voices and began addressing women's issues through education and advocacy. WWV is engaged in a variety of activities, from providing lectures and workshops to lobbying.

Organizations such as WWV and *ICORU* have a long history in Japan. Dating back to at least the turn of the twentieth century, women in Japan have formed grassroots groups that tried to foster social and political change through education and advocacy, even when it was illegal for women to participate directly in political activities (Simpson 1985; Molony 1991; Nolte and Hastings 1991; Liddle and Nakajima 2000; Mackie 2002, 2003; Broadbent 2008).[6] Representing right, left, and centrist political orientations, these groups held educational forums and published their own materials to raise awareness and spur public debate on issues such as prostitution, expanding education for girls, working conditions for factory women, motherhood protection legislation (e.g., restricting work hours and conditions for women to protect their childbearing and childrearing functions), attaining voting and other political rights for women, and mobilization of women to support or oppose Japan's involvement in regional imperialist wars of that era as well as World War II. In the second half of the century, women's advocacy groups also engaged in direct action, lobbying, and "Get Out The Vote" campaigns—along with the familiar range of educational activities—as they focused on such issues as consumer and environmental safety, protesting nuclear development, the Vietnam War, the US military presence in Japan, and globalization, and promoting equality in the workplace for women, people with disabilities, and other minorities (see, for example, AMPO 1996; Gelb 2003; Mackie 2003). *ICORU* and WWV are part of the latest wave of advocacy groups that seeks to empower working women—through engagement with these sorts of activities—to personally and collectively confront the problems they face on the job.

"Our goals are to empower working women, who are often isolated and oppressed by unfair working conditions, by providing both information on the law and consciousness raising and emotional support," Naruse said. "We thus will offer counseling and worker education for women and also participate in movements for enactment of equal employment and other legislation."

Working Women's Voices has about eighty members, including women employed in a variety of formats, from full-time regular positions to temporary, contract, and dispatch workers. The organization is managed by a seven-member secretariat and holds bimonthly secretariat meetings and monthly internal study sessions. Membership dues run about $10 per year. The group has no full-time staff.

Beyond holding lectures, WWV's activities include holding hearings and submitting an opinion on a local ordinance calling for gender equality, submitting recommendations for revisions on the guidelines on working conditions for part-time workers, taking part in the nationwide actions to promote gender equality, and conducting a study on changes in women's working conditions as employment patterns become more diverse.

As for organizational problems, Sazaki and Naruse agreed that the group would benefit from a more clearly defined mission and stronger ties to unions and other labor organizations in the region. "Thus far, we have provided information on working women's issues through carrying out studies and offering lectures and workshops, but we have not clearly, concretely defined the direction in which we are seeking to go," Sazaki and Naruse said in their joint statement. "Thus, our activities have tended to be unfocused. Also, we have few ties with existing organizations in Fukuoka (the Fukuoka local of Rengo, the Japanese Trade Union Confederation, or the General Union, for example), or with women who are suing under the labor law, and our activities are not expanding. These are problems." But they presented these deficits as areas for improvement rather than as serious obstacles that have held them back: "We are not, however, drifting. We are confident that we have acted on the issues we should, to the full extent that our membership permits, after recognizing that secretariat members hold differing views on women's labor issues and reaching a consensus. Thus, we have been able to continue to address the problems of working women as a grassroots group in Fukuoka."

Organizations such as *ICORU* and Working Women's Voices showed the potential for alternative structures to help address women's concerns. One point that was not made directly that first day, but that I hoped the next day's discussion would flesh out, was that although virtually all grassroots women's organizations face resource shortages and other difficulties, the situation for groups such as WWV and *ICORU* is not as immediately dire as it is for the women's unions. Support groups, including WWV, do not have the constant influx of new women with new grievances that need immediate and intensive intervention. When women come to women's unions for help, they generally have or are on the verge of losing their jobs, and are usually suffering severely on an emotional if not physical level. It is this ever-increasing demand for immediate help with no commensurate increase in skilled members to provide it that puts many women's unions in danger of collapsing in on themselves. When a new member joins WWV or *ICORU*, they do not immediately add to the workload. A new member might mean another seat taken in a lecture hall, another body at a march, another set of eyes to proofread the newsletter, or another set of ideas brought to a research project or study meeting. In cases such as this, new members add to the organization's strength, whereas every new member of women's unions, as currently structured, significantly increases the union's workload without increasing the union's resources.

The day's presentation had taken us a long way toward understanding what we all had in common, what special challenges each side faced, and how we might move forward to work together on our common goal of promoting women's equality at work.

The End of a Long Day

As we packed up at the end of the first day's presentations, Heidi and I felt confident that the sessions had laid the groundwork for some good, meaty discussions. Now the question was: Would the women dive deeper into the dialogue during the off-hours or would they go back to their separate corners to chew over what they'd heard? Although there is certainly a place for processing a wealth of new information, we thought it would be a very good sign if the women felt confident enough to cross cultural and organizational boundaries and start making their own connections and pursuing their own questions. Would they take the initiative to go beyond the guided tour provided by the presentations and see what more they might be able to learn through direct dialogue?

We did not have to wait long for the answer. When we arrived at the conference room that morning, we had filed in individually or in small groups. But when we walked out that night, it was as one very loud group, with everyone talking animatedly and all at once about the day's revelations. The US participants were flat-out astounded by what they'd just witnessed. Bear in mind these were not casual observers of labor. They were highly regarded activists and researchers who keep one ear to the ground at all times and are used to being in the know about major developments in the world of labor. But as we walked out together, several of these women expressed their utter amazement about what was going on inside Japan: reputedly docile Japanese women are launching a major offensive against a profoundly gender-segregated employment system and unapologetically male-oriented labor institutions, and yet virtually no one in the West knows about it. Moreover, the Japanese are experimenting with new ways of organizing minority workers to ensure that the concerns of one demographic do not dominate the entire labor movement. These were exactly the questions that US labor activists were struggling with, and yet, until now, no dialogue was taking place between the two sides.

On the Japanese side, Cobble's talk and the accounts of US women's within-our-lifetime struggles that we heard from CLUW, UAW, and 9to5 shook the

Japanese women's reserve in such a way that they began interacting with us with an openness that suggested the us-them dividing line had momentarily receded far into the background. I think what had touched the Japanese women so deeply was the revelation that US women really do know the pain and frustration of gender discrimination. We know the financial and spiritual poverty that comes from being funneled into low-skilled, dead-end jobs. We know the anger and humiliation of sexual and power harassment. Despite the radical broadening of the range of opportunities open to women in the United States, there are still women who know what it's like to be stuffed into gendered roles that stunt their growth and inhibit their ability to fully develop into the shape they were meant to be. In that moment of realization, the barriers between us seemed to melt away and we talked easily and without feeling the weight of all the social and historical inequalities that so often complicated our relationships. It was not a permanent fix. Time and again we would get stuck in that same quicksand and have to painstakingly work our way out before we could move forward. But the day's presentations reminded us that such moments were possible. That grounding in hopefulness got us through a lot of sticky and frustrating moments over the next few years.

I think the best measure of the day's success was the excitement with which people mingled that night. We were all alive with discoveries: of the exciting new organizing going on in Japan, of the possibilities that working together could open up for both sides, and of the potential for making a significant contribution to Japanese women's efforts to create a new movement based on a concept of labor feminism. That night at the conference dinner, everyone was brimming over with questions and stories and expressions of amazement at the efforts of the other side. Eavesdropping as best I could, I could hear Yakabi telling the US organizers about her long-running lawsuit, the first of its kind in Japan. I could hear Ban talking about the part-time workers' union she belonged to, and about the severity of the wage discrimination part-time workers face. Linda Meric was deep in conversation with several Japanese activists who were peppering her with questions about 9to5's success at projecting a positive image as a workers' organization that women would want to join. That was particularly gratifying to me. Before the conference started, the Japanese participants were a little starstruck at the idea of meeting the executive director of "the famous" 9to5. But Linda is so warm and approachable, so genuine, that the Japanese women were talking to her with ease. In Japan, it can be considered rude to ask a lot of questions because it puts a burden on the person being questioned. But no one seemed to be holding back that night. The only obvious factor inhibiting cross-national discussion was the language barrier, but our bilingual members and graduate student helpers did a much better job of facilitating conversation than our professional translators had done during the day.

Equally important as the cross-national connections, the Japanese women (and their organizations) were forming new ties with each other. When I first met up with the WUT, it was clear that part of the problem was that most of these women's groups were operating in isolation from each other. Part of that was that they simply had not had the opportunity to meet face to face, drink tea, and develop ideas about how they might be able to help each other move forward. For the Japanese women, this project was at least as much about forming a network among themselves as it was about forming ties with US activists. Indeed, from their perspective, developing national ties was more important in the long run. Whereas meeting with US activists would give them access to new resources, help them analyze and address organizational problems, and learn new teaching techniques, forming permanent ties with each other would be the key to effecting and enforcing long-lasting change. From the perspective of the project as a whole, all of these new bonds were crucial as our tasks would become increasingly interdependent over the next few years.

Yet, for all my eavesdropping, I think what struck me most was what I *didn't* hear. I did not hear anyone lecturing or pontificating. No one was holding court, spouting great truths, or beating the drum for their particular organization or philosophy. Anyone who has attended academic or political conferences will know how rare this is. Instead, the conversations I heard were true dialogues, with parties on both sides asking questions that suggested sincere interest in finding out what the other side might have to teach them.

Looking Ahead

Despite the long day, jet lag, and a brief stop-off at the requisite party-after-the-party that the Iron Women of Japan were holding in the common room downstairs, I was too wound up to sleep that night. I was excited, relieved, and grateful for the bonds that seemed to be forming among us. I felt as though we were on the verge of seeing a dream we had worked so hard for beginning to take shape. But there was apprehension as well. The next day was going to take us into trickier waters. As we began to move into the trouble-shooting phase of the workshop, these creative, outspoken, experienced activists would begin mixing it up, challenging each other's assumptions, calling particular structures into question. Debates would inevitably break out—after all, that was the whole purpose of the workshop—but how those debates would unfold, and how they would affect the tender shoots of our budding solidarity, remained to be seen. I truly believed that the fate of the project rested on what would happen on the second day, and that was by no means a sleep-inducing thought.

UNDER THE MICROSCOPE

Several months prior to the workshop, Heidi and I asked the WUT to conduct a thorough, systematic organizational self-analysis and present their results at the meeting in Detroit. We chose this form for several reasons. In the two years leading up to Workshop I, the WUT members and I had talked over these issues countless times, but usually in informal conversations that took place over dinner after negotiation sessions, on the train coming home from union meetings, or at the late-night drinking parties that punctuated long days of brainstorming at the union's summer retreat. In most cases, we were talking from our own experiences and observations, without any formal data in front of us. These impressionistic conversations were useful in many ways; they were, in fact, the catalyst for the project. But to engage in the kind of meaningful problem solving we had in mind for Workshop I, the participants would need a more thorough and accurate understanding of the big picture challenges (such as lack of educational resources and chronic underfunding), as well as the day-to-day difficulties that are sometimes symptomatic of much larger issues (such as the problems that grow out of the individual-membership model) that the WUT faced. They would also need to know with specificity what kinds of help the WUT was looking for.

We liked the idea of an organizational self-critique for several reasons. First, we wanted the members to decide for themselves which issues they wanted to focus on in the problem-solving segments of the project. Second, we thought they might be more open to considering new ideas if we were working to solve problems they had identified for themselves. Also, we hoped that our request for a formal self-analysis would encouraged the WUT to include systematic, verifiable data in their evaluation process.

The union held a series of meetings to ensure that the study would be as democratic and inclusive as possible. They gathered input from members, past and present, and held discussions to collectively analyze the organization's strengths and weaknesses. They also used data collected by sociologist Sachi Kotani, then a graduate student conducting research on alternative unions in Japan. Kotani's (1999, 2013) research included measures of overall efficacy, retention rates, reasons for joining and leaving the union—exactly the kind of objective information necessary for a realistic evaluation of the union's strengths and weaknesses. For example, the union leaders assumed that women who participated in collective bargaining were the most likely to stay on as long-term active members because they would be empowered by the experience. But Kotani's data suggested it was the other way around. Women who experienced collective bargaining were less likely to maintain their union membership than women who did not. The union's leaders were shocked by this finding. All along, they had interpreted the low-retention rate as a sign that women needed more exposure to the empowering effects of engaging in negotiations. But once they saw the data, they became much more open to considering alternative explanations for what was causing the high drop-out rate, and alternative approaches to solving the problem.

At the end of many difficult months of organizational self-evaluation, the union members compiled an inventory of the many ways the WUT was not operating in the way the founders had envisioned. On the second day of the Detroit meeting, Tani presented their findings along with an invitation to the workshop participants to help the WUT develop strategies for breaking down those newly identified barriers.

Barriers to Union Growth
Low Retention Rate

The union's retention rate is only about 30 percent. According to union records, 821 women joined the WUT between 1995 and 2003. By January 2004, 578 members, about 70 percent, had withdrawn from the union. Also, membership reached a plateau of about 250 members in 1997 and had remained constant since then. "That number, one-third, is not seemingly a bad number compared to other labor unions based on individual affiliation in Japan. However, we found that this fact reveals various issues in the WUT," said Tani.

Particularly alarming for the WUT leaders was the finding that the retention rate was higher among members who did *not* engage in bargaining than among those who did. "It is very clear that most WUT members tend to withdraw from the WUT after the settlement of their own issues or to participate in union activities less frequently, and that the withdrawal from the WUT is only a matter of time for those who have settled their own issues," Tani said. "In other words, the continuity to share their own experiences with one another is poor." The main reason women gave for leaving the union is that they can't afford the membership dues.

> The biggest reason that members cancelled their membership was a financial reason, for instance they could not find a new job and were unable to pay for the membership fee. Recently, there were some WUT members who [could not] pay the membership fee because of low wages for women, especially under the progression of nonpermanent employment and the degradation of working conditions year after year. In these cases, the WUT considers exemptions of a membership fee individually. However, the WUT has its limits as to the measures it can employ to financially support these members, since the WUT itself is run only on union dues and donations.

Other women said they left because they weren't getting enough out of the union. It's the classic downward spiral understaffed organizations often face: chronic lack of human resources makes it difficult for the WUT to provide training and activities to empower individuals and build solidarity among members, but failure to empower and create solidarity among members leads to high drop-out rates, virtually guaranteeing continued understaffing. The core members want to provide the kinds of educational opportunities that help members see the link between their individual troubles and the larger social issues that will continue to affect them in their work and home lives as long as Japan remains a gender-unequal society. Such opportunities provide the logic for becoming a long-term active member. But the shortage of members who have the training and commitment to foster such opportunities—coupled with the overwhelming demand for help with individual grievances—means that active WUT members have little time for anything beyond job counseling and collective bargaining. According to Tani:

> The WUT works under pressure in settlements of difficult cases most of the time, and this situation makes it hard to develop union activities besides a labor advisory service and bargaining. Even after settling original issues, many WUT members still have varied problems such as unemployment, change of job, poverty, and illness. However, the WUT cannot carry out enough activities to meet the needs of these

members . . . . For example, there are some members who need to raise their self-confidence, to be trained in business skills and manners, and to promote their own businesses to utilize abilities of their own that might not be useful in a general workplace.[1]

Nor can the union provide much in the way of recreational activities that could help refresh members' spirits and allow them to form bonds of friendship and solidarity. "Although the WUT deals with deep and serious issues, we also need to create the moment of enjoyment and relaxation in the ways of counseling, bargaining, and discussion."

The issue of recreational activities is a good example of how resource shortages feed on each other. Even if the union could somehow come up with the resources to offer much-needed recreational activities, most members still wouldn't attend. Without some sort of educational program to explain the larger purpose of such activities, many women would write them off as just another social activity they have no time for.

The union is also hampered by limitations of time and space for holding membership meetings. Limitation of space is not just a problem of cramped offices, although that is a habitual challenge for most of the women's unions I spoke with. It is also a question of limited venues for holding regular union meetings and activities. Most of these fledgling unions can afford to keep only one office, which means members could have extremely long, cumbersome commutes depending on where they live or work in relation to the union's office. This is particularly a problem in an enormous city such as Tokyo. The WUT's only office is located in central Tokyo, but since the union draws women from all over the metro area, it takes some members well over an hour by train to get there. For a lot of women, that alone precludes regular attendance at and participation in union activities.

Information Gap

The proliferation of employment patterns (full-time, part-time, contract, dispatch, etc.) and the changing laws around them mean that many women do not know the specific terms of their employment, nor which laws apply to them. The union does not have a research department and must rely on union members to gather the information necessary to pursue their cases. This system is slow-going and not very effective for the same reasons the union has trouble getting volunteers to answer phones: not enough people, not enough training. And the situation is getting worse as longer work hours mean even fewer women have time to track down information that companies do not make readily available.

The WUT also lacks resources and strategies for communications and information sharing. The union does not have the financial resources to undertake direct mailings or other expensive forms of print communications to keep members who cannot attend regular meetings informed. The WUT newsletter is a spare, black and white, in-house production that comes out once a month. Beyond the newsletter, the union relies on its website, message board, and e-mail distribution lists. For some members, web-based communications work very well and, in fact, are a preferred method for information sharing. But for those who lack access to computers or, more commonly, lack the skills or confidence to use the Internet, web-based communications leave them out in the cold. This point was brought home to me later in the project when I was soundly scolded by members of women's unions in other cities. I had sent e-mails to all of the participating unions to solicit members' input on what our next workshops should include. In response, some of the women complained that too much of the planning dialogue was being conducted online and they didn't have the time or access to a computer to participate.

The self-study concluded that the union's web-based communications were reasonably effective in helping core members stay in touch with each other and members of other women's organizations, but only marginally inform—and in some cases alienate—more casual union members. Core members routinely use the Internet to keep each other apprised of upcoming events and emerging issues, and to share ideas and planning tasks, without having to be physically in the same room. But the union's online communications have had little effect on the participation and engagement of members outside the core, in part because the union does not have enough staff or volunteers to provide detailed, up-to-date content, such as discussions of impending legislative initiatives, updates on cases and campaigns, and summaries of union meetings, on a regular basis.

Shortage of Funding Sources

Wary of accepting funds that might come with strings attached, the WUT relies almost exclusively on membership dues. But at approximately $20 a month, their dues do not provide enough revenue for the union to develop all of the activities and programs members want and need, particularly when every new member comes with a grievance already in hand. According to the report Midori gave on the first day of the workshop, the union's annual budget was 10,000,000 yen, which at that time was approximately $91,000. The union received 4,800,000 yen ($44,000) in membership dues; 3,000,000 yen ($27,000) in donations; and 500,000 yen ($4,500) in corresponding membership fees, leaving a 1,700,000-yen ($15,600) deficit. Tani said the union would like to develop projects that could attract grant money, such as job-skills training or seminars to help women promote their own businesses. But, once again, it is a question of lacking the resources to develop such programs.

Individual Settlements Not Leading to a Larger Movement

The founders' goal was to create a union that would be a catalyst for a larger women's movement, which would in turn promote broad social change in the workplace, the home, and society at large. But so far, the WUT has had little success in converting new members' initial focus on individual grievances into a broader social justice perspective.

"The reality that many WUT members disengage from union activities or withdraw from the WUT after the settlements of their own issues shows that the settlement of individual labor issues has not led to [a] movement to establish women's right to work," Tani said. The members identified what they believe are the main reasons the union has not been successful in stimulating a larger movement.

INABILITY TO BUILD SUPPORT AMONG COWORKERS

Many of the individual cases that women bring to the union are, in fact, problems for other people in the same workplace. For example, if one person is being forced to work unpaid overtime, other employees are almost certainly under the same pressure.[2] But, for unions based on individual affiliation, there is little opportunity and few mechanisms for developing awareness among the other employees that the union member's fight is their fight, too. "In most cases it is impossible to make an individual struggle into the struggle of the entire workplace," Tani said.

INABILITY TO OVERCOME ISOLATION AND PROVIDE PROTECTION IN THE WORKPLACE

The WUT is unable to protect members from harassment and retaliation in the workplace. In a traditional union situation, in which a large block of the workers belong to the same union, the members (ideally) would stand together and support the woman in the face of harassment and bullying. But when a WUT member decides to fight back, there usually are no other union members in her workplace to back her up. "The reality is that the employee who stands up and exercises her rights becomes isolated in the workplace," Tani said. "It would be difficult for the member to keep fighting against unreasonable treatment from a company if the WUT cannot support such a member enough. This is a common issue among labor unions based on affiliation."

A related problem, which the self-report did not mention, is that individual-membership unions have little power to stop violations *before* they happen. With a strong union presence at the worksite, bosses sometimes check their own worst impulses to avoid costly showdowns with the union. But in the case of the WUT, there is nothing to stop management from committing violations. All the union can do is help members take action after the fact, by which time the damage, to the employee's health, safety, dignity, and so on, is already done.

DIFFICULTY DEVELOPING "UNION SPIRIT" AND COMMITMENT TO SOCIAL CHANGE

The self-analysis also revealed a persistent "lack of harmonization" between members' goals and the underlying philosophy of the WUT. While the leaders hope the members will come to see the union as a vehicle through which they can wage a broad-based fight for women's rights, most members continue to "consider the WUT as a rescue organization to solve [their] problems."

Once again, it's a problem of resources. Demand for job counseling and collective bargaining leaves core members little time to conduct activities that would help new members see their individual issues as part of the bigger picture of gender and class inequality, and inspire them to join a broader social justice movement. Core members see the connections between the individual grievances and larger labor trends, the relationship between women's position in the workforce and persistent gender stereotypes and gender-role expectations in society at large, and that making significant improvements in women's working conditions and their ability to participate as equals in the workforce will require profound social change. However, such goals are light-years away from what most women come to the union hoping to achieve. Most women come to the union seeking a solution to their immediate problems and a quick return to a more normal (less conflict-ridden) existence. Getting them to sign on to an even larger struggle takes a great deal of education and internal organizing, much more than the WUT is able to provide. To make matters worse, even when the union does manage to host solidarity-building activities, they are typically conducted under such a cloud of exhaustion that they are neither inspiring nor do they project a sense of empowerment that could capture members' imaginations and hearts.

Finally, the lack of internal organizing and solidarity-building activities means that members rarely interact with anyone outside of their own bargaining team. Since the union is limited in the number of events it can offer and attendance at such events is low, new members tend to communicate only with the members who are helping them with their case. New members have little opportunity to hear the thoughts and stories of other women, which could help them to develop a bigger picture understanding of their own grievances as part of a much larger social problem. "It is very important for a labor union based on reciprocal help to improve communication among the union members. Unfortunately, the WUT has not yet created sufficient organic networks among the members," Tani said. The union's monthly case-study meetings were intended to stimulate discussions among members with active cases, so that they could discover similarities and common purpose. But, as with other union activities, the members who need that experience most are the least likely to attend. "Members who attend bargaining cannot afford to make time for a meeting to share experiences or reflect on cases."

Limited Impact on Public Policy

Linked to the union's inability to fuel a larger social movement, the WUT has not been able to play nearly as large a role in shaping public policy as the union leaders would like. Women's movements in Japan have historically sought change through legislative and other policy initiatives. Such strategies are especially important for individual-membership unions, which do not have access to the traditional source of labor unions' power. Individual-membership unions, like other social advocacy groups, must focus their efforts on changing public policy, public opinion, and the law. "Indeed, the WUT needs to work more actively on making public comments for deliberation councils and workshops, making proposals to relevant levels of government, and submitting reports to international machinery such as the International Labour Organization, in order to play a role of policymaking based on the analysis regarding the current situation of women workers," Tani said.

Japan has a variety of mechanisms for bringing civil society groups into the deliberations over pending legislative and policy decisions, and the WUT does participate in such dialogues. However, the union is not able to devote nearly as much time and energy to these efforts as the members would like—or as their movement needs—in order to counterbalance the weight of corporate interests. Originally, the founders thought that in time they'd be able to pass the responsibilities of union leadership on to the next generation, freeing themselves to devote more time to lobbying and other political activities. But so far, the union leaders have had no time to train or motivate their own replacements.

Lack of Effective Advertising

The WUT membership expressed a strong sense of obligation to ensure that "women who are suffering in their workplaces" know about the union and how to get in touch, and deep disappointment that, although the union had been in operation for nearly ten years, few women outside their small circle had ever heard of the WUT. The members say they have been unable to develop sufficient methods for advertising the fact of the union's existence, nor have they developed methods and materials for promoting a positive image of unions and feminism in general.[3] This is a primary concern among core members because they know very well that even women who have heard of the WUT and are in need of its services might be reluctant to join because of the negative image that both unions and feminist groups have in Japan. Unions are often thought of as weak, ineffective, conflict-ridden anachronisms. And groups linking themselves to the "F-word" strike younger people especially as being hopelessly old-fashioned. As one young gender-studies student put it, "To young people like me, these groups smell of red rust." What that statement lacks in charity it makes up for in pithy accuracy. The WUT really does use outmoded language, outmoded methods and media, and, in some cases, even outmoded analyses. The members know this but, without input from younger people, they don't know how to change it.

Re-creating Hierarchy

Perhaps the most distressing revelation to come out of the self-analysis—certainly the most painful to admit—was that although the WUT was designed to break down traditional union hierarchies and replace them with democratic practices, lack of resources has forced the WUT to operate in ways that inadvertently reproduce the same kind of hierarchical power structures found in male-oriented unions. Beyond undermining Midori and Tani's vision of a self-sustaining, person-to-person union, the pooling of knowledge inadvertently reproduces the type of top-down power relations the WUT hoped to break down, and puts the union in danger of dying out once the founding generation retires. Moreover, the lack of time, energy, and resources—and the dearth of opportunities for members to interact with each other away from the bargaining table—means new and experienced members have little chance to get to know and trust each other. Experienced members become reluctant to hand off union operations to undertrained new members. New members feel intimidated about taking on responsibilities they haven't been trained to handle. The result is that the membership divide is again reinforced, with a layer of "experts" coming to the aid of "suffering women" who need their help. This is exactly the dynamic the WUT founders wanted to break down.

Part of the problem was that the founding members didn't realize how much training is necessary to properly prepare people with no union or activist background so that they could (and would) become fully participating members. "I thought union activities were nothing special, no special skills were needed," Tani said. "I thought if we could share experiences there would be no difference among us, staff and members. But that did not happen. The difference in experience always remains and becomes a gap between members and staff. It created hierarchy and could not be overcome."

Building Participation through Education

After the previous day's celebration of success stories, Tani's report was stark, sobering and more than a little overwhelming. And yet, it was unequivocally the centerpiece of the Detroit meeting because it laid out, with brutal specificity, the exact problems that we as a group were here to address. We already knew from our discussions during the planning phase that the best way we, as US activists, could support the JWUs was to help them develop their own educational programs. Now we had a much clearer picture of exactly what the Japanese groups needed those programs to accomplish. The next step was for us to help the Japanese women gain a more concrete understanding of what labor education is, how some nontraditional unions in the United States have used it to overcome their internal challenges, and how the JWUs might use it to address some of the deficits mentioned in the WUT report.

In the afternoon we heard from two nontraditional unions that have been particularly successful at building and maintaining democratic practices and strong membership participation through labor education: the United Electrical Workers (UE) and UNITE HERE Local 34 clerical and technical workers' union at Yale University. The UE was founded in 1936 as a grassroots, rank-and-file controlled union. Many of the unions that emerged during the 1930s—those heady days after FDR granted workers the right to organize into unions in Section 7(a) of the National Recovery Act—initially embraced the idea of keeping power in the hands of the membership, but over time ossified into the kind of top-down corporate structures that dominate the union landscape in the United States today. But the UE has been fairly successful at maintaining its more democratic practices and orientation. Organizer Leah Fried told us that the UE didn't do it by relying on the goodwill and intentions of its leadership. It did it by adopting an organizational structure that was designed to ensure that power stayed in the hands of the members. Under the UE's bylaws, each workplace forms its own, independently run local union which elects its own leaders and votes on all local matters, such as contracts, dues, and calls to strike. Each local maintains its own treasury and elects representatives to the district and national levels.

The locals are empowered to handle as many union functions as possible. However, some functions are so resource-intensive, such as providing educational programming, that it makes sense for locals to pool their resources at an intermediate level and share the burden of providing them. The intermediate level, called the District Council, coordinates education and solidarity activities among locals within a given region. In addition to educational programs, the District Councils also help with mobilizing people to attend rallies and support picket lines, to participate in organizing drives, and to help with financial support for struggling workers. The District Councils also have their own treasuries and meet three times a year to vote on activities and allocation of funds, and to share ideas and experiences.

The third level is the National Union, which provides the even more expensive functions, such as legal assistance, research, and international solidarity. It is also responsible for enacting national policy set by the delegates to the national convention (and subsequently voted on by members at the local level).

Since the locals are largely autonomous, it is especially important for members to have access to a well-developed educational program to help them acquire the skills they need to run their own union. The UE's educational program includes national- and district-level workshops, monthly training for local unions, a steward's newsletter with advice on how to fight for justice in the workplace, a kit of materials for stewards, and a Leadership Guide, described as "a complete how-to for local unions on everything from balancing the books to new organizing." To all of us, these sounded like exactly the type of materials the women's unions were hoping to develop. The content might differ significantly, but the idea of a how-to handbook that would be the repository of activists' experiences and advice was right on the money.

We also heard from Laura Smith, president of UNITE HERE Local 34, which represents the clerical and technical workers at Yale University. Local 34 gained a kind of rock-star status in labor circles in 1984–85, when the predominantly female workforce scored an against-all-odds victory over a notoriously anti-union employer in the profoundly hostile years of the Reagan administration. Several unions had tried to organize Yale's clerical and technical workers (C&Ts) in the past but each time had been defeated by Yale's aggressive anti-union campaigns and the logistical difficulties of organizing campus-based clerical workers. At the time of Local 34's organizing drive, Yale had approximately 2,600 clerical and technical workers, spread out across some 250 buildings, with work groups typically consisting of four or five people. Most unions simply do not have enough professional organizers to reach every corner of such a large, geographically dispersed workforce. As one union member put it, "[T]hirty people simply can't organize 2,600" (Gilpin et al. 1988). So Local 34 didn't try. Instead, the union's professional organizers trained approximately 450 C&Ts in organizing and basic union skills so that they could organize their coworkers, run the union election campaign, and later negotiate their own union contract. Although an organizing committee of this size was at times unwieldy and eventually had to be broken into smaller, targeted committees, it enabled a union—for the first time—to get its message to virtually all of the workers in the potential bargaining unit. It also gave a large percentage of the workforce the education and skills to build and run an effective, democratic union.

A second reason for Local 34's success was that other unionized workers on campus supported the C&Ts efforts to organize. Local 35 (representing Yale's electricians, carpenters, plumbers, groundskeepers, dining service, and other campus maintenance workers) provided invaluable financial, strategic, and emotional support to the struggling C&Ts during the organizing drive and subsequent strike. Local 35, which had been organized for decades, recognized that, over the years (as manufacturing jobs disappeared from the region and the university became one of the few major employers in the area), Yale was acting less like an institution of higher learning and more like a for-profit corporation whose sole interest was its bottom line. With each new round of contract negotiations, Local 35 members had to fight harder and longer to win ever smaller gains at the bargaining table. The union realized that the only way to fight this trend was to organize more of the workers on campus. Although there was some bad blood between Local 35 and the C&Ts, Local 35 members were well educated in union matters and understood that it was in their best interest to organize as much of the campus as possible.[4]

The union also built local and national support through community outreach and education. The C&Ts framed their dispute as an appeal to basic fairness. By juxtaposing Yale's reputation as a venerable institution of enlightenment and progress with its actions as a tight-fisted corporation that treats women employees like second-class citizens, Local 34 won the support of the faculty, students, and much of the New Haven, CT community. The union built support in the community by running a campaign that focused on demanding fairness, gender equality, and for the employees to be treated with dignity and respect. The union also called on Yale to be a good neighbor and share the wealth with the surrounding community that supports it. Following the loss of heavy industry in the region, New Haven was becoming an increasingly economically depressed area. The entire community was suffering as crime and other poverty-related social ills were on the rise. As one of the major employers in the area (one out of every four jobs in New Haven was a Yale job), Yale could make a significant contribution to stabilizing the local economy by paying employees a decent wage. Instead, it was spending its vast resources to keep underpaid workers ever more firmly under its thumb. The local population did not take kindly to this kind of robber baronism. Soon, yard signs and bumpers stickers chiding Yale started appearing all over town, and news of Yale's bad corporate citizenship got national and even international attention. On January 19, 1985, after a three-year organizing drive, eighteen months of negotiations, and a ten-week-long strike, Local 34 won its first union contract.

The union's greatest achievement has been in maintaining high levels of membership participation and its alliances on and off campus, long after the first contract was settled. The members of Locals 34 and 35 were well aware that if they let down their guard, if they let the union get flabby between contracts, Yale would immediately start chipping away at the gains they had won. They understood that, in order to protect their jobs, wages, and benefits, they needed to continue to organize internally, to keep their own members sharp and active, and they also needed to support other campus employees, such as graduate students, researchers, adjunct teachers, and the hospital workers in the medical school who were trying to organize.

From start to finish, Local 34's success was a victory of education. The original members won their union by educating themselves, their coworkers, the campus community, and finally the New Haven community at large about the need for a C&Ts union at Yale. And they did it through the kind of person-to-person outreach that the WUT founders had envisioned but not been able to get off the ground. It was clear that, like the story of 9to5 the day before, the story of Local 34's organizing success struck a chord with the Japanese women who were present. It was starting to click: women working in pink-collar occupations, in distributed work settings, and in politically hostile climates were nonetheless successfully organizing and overcoming inherent deficits while empowering members through skills-based education.

Like most unions, the UE and UNITE HERE have their own in-house educational programs. But there are other types of programs that exist independent of specific unions, such as university-based labor education. Emily Rosenberg, director of the Labor Education Program at DePaul University, gave us a brief overview of university-based labor education, which provides skills and leadership training to union members, leaders, and staff. University-based programs typically offer workshops, short-term courses for nondegree students, and semester-long classes for degree-seeking students. Some programs, such as the DePaul Labor Center, also offer multi-year curricula to train union leaders. Typical courses include organizing, grievance handling, collective bargaining, workers' rights, health and safety, labor law, labor history, economics, arbitration, politics and labor, and current issues that are relevant to labor, such as the effects of trade agreements on US workers. Labor education programs in public universities are usually funded through the state. Programs in private universities rely on funding from the university itself and on fees from unions that use their services. Unions and labor activists have had to fight hard to protect funding for education programs, as union membership and public support for unions in general has waned.

Although Japan has no equivalent university-based programs and the Japanese participants could not imagine their government providing funding for such programs, Emily pointed out that public funding for university-based programs in the United States was a political victory, won by organizing and leveraging political power. And while university-based education is clearly not an immediate solution for JWUs, it is important to consider for two reasons. First, because this sort of education system could possibly be won through political struggle if Japanese workers decide they want it. Second, because it reminds the participants to think outside the box. Labor education doesn't have to come only from the unions themselves. With the right incentive, society can create entirely new, previously unimagined structures and institutions to handle pressing social needs.

Tess Ewing, an educator at the University of Massachusetts Boston Labor Extension Program—and with the Women in Leadership Development (WILD) program—introduced yet another type of educational structure, union women's schools, which focus on the special needs of women as a minority population within the labor movement. Women's schools (which are actually more like annual conferences or workshops than traditional "schools") were developed as one way of addressing the unequal distribution of power between male and female union members. The idea was to empower women by enabling them to build their union skills through the process of participatory education. Typically, women's schools meet on university campuses during the summer and offer classes on collective bargaining, grievance handling, public speaking, and other basic union skills. Many also offer workshops on current events and how they relate to working people and women.

As an example, Tess described the women's union school she works with, WILD. Its mission is to help women develop the skills and confidence they need to assume leadership positions within the labor movement. The WILD program also seeks to promote more democratic and inclusive unions, and to raise awareness about racism, sexism, and homophobia in unions and in the labor movement as a whole. The Japanese women were very enthusiastic about union schools as a model for the kind of program they would like to build. Their smaller scope and scale make weekend schools such as WILD a more realistic model for the small, under-resourced JWUs. And the Japanese women saw the potential for creating a curriculum that was specifically designed to empower women.

The concept of labor education was so new to the Japanese participants that we couldn't possibly fill in all the blanks in a single afternoon. Still, the presentations provided enough to get everyone thinking creatively about how the Japanese groups could use education to address the kinds of problems the WUT members identified in their report. We had agreed from the outset that Workshops II and III would be devoted to helping the Japanese groups create three educational modules on the topics of their choice. We spent the rest of the day brainstorming ideas about the kinds of skills the JWU leaders would like their members to acquire, and imagining respectful, engaging, and empowering ways to teach those skills. Our hope was that the Japanese groups would take those ideas back to their own members and continue collectively riffing on those themes until they were ready to choose the three topics they wanted to focus on at our next international meeting.

Summing Up: Positive Outcomes of the First International Meeting

If sparking new and lasting activity is the sign of a successful workshop, the Detroit meeting was an unqualified success. Our concrete goals were to educate each other about our organizations, build national and international ties among our organizations, and begin mapping out a plan for developing basic resources that Japanese women's unions need to move beyond their current plateaus. We did that. But even more importantly, we came away with specific plans and procedures—developed by the participants themselves—for continuing the discussions and getting started on the tasks we committed to during this first workshop. This was especially significant for the Japanese groups for two reasons. First, after just one meeting the Japanese groups were already working collectively, innovating, and solving problems collectively, and they were looking to themselves to create a fair and democratic process for moving the project forward. Second, in doing so, the Japanese groups were gradually taking control of how the project would develop over the next two years. As the official conference planners, Heidi and I had taken responsibility for determining the content and format for Workshop I, but the goal was for participants to increasingly take over the role of directing the project based on the insights and innovations that grew out of their interactions. That can be a difficult transition, as logistical and administrative difficulties, not to mention inertia, make it easier to just let those in charge stay in charge. But, by the end of Workshop I, it was clear that the Japanese women were stepping up to the challenge sooner and even more definitively than we dared to hope.

Building a Shared Knowledge Base

Despite truly abysmal translation services, the participants managed to educate each other on the problems working women face in each country; the history, structure, and goals of the organizations we've built to address them; and the legal, economic and political climates in which we, as workers and as activists, operate. I was truly amazed that, in just one weekend, the women were able to convey and absorb so much information that we all walked away with tremendously enhanced understandings of the similarities and differences in our circumstances. We learned about significant differences in employment practices, and how those differences shape the particular ways each country's employment system limits opportunities and rewards for women. This was a crucial step in the project because we needed to know exactly what discrimination looks like and how it is perpetuated in each country before we could engage in meaningful problem-solving and strategy discussions.

Unquestionably, the most significant and groundbreaking achievement of this first meeting was the dialogue that was opened through the WUT's self-report. The union provided enough detail about its internal operations that we could begin asking deeper questions about *why* it wasn't able to grow beyond its current level. We could look beyond individual and psychological explanations and begin considering how the organization itself might be creating or at least perpetuating some of its own worst problems. The WUT's previous conclusions, "We just have to try harder" or "We aren't doing enough to empower our members," were dead ends. They didn't open any space or provide any ideas for trying something new. But, by laying bare its internal operations, the WUT opened the question to a larger assembly of experienced activists, and gave us the information we needed to analyze the situation, find the roots of the problems, and develop workable strategies for helping JWUs break through the barriers that were holding them back.

Of course, that was our expected outcome. We had asked the union to undertake and present an organizational self-study because we thought it was an essential step in our larger problem-solving agenda. What we hadn't counted on was how powerful the self-report would be in building solidarity. As we listened to Tani present the union's findings, it became increasingly obvious just how difficult this task was for the WUT members. We could see in their faces just how much courage it took for these women to examine their organization with brutal honesty (and with egos admirably set aside), itemize its failings, and then admit those failings to a roomful of strangers. Not a task anyone would relish, but they did it because they put the union's success above everything else. And we understood that by sharing their findings with us, the WUT members were placing enormous trust in the rest of us, the other Japanese groups as well as the US participants present. They were trusting us to respect rather than ridicule, to enhance their efforts rather than undermine them, and to help them achieve their vision rather than trying to impose our own. The room fell very still as Tani spoke, I think because we were feeling humbled by the courageous act we were witnessing, and because that was the moment that solidified our commitment to each other and to the project.

Aside from the shared benefits of the Detroit meeting, each side also came away with insights that were unique to their situations. The Japanese participants were introduced to a variety of organizations and new forms of organizations that exist in the US to educate and empower members, including: university-based labor education programs; women's union schools; in-house empowerment institutions such as the UAW Women's Department; and free-standing organizations such as CLUW and 9to5. They also learned about the tradition of labor feminism that has existed in the United States for more than a century, as well as more recent efforts of progressive US activists to reject bureaucratic, service unionism in favor of social-movement unionism. And they had the opportunity to talk with representatives from two progressive unions, the UE and UNITE HERE Local 34, which rely on strong labor education to build and sustain organizations that are in many ways similar to JWUs.

The Japanese women also came away thinking about education as a way to build commitment among members and for injecting a broader social justice vision into the movement. In the beginning, their interest in building an educational program focused on the need to transmit knowledge and skills to new members for their own empowerment and so they could help shoulder the work involved in running the union. By the end of the workshop, the Japanese women were also talking about education as a form of internal organizing and a first step in the long-term goal of building a more encompassing social movement that seeks to humanize life for men and women alike.

For the US participants, finding out about a whole new world of women's activism was worth the price of admission. Activists and academics alike reacted with surprise and delight as we learned about the many kinds of alternative organizations that are springing up in Japan. We also came away with a better understanding of the unique barriers embedded in the Japanese employment system, the unique challenges to women those barriers produce, and how those challenges have in turn shaped the unique organizations Japanese women have created. I think it's also fair to say we came away with increased respect for Japanese women and workers whom, we learned, are not so docile after all. We were all struck by the enthusiasm, creativity, and tirelessness of the Japanese women. At home the Japanese women talked about being tired and burned out—and no doubt they were, physically. But their ideas were so fresh and their hopes so high that they seemed mighty twinkly to those of us who work in or with well-established institutions. Several of the US activists said they felt a renewed sense of possibility and purpose, as well as renewed energy for creating fresh, new ways to engage with members and the public, and fresh, new ways to fight back against the boss.

Building International Ties

The Detroit meeting also succeeded in creating networks among US and Japanese women's groups and stimulating a desire for ongoing information exchange. Despite language, cultural, and experiential differences, we eagerly engaged with each other, sharing our knowledge and ideas while also building organizational and personal ties. Some of the Japanese activists organized US participants to support cases they were pursuing at that time. The Japanese participants also expressed interest in continuing their dialogue with the US labor educators. Since both the concept and methods of empowerment-centered education were extremely new to the Japanese groups, they wanted more input from US educators before undertaking the task of writing their own system. In particular, they asked for concrete (written) examples of empowerment-centered educational methods and materials to begin conceptualizing their own program. They also requested online discussions with US educators as they worked to develop their ideas about the style and content of the materials they would create over the course of the second and third workshops. That turned out to be tricky because of the language gap, but we took it as a good sign that the Japanese women would be interested in an ongoing discussion—if we could figure out a way to make it happen.

Building Ties among Japanese Groups

The US-Japan Project in fact comprised two simultaneous exchanges, one between the US and Japanese participants, and the other among the Japanese groups. From the very beginning, Midori and Tani made it clear that the Japanese groups needed time and interaction with each other at least as much as they needed interaction with groups outside Japan. Since the project provided a rare opportunity for Japanese women's groups to be in the same place at the same time, they used the opportunity to hold a separate, Japanese-only meeting (after a full day of workshopping) to discuss things that were beyond the scope of the international exchange. As it turned out, the Japanese-only meeting also proved to be a fruitful forum for extending the discussions that were generated by the workshop, for developing plans for disseminating the ideas and insights that emerged during the workshop, and for developing a democratic process that would bring as many Japanese voices as possible into the discussion of which topics we should focus on in Workshop II.

The Japanese groups also decided that upon returning home they would each hold informational meetings for their own members and members of other women's organizations in their area to share what they learned in the Detroit workshop. Following these informational meetings, they would hold a series of local, regional, and national planning meetings to choose three topics for educational modules that we would work on at our next international meeting.

They also established an online discussion forum to enable geographically dispersed groups to continue working together between meetings and after the workshops series concluded. The Japanese participants used the forum to plan their regional and national meetings, to discuss ideas for our second international workshop, and to disseminate information about their activities and relevant community events, speakers, and so on. For example, women from a variety of organizations engaged in a lively online discussion of Paulo Freire's theories of education and how they might relate to the Japanese organizations' educational goals.

These were significant developments because they were not part of the original plan. The Japanese women were already innovating new communication processes in response to questions that grew out of our collective discussions. And their innovations reflected their commitment to democracy and inclusion. Instead of simply choosing the three topics among themselves, the Japanese participants decided on this far more costly (in terms of time, money, and effort) plan because it would bring more women into the decision-making process, and because it would provide opportunities to further develop the organizational connections they made during the first workshop. Their meetings also extended the benefits of the international meetings by providing opportunities for the Japanese activists to process and adapt ideas they encountered in Workshop I. The groups also used the national meetings as an opportunity to jointly strategize responses to issues that were arising at that moment, such as organizing a united campaign around proposed revisions to the Part-time Workers' Law.

Lessons Learned the Hard Way

We also made our share of mistakes, some of which we could learn from and address, or at least be mindful of, as we moved forward; others not so much. I discuss our notable blunders in more detail in the final chapter, but for now I want to mention a few that were especially troubling because they reinforced existing divisions within the group and created rifts that we were never quite able to overcome.

Reproducing Inequality: Introductions

On the first day of the workshop, I made the fundamental mistake of skipping over the Japanese custom of self-introductions in the interest of saving time. At the first break, Midori told me that the Japanese participants were very uncomfortable because we hadn't started the meeting with a round of self-introductions. I had cut that segment out of the schedule because we were in a terrible time crunch and everyone wanted more time for the speakers. But Midori explained that, for the Japanese participants, self-introductions are necessary for creating a sense of belongingness and shared purpose. As with drinking tea, self-introductions at the start of meetings are an important part of establishing harmony, which is a necessary social condition for moving forward as a group united in a task. Moreover, if only those who come to the podium get introduced, only the "famous" people have identities; audience members remain anonymous.

But that was not the only way we blundered on introductions. The way we introduced the speakers inadvertently reproduced, and even amplified, the class inequality that existed among us. Heidi and I had not discussed introduction styles in advance. In fact, with everything else that was going on, the question of introducing speakers hadn't even crossed my mind. It wasn't until the first morning of the workshop that we hurriedly decided that Heidi would introduce the academics and I would introduce the activists. (There were a few exceptions on either side but this was basically how the split came down.) Since we hadn't discuss introduction styles beforehand, we each introduced people in the way we were accustomed to, I in the style of a union meeting and she according to academic custom. The result was an embarrassing mismatch that radically highlighted the status differences among us. Recapping academic speakers' illustrious careers—their latest books, prestigious appointments, and profound influence on their fields of study—Heidi sounded like she was introducing nominees for a lifetime achievement award. I, on the other hand, sounded more like a bailiff calling out the next case on the docket—just name, affiliation, and topic of presentation with very little fanfare. In another context it might have been funny, but in our case it undermined our efforts to manage a difficult balance that was essential to the success of our project.

And yet, even if we had harmonized our introductions in advance and adopted the typical academic style of introducing speakers by listing their credentials and accomplishments, we would have had the same problem. Introducing people by their achievements is useful in that it provides context for the audience and serves as a sort of quid pro quo; public praise as a way of thanking the speakers for sharing their expertise. But again, it can't help reproducing inequality because the outcomes associated with elite occupations tend to be more glamorous, more highly valued, and more likely to be tallied than the outcomes of the work people in "ordinary" jobs do.[5] When academic speakers came to the podium, we heard how many books and articles they had published, which prestigious awards they had won, which elite institutions they were associated with, and how important they were in shaping the world we live in. But there is no score-keeping equivalent for nonelite workers. No one keeps track of the number of floors a janitor has washed or patients a nurse has cared for; there is no universal system for quantifying or even recognizing the impact many types of workers have on people's lives. Their achievements and contributions may be just as or even more important than those of elite professionals, but they are invisible in this form of introduction. We would have been much more successful at fostering participation and openness if we had asked everyone to introduce themselves in the beginning and then step to the microphone as one among equals when it was their turn to talk.

Reproducing Inequality: Accommodations

Class haunted the project almost as much as nationality. Workshop I ended up being the most expensive of the three international meetings, in part because of the extra costs associated with hosting academics and other middle-class profes-sionals. Because of the nature of the Detroit meeting, we had quite a few more academics among the participants than we would in either of the subsequent workshops, and that inevitably affected our decisions about the kinds of accom-modations we needed to provide.

At one level the controversy over accommodations was one of misperception. We were staying in a B&B across the street from campus. With its richly deco-rated interior, it appeared to be a much more expensive establishment than it actually was. In fact, it was the most economical option we could find. The room rates were comparable to basic business-traveler hotels in the city, and its prox-imity to campus saved us the cost and hassle of transporting forty people to and from their hotels every day. I repeatedly explained this to the Japanese women when they fretted about the cost, but the visual cues won out. They could not reconcile all the space and luxurious-looking furniture with the modest price. Two years later, when we were scrimping and stretching to cover expenses for the final workshop, I was still getting blowback for overspending on our fancy accommodations in Detroit.

But while the issue of the B&B in particular was largely a cultural misunderstanding, the cost of accommodations in general reflected concessions to class that cut across nationality.[6] Although the B&B was no more expensive than any other hotel that we would be willing to consider, if this had been a gathering of activists only, we might not have been considering hotel options at all. Travel for grassroots activists looks a lot like travel for college students: lots of sleeping on people's couches or sharing rooms at highway-exit motels. But none of us would have been comfortable putting up the academics in sub-prime lodgings.[7] Our hands were tied by social conventions of politeness and hospitality: the academics were doing us a huge favor by giving us their time and knowledge with no remuneration or direct quid pro quo. It would have been rude to ask them to do all that and then not host them in a manner that was customary for middle-class professionals.

We ran into the same problem with the conference dinners. We held them at restaurants that were absolutely standard issue in academic circles, the kind of places every visiting academic or job candidate is taken to after giving a talk. Many of the activists, on the other hand, were well outside of their comfort zone. Although they enjoyed the dinner, and even more the opportunity to interact with everyone, the prices and relative finery left a bad taste in their mouths. Some of the Japanese women later told me they felt guilty and a little resentful because we were spending money on luxuries instead of using it to, for example, invite one more activist to join the project.

Institutional Barriers

During a break on the first day of the Detroit meeting, several of the Japanese women suggested to me that, instead of having three international workshops as originally planned, it might be better to hold two international workshops with a series of smaller, national workshops in Japan in between. This would give the Japanese women more time to prepare and refine their ideas for a final international meeting. I was excited by their suggestion. Not only did it seem like a good idea to me, it also seemed like a sign that the Japanese women had been stimulated by what they heard so far and the connections they had made, and they were eager to take the ball and run with it. That kind of organic innovation was exactly what we were hoping for. Unfortunately, we ran into an institutional barrier I had not foreseen. When we were writing the grant proposal, I understood it to be a working model for how the project was likely to unfold, with the understanding that the participants would be free to reshape future elements of the project based on insights that emerged over time. I thought I had written that very clearly into the project's description. But when the Japanese women raised the idea of changing the format, Heidi was in the unenviable position of having to inform us all that under the terms of our grant, we had to follow the plan exactly as specified in the original proposal. For me, that was the first moment when I really felt the restricting presence of the supporting institutions. We had had some minor spats with the Wayne State University accounting office, which was administrating the grant, but this was the first major instance of an outside institution directly impinging on the shape of the US-Japan Project. It was a painful and embarrassing setback, and it was the first appearance of yet another problem that would dog us throughout the collaboration.[8]

Looking Ahead

For all the challenges this meeting faced, we had indeed accomplished quite a lot for our first encounter. We now knew that our long-term goal was to help the Japanese groups develop their own curricula for three membership-skills workshops. Between the end of the Detroit meeting and the start of the second meeting (place and time as yet unspecified), the Japanese women would be responsible for choosing three skill areas they wanted to focus on (in essence, to identify the three most immediate skills members needed to participate meaningfully in their union). Once Japanese women had named the skill areas they were interested in, the US labor educators would develop custom training-the-trainer curricula designed to introduce the Japanese participants in the second international meeting to the methods and materials US activists use to teach skills in each of the three areas. These training-the-trainer workshops were not meant to provide ready-made educational materials and methods that the Japanese women could adopt directly. Instead, they were meant to provide concrete examples of both a new style of education (participatory adult education) and content (the nuts and bolts of teaching particular skills). Our hope was that these examples would provide a jumping-off point for the Japanese women to create educational materials of their own. But first the Japanese activists—from so many different groups and regions—had to collectively decide on their three skill areas, which meant initiating a national debate and decision-making process among women's organizations in just a few months. This step was important because it ensured that going forward our efforts would be focused on teaching the skills the Japanese activists judged to be their first priority. But more importantly, this stage of the project was intended to be the occasion for the Japanese women's groups to start building the infrastructure for their own national network. Over the next several months, the Japanese women would need to develop personal and organizational relationships and new communications practices; they would need to educate the women around them who were not able to attend the Detroit meetings and find ways to bring these women's voices into the discussion; and they would need to meet at the national level at least once to finalize the details of a project that would keep them working in tandem for at least the next two years. In other words, the US-Japan Project had created conditions that necessitated the Japanese women's groups' operating as a national unit.

Over the years I had seen a number of activist groups try to establish coalitions by having groups sign up first, then later try to fill in the blanks of what their on-paper organization would really consist of. That always seemed backwards to me or, at the very least, like trying to fill an inside straight. Instead, we set the Japanese activists to a task that required cross-organizational cooperation, and in the course of completing that task the Japanese women would organically create the structures and practices that became the foundation for their national network. That was our theory anyway. Whether or not it would come to fruition depended entirely on what the Japanese women would or could do over the next few months. The ball was in their court; we could do nothing but sit back and see where our Japanese colleagues would take our evolving project.

CRISIS OF DIFFERENCE

The Japanese women wasted no time in making good on their plans to share what they'd learned in the Detroit meetings. The WUT held its first satellite meeting in mid-October. Those who had participated in the Detroit meeting gave summaries of the US participants' presentations, with particular emphasis on Dorothy Sue Cobble's talk on the history of labor feminism in the United States, and Tess Ewing's and Emily Rosenberg's presentations on labor education. Longtime WUT member Miyako Ōga, who gave a presentation on Cobble's talk, told me before the meeting that some of the women had been so excited by Cobble's discussion of US labor feminism that they ordered her book, *The Other Women's Movement*, hoping that they would be able to read it with the help of computer translation programs. They quickly found out their *denshi jisho* (electronic dictionaries) didn't have the muscle to keep up with an academic's vocabulary, Ōga told me with a laugh. But the women were still happy with their purchase because the big, meaty book of working women's accomplishments is still an inspiration and a reminder of the energy they felt as they listened to Cobble's talk. They also studied the presentations by 9to5, the UE, and UNITE HERE Local 34 because those organizations are similar to the WUT in goals and values yet have been more successful in addressing high turnover rates and stimulating membership participation. Similar meetings were held in Fukuoka, Hokkaido, and Osaka to share what they learned in Workshop I, to spread the word about the US-Japan Working Women's Network Project, and to invite others to join us in our goal of developing a membership skills education program for Japanese women's unions.

In November and again in March, representatives from the expanding pool of participating women's organizations met at Waseda University in Tokyo for a national two-day seminar to begin choosing the topics for their first three educational modules. Like the regional meetings, the Waseda meeting was run entirely by the Japanese activists. I was invited to attend as a participant and to answer any logistical or substantive questions about the project that might arise. My primary role, however, was to relay the Japanese women's conclusions back to the US labor educators who would custom design sample modules that they would then present at Workshop II.

Prior to the November meeting, the Japanese groups had agreed that Workshop II should consist of three, small group skills-development workshops, one of which should focus on organizing skills. Our tasks for the two national meetings were to choose the other two skill areas we would focus on, and then begin the process of specifying exactly what the content for the three small group workshops should include. To keep the process democratic and to help avoid culturally based assumptions, the Japanese women held brainstorming sessions to give everyone a chance to share their ideas about what each skills module should include and accomplish. For example, the women brainstormed endings to the sentence: "We want our organizing module to . . . ." The members came up with endings such as: "be interactive and discovery-based," "win the hearts of free-riders," "develop more effective ways to talk to young workers," and "promote good feeling, not gloom." The women then compiled their answers and created a "wish list" for each module that the US educators could use to customize the workshops they would conduct at the second international gathering, which was slated to be held the following July at the International Christian University (ICU) in Tokyo.[1]

After much debate, the Japanese participants decided that, in addition to a small group workshop on organizing skills, Workshop II should include small group workshops on basic communications and empowerment skills (as defined by their wish lists) as well as a plenary workshop on networking among Asian women.[2] The women asked us to invite Emily Rosenberg to conduct the communications workshop, Tess Ewing to facilitate the empowerment skills workshop, and a longtime organizer and friend of the WUT, Mabel Au, to conduct the workshop on networking among Asian women.[3] As for the organizing workshop, initially the then-director of the AFL-CIO Organizing Institute (OI) was to be the facilitator. She and I had numerous phone conversations to get her up to speed on the project and on cultural issues she should be sensitive to when customizing the curriculum she would present. All seemed to be going well in that department until, out of the blue, I heard through the grapevine that the OI was sending a different facilitator entirely to head-up the workshop. A major shake up was brewing within the AFL-CIO and the leadership wanted all hands on deck to respond to the situation. So, with only a month to go before the workshops began and without informing me, the OI decided to send someone else—someone with no familiarity with the project—to conduct this highly specialized workshop. The good news was the person they chose was the highly respected OI organizer and educator Carol Edelson; the bad news was that, despite her expertise in the area, this was not a situation anyone should walk into without sufficient prep time. Through no fault of her own, this unique task suddenly dropped in her lap and she did a remarkable job of responding to the challenge under the circumstances. Still, the lack of lead time meant she was at a significant disadvantage compared to the other facilitators, all of whom had history with the project, and, as we would soon learn, that made what we already expected to be the most emotionally charged workshop even more difficult to pull off.

Workshop II Begins

Once again, the days leading up to Workshop II were among the most stressful of the project. It was mid-July. We were well into another sweltering Tokyo summer. And we had been embroiled in one administrative hassle after another since the end of Workshop I. The WUT women were frustrated with all of the financial snags, and I was feeling beaten about the ears and ego from all the criticism about issues beyond my control. (Even my colleague at ICU, who speaks nearly perfect English, could not understand why I wouldn't just turn the money over to the Japanese groups and let them decide how to spend it. I repeatedly tried to explain to her that I would have happily handed over the money for them to allocate in the way they saw fit, but grants don't work that way. I did not have direct access to the money, and even if I did, we were bound by the terms of the contract to spend it in particular ways.) On the night before the others were to arrive, we held a final meeting to square all the last-minute details. We all looked so strung out and frazzled I couldn't help wondering if the Tokyo contingent would be able to muster the energy we needed to participate in the workshop. But the gloom dissipated like morning fog when the out-of-towners starting showing up the next day. Their bright, expectant faces and positive energy helped to shift our focus away from all the bureaucratic absurdities that had been bogging us down and back to the sense of hope and possibility that brought us together in the first place.

We gathered in the lobby of our "businessmen's hotel," a happy medium between the faux opulence of the B&B in Detroit and the true grit accommodations at Waseda University. Our complimentary breakfast had turned out to be coupons for pre-made sandwiches at the chain café adjacent to the hotel. Not much on nutrition, but at least the coffee creamer didn't come out in lumps. We cabbed en masse the short distance to the International Christian University. The entrance to ICU is well known in Tokyo because of the long stretch of cherry trees that line both sides of the wide lane, magnificent in April when the trees are in bloom. By late July the blossoms are long gone but, even in the early morning hours, the pedestrians are grateful for whatever shade the thick black trunks and sprawling branches can provide.

When we arrived at the main conference room there was no gleaming coffee urn or heaping tray of pastries awaiting us. It was a much more bare-bones affair in terms of refreshments and other niceties. On the other hand, the equipment was better in the sense that the large, comfortable conference room had a built-in simultaneous translation booth, freeing us from the burden of having to rent an expensive sound system like we did in Detroit. We were also able to cut our interpretation budget—while at the same time guaranteeing more accurate interpretation—by hiring professionals who were also active in women's movements. Not long after the Detroit meeting, Midori had told me we should hire professional translators and interpreters who were also activists in the women's movement. At first I thought she was joking; what were the chances of finding people with those specific credentials? But it turns out that, even in a city as mammoth as Tokyo, the activist community is a small world and the WUT members knew several women who fit the bill. Mika Iba and Hwa-Mi Park turned out to be invaluable additions to the project. Their skills propelled us to a level of communication we would never have been able to achieve if we had relied on the kind of mainstream interpreters I had assumed were our only choice.

After the introductions, we split into three groups and adjourned to separate classrooms for the skills-development workshops. My role in this workshop was different from the last. Instead of being a full-time participant, I split my time among the small group workshops, observing when I could, fielding problems when I had to. I was tied up with bureaucratic issues for part of the morning, but when I got free I started with Emily's communications workshop because, not surprisingly, there was an appealing commotion coming from that end of the corridor. When I walked in, the session was already in full gear. People were laughing and talking and sharing ideas in rapid-fire fashion. One woman was standing as she spoke because she was so pumped up. All the while, the tireless Park was providing line-by-line (instead of simultaneous) interpretation in her unique style. Most interpreters simply render the words of the speaker they are translating for. With her boundless energy, Park delivers each line exactly the way the speaker did, with the same emotion, intonation, and body language. Hard enough to do when you are translating for one person, but to capture and relay the personalities and styles of expression of twenty different people is completely beyond my comprehension.

Emily's workshop was, by its nature, the feel-good workshop. The participants learned new skills, and they experienced for the first time the kind of interactive, discovery-based teaching methods they'd been searching for. But on top of all of that, Emily's workshop was a lot of good, clean fun. Since one of the goals was to explore using the arts to get your message out, Emily's workshop included hands-on art projects that allowed the participants to tap into their own creative abilities. And, for the segments that were a little more nerve wracking, like practicing public speaking, the goodwill and familiarity among the members created a safe, supportive environment that enabled the women to take some chances.

The atmosphere in Tess's Empowerment Workshop was equally positive. The women were working in small groups on a task to help them identify their strengths and think about how best to use them in their activism. In short, in the communications and empowerment skills workshops everything seemed to be humming along fine. The atmosphere in both rooms was relaxed and happy. Everyone seemed to be having a good time as they took part in the creative, interactive activities that Emily and Tess had chosen to help them develop important new skills. But when I joined the organizing skills workshop, I found an entirely different situation. It was immediately obvious that the workshop had gotten off to a rocky start. We were only an hour or so into the first session and already the atmosphere was tense and lips were pursed. No one looked happy to be there and it only got worse as the day wore on. In the following sections of this chapter, I discuss the skirmishes that broke out in some detail as they revealed critical tensions within the project, and in doing so provided opportunities for us to address previously unidentified differences in our philosophies and missions.

Organizing Workshop

The purpose of this workshop was to introduce the Japanese participants to US organizing strategies and the methods we use for teaching them. Carol created a customized workshop based on the wish lists the Japanese women had compiled— and on the problems that WUT members had identified as their most serious challenges in the union's self-analysis. The curriculum centered on introducing one-to-one communication skills that have proven effective for union organizers in the United States. It included a discussion on the importance of one-to-one communication in organizing, an introduction to the goals of a one-to-one organizing conversation and the elements it should include, and various activities for practicing one-to-one organizing techniques. In the United States, many of these activities are used for organizing inside the workplace, but we felt they could also be adapted for organizing women in different contexts, including organizing women who were already members of the union to be more active and to remain members after their grievances were resolved. We had discussed in advance that the strategies Carol would introduce might not be directly applicable to the JWUs' situation but could still be valuable as food for thought.

I had read through Carol's materials before sending them to the translators and thought she had done an outstanding job of fashioning a program that met the parameters the Japanese women had spelled out in their wish lists. Even so, we knew that the organizing workshop had the potential to be stressful because the Japanese women were already divided in their opinions about the possibility for and effectiveness of workplace organizing. Some, such as Midori and Keiko Kondō from the Sapporo Women's Union, considered workplace organizing impractical if not impossible given the realities of the Japanese workplace. Others, like Tani, argued that, where possible, workplace organizing would increase their power and help cut down on the number of cases the union has to take to the bargaining table. By building a strong presence within the workplace, members could deal with issues through on-the-spot direct action instead. Although everyone recognized that workplace organizing might not be a workable strategy in all cases, Tani argued that when the conditions are right it should be the union's go-to strategy because it puts more power in the hands of the members, it reduces the need for bargaining, and it creates a lasting presence in the workplace to counterbalance management's previously unchecked power.

Despite these differences, I was comfortable with our plan because, after all, the Japanese women had requested a workshop on organizing skills, and they had spent several months specifying exactly what they wanted that workshop to address. Nevertheless, success hinged on everyone keeping in mind that the workshop was not intended to provide ready-made solutions. Carol's job was to demonstrate US methods and invite the Japanese women to try them on, walk around in them a little bit, and decide for themselves what fits, what doesn't, which methods can be adapted, and which are so culturally specific they don't apply in any way. We all agreed at the outset that this was the only reasonable and proper way to proceed, but when it came down to actually putting it into practice, the process was less straightforward, and far more emotionally fraught, than any of us had imagined.

Blindsided

The workshop started off exactly as expected. After taking some time to get acquainted, Carol opened with a quick review of the history of direct organizing in the United States. In the days before workers had a legal right to union represen-tation or collective bargaining, the only way workers could unionize was to get all of their coworkers to agree to walk out if the company wouldn't voluntarily recognize the union. That strategy required rock-solid unity, which they were able to build and maintain through direct, one-to-one organizing. And it proved very effective. During that period, US workers used direct organizing to build the mass labor movements that eventually led to the adoption of the National Labor Relations Act (NLRA), the Fair Labor Standards Act (FLSA), and many other innovations of the New Deal era, including pension systems, Social Secu-rity, Medicare and Medicaid, and Workers' Compensation.

After union rights became institutionalized, however, US unions started mov-ing away from direct organizing and direct-action unionism, Carol explained. Instead of relying on a solidly organized membership that could act on its own behalf, unions began to hire professional staff to negotiate and enforce the union contract and provide legal assistance when workers' rights were violated. Work-ers got out of the habit of using their own collective power to protect their rights. They called instead on union business agents or lawyers to handle problems for them. This reliance on an outside agent weakened unions, she said, because it undercut the true source of any union's power: the workers' willingness and ability to act collectively to protect their interests. Workers stopped thinking of themselves as the union, seeing it instead as an outside entity, like an insurance company or a law firm that they could call on to protect their rights for them. In other words, workers had virtually lost the sense of the union as an expression of their own solidarity and the power they could wield by acting collectively. Over time, the shift away from direct organizing to service unionism, with the accom-panying loss of solidarity and membership participation, sapped US unions and the US labor movement as a whole of much of its power and vitality. Now, hav-ing recognized the problem, many US unions have returned to the more direct methods. From Carol's perspective, she was simply providing the rationale for why the OI teaches the particular methods she was about to introduce, but already a few of the Japanese participants were shifting uncomfortably in their seats.

Next, Carol tossed out a few easy questions to the audience. "Why is it impor-tant to reach out to prospective members?" "What are the disadvantages of relying on written materials?" "What are the benefits of talking to people face-to-face?" These were just a few icebreakers to remind us of our common ground before heading off into a deeper conversation. But those softball questions turned out to be lead balloons. The Japanese participants sat staring at her tight lipped, offering little beyond an occasional curt reply. Surprised but intrepid, Carol persevered. She prodded a little, asked a few more questions, and got uncomfortable silences in return. Eventually, the non-Japanese participants started offering a few answers in the hope of getting the discussion rolling. But the Japanese women remained inexplicably aloof. For some reason, they were unwilling to concede that one-to-one communication was an important part of organizing, despite their frequent requests in the past for training in one-to-one organizing. Over anxious glances, Heidi and I wordlessly agreed to let things play out for a while and see if the problem would resolve itself. Maybe it was the translation, maybe they just needed time to warm up to Carol; she was not at the Detroit workshop, so they were meeting her for the first time. Maybe they just needed a little time to settle in.

Next, Carol introduced the idea of using a structured conversation to help current members talk more effectively with prospective members. Over the years, US organizers have learned that successful organizing conversations tend to follow a familiar pattern that pretty much follows the logic of any sales pitch. The OI used that knowledge to develop a simple script that takes organizing trainees through the steps of a successful conversation, including establishing trust and rapport, encouraging the person to talk about her work issues, offering a vision of how things could be different with a union, and dealing with her fears and concerns before finally asking her to take some action. The script is a powerful learning tool because it identifies the steps of successful conversation, explains each step so that new organizers know what to expect, and gives them a way to practice conversations before going out in the field. Even if you don't plan to use the script in the field, it is still extremely useful for teaching organizers how to have a positive conversation with potential members and how to help them move beyond their fears so they can take action.

If the first segment came off like a lead balloon, this one was heading more toward Hindenburg territory. One part of the structured conversation focuses on the importance of letting workers tell us their stories before we tell them about the union. For most activists that's hard because we are helpers by nature. When someone tells us they're having problems at work, we want to jump right in and start offering solutions. But good organizers know that it's important to let the potential member tell her story, first because she probably needs to get it off her chest, but also because by telling us her story she is essentially making the case *to herself* for joining the union. But even so, most activists need practice to overcome our instinct to offer solutions, Carol said. She asked the women to break into groups and role-play an organizing conversation, with the stipulation that those taking the organizer role were not allowed to talk about the union until they had gotten the "worker" to talk about herself. I sat in on several of the role-plays and was shocked by the outcome. The Japanese women no longer seemed merely resistant. Now they seemed outright angry. Something about this lesson had offended the Japanese women to the point where they seemed to be shutting down.

When we broke for lunch I talked with some of the participants to see if we could pinpoint the cause of the tension, but all I could get out of them were curt rebukes. "This isn't working!" "Those methods won't work for us!" "She does not understand the Japanese situation!" It was all so confusing to me because, again, I knew these women; they were my friends. I knew how deeply committed they were to bringing other women into the union. Yet, suddenly they seemed resistant, even hostile, to a fellow activist who had come halfway around the world to share her experiences with them. True, there was nothing unusual about them engaging in a little knee-jerk nay-saying when confronted with a new idea. Nay-saying does seem to be a favorite indoor sport for much of Japan. But the intensity of their reaction went well beyond customary skepticism. Something much bigger was going on here, but I couldn't yet identify the source of their anger.

We fared no better in the afternoon session. Carol asked the women to role-play the final part of the structured conversation, in which the organizer answers the potential member's objections then asks her to take some specific action. This is usually the hardest part of the conversation because, at this point, potential members typically raise a hundred and one reasons they can't possibly take any kind of action and organizers respond by challenging them to think about the consequences of not taking action. This is the moment the conversation can become confrontational, and it's the moment when US organizers tell potential members they have to make a hard choice. Of course, we knew that a Japanese version of the conversation would need to take on a softer tone, but we thought that it would be beneficial to practice responding to objections because if there is one universal in organizing, it's that people will always come up with a list of reasons they can't take action, and organizers have to be able to field those objections to move the conversation forward. At first I was encouraged, because the women who were playing the role of prospective member were finally letting down their hair and having a little fun with the exercise. In fact, they were having so much fun shooting down the organizers' advances that I wondered if they weren't inadvertently taking out the morning's frustrations on their fellow role-players. But those taking the role of organizer were having no fun at all. They were tense and angry and nothing at all like the women I had known for the past several years. The problem wasn't that they were uncomfortable with role-playing per se. I had seen them successfully engage in role-plays in other contexts, so it wasn't the technique itself that was bothering them. But something about this exercise was, and to a degree that baffled me.

I hoped that the debriefing session that followed the role-plays might give us a clue about where all the tension was coming from. But instead it only added to my confusion, because it was then that the Japanese participants categorically declared that Japanese women can't organize; that's it, end of discussion.[4] Carol, Heidi, and I were stunned. Where do we go from there? And what did it mean to say that Japanese women "can't organize"? They *have* organized in the past and many of the women sitting before me had seen it with their own eyes. Moreover, this is what they told us they wanted to learn. Earlier in the day Tani had said, "All the things we need are things that face-to-face organizing can help us with. I want to know what are the strategies in the United States for person-to-person organizing and how to translate that into the Japanese way." And yet here we were, being accused of trying to impose our ways on Japanese women. Some of the women were so frustrated they started throwing up the "We're different" roadblock. It's a favorite rhetorical strategy I often heard Japanese people use to end uncomfortable conversations with foreigners. Basically they were saying, "It's a Japanese thing; you wouldn't understand." The organizing workshop might well have ground to a halt at that point if it hadn't been for Mabel Au.

Mabel was slated to facilitate the plenary session on networking among Asian women later in the program. Fortunately, she had also agreed to participate in the organizing workshop.[5] As an Asian woman, and as a person who has organized women in a variety of Asian countries, Mabel was able to speak to the Japanese women with an authority that none of the American women had. She acknowledged the parts of their "we're different" arguments that were legitimate but also pointed out that women everywhere, and under far more severe conditions than those in Japan, find ways to organize when they want change badly enough. If I had made the same argument it would have had little impact, but coming from Mabel it was enough to break the impasse and allow the discussion to move forward, if begrudgingly so.

The rest of the day was rough going for everyone. No one truly understood what was going on and why there was so much tension in the room. What fascinated and frustrated me most was that the Japanese unionists were voicing the same objections we hear from employees during organizing drives: "We can't do that," "I don't have time," and "That would never work here." These are all objections that organizers hear as a matter of course whenever they start talking to a new group of workers. It wasn't until later that I realized that was an important clue. As organizers we know that the first reasons people give for not taking action (whether it's about joining the union or starting an exercise program or signing up for a class) are almost never the real reasons. Those roll-off-the-tongue objections are usually masking something bigger, something harder to articulate, and it's the organizer's job to find out what is really holding the person back. Something was holding the Japanese women back and it was our collective job to figure out what it was before the workshop imploded.

By the time we broke for dinner, we were all exhausted, frustrated, and confused. And seeing the members of the other two workshops emerge bubbly and joyous from their sessions did nothing to help matters. I was glad to see they went well, of course. But I feared the obvious success of those workshops would make our group even more resentful about the day we'd had. Our ICU hosts had arranged for us to have dinner and a reception in the school cafeteria that night. I hoped to use that time to talk individually with the women from the organizing workshop and see if we could unpack what had happened during the day from their perspective in the hopes that that would help us get back on track.

Under Attack

At the reception following dinner, while the rest of us sang songs, drank beer, and clowned around at the open mic, the participants from the organizing workshop sat huddled around a table toward the back of the room, talking ominously among themselves. As snatches of their conversation wafted over to me, I realized the situation was even worse than I had thought. The women were so upset they were making plans to confront Carol the next morning and demand that she either change the program or they would quit her workshop and join one of the other two. I couldn't help smiling at the irony. The very women who claimed Japanese women can't organize or be confrontational were doing a pretty darn good job of exactly that. But, at the same time, it sent a chill down my spine because I knew there was no way to change the program on the fly since we couldn't instantaneously translate a new set of materials. And even if we could magically produce new materials, I doubted that the content itself was the problem. There was something behind all the tension that we couldn't quite put our fingers on, and now time was running out. We had to come up with a solution by nine a.m. the next morning or the organizing workshop would collapse.

I made my way to their table, hoping to join the discussion. For a moment I was concerned they might clam up because they would consider it impolite to complain in front of me. I needn't have worried. My Japanese colleagues were angry enough that their customary aversion to conflict gave way to their need to make me understand how the day's events had looked and felt to them. And they were unequivocal. The conflict wasn't fundamentally about the US model not being a perfect fit. It wasn't fundamentally about Japanese women being different from US women. The real source of the day's tensions was that, for the Japanese women, Carol's entire presentation struck them as an attack on the very concept of individual unionism. As I listened to my colleagues adamantly defending their organizations, I realized that somewhere in the assumptions underpinning the concepts we thought we agreed on lay some great but unexplored gap between us, and it centered on how "the individual" figured into our different systems.

All along, I had understood the JWUs' focus on individuals to be a practical, strategic decision based on the fact that Japanese women work under conditions that are less conducive to organizing than those in traditional industrial work settings. But the vehemence with which they were now defending their focus on the individual made me realize I had gotten it wrong. After all the time we had spent together, I finally realized that JWUs focus on individuals on principle as well as for practical considerations. Where US unions are, first and foremost, organizations for building and wielding the collective power of labor against capital, JWUs see themselves as caring, supportive organizations whose purpose is to catch vulnerable women who are slipping through the cracks of a system that was never designed to serve them. That difference leads to radically different strategies, tactics, and even basic values. In the United States we push members to stand up and be counted. When people tell us all the reasons they can't join a union, we challenge them. We say, "You can stay where you are or you can work to change it," because we believe that's what working people have to do to win meaningful change in the workplace. But that approach must have sounded heartless to organizations whose first priority is to "address the extra damage that is done to women working in a 'man's world.'" In that light, the conflicts of the day began to make sense to me. I flashed back to the session on organizing in the workplace when one of the Japanese women told us most plaintively, "The women who come to us have tried everything they could do and it didn't work. So they come to us. We cannot tell them to go back to work and make their case [to their coworkers]. They come to women's network for support. We help them recover mentally and physically." That seemed like strange talk coming from a unionist. But not strange at all if their definition of "union" means an organization whose first job is to help women heal.

But that still left me with the question of why JWUs were so adamant about foregrounding the individual. Why would organizations that recognize and seek to change the structural underpinnings of inequality and discrimination be first and foremost centered on the individual? My hypothesis that night was that the answer in part stems from the differences between the labor unions' and feminist organizations' core missions. Typically, labor unions seek to critique the ideology of individualism, and enable members to recognize first, that they are part of a class and second, that they can improve their life chances by acting as a class. Feminist organizations, on the other hand, tend to emphasize empowering women to claim their status as full and equal individuals with the right to pursue self-actualization and full participation in society. Even in the United States, many women feel guilty about tending to their own needs because we are expected to take care of everyone else first. In Japan, the situation is even more extreme. Japanese women, and therefore Japanese women's organizations, still have a long way to go to establish in practice women's right to full personhood. And it is in that context that the individual gets such a prominent place in a collective struggle.

With that distinction in mind, I read over the materials from the day and was appalled by how they appeared in that light. The practices that I, and most US unionists, fully support could indeed sound very much like the argument Japanese women were used to hearing from company unions: put the individual aside and do what's best for the union. That strategy is great if doing what's good for the union is ultimately a pathway toward improved conditions for all members. But, if "do what's right for the union" is simply code for "accept your inferior status"—as is often the case for women in enterprise unions—that's a whole different ball game and certainly not what we were suggesting. But at least now I was beginning to understand the Japanese women's reaction, and that gave me a starting place for opening a dialogue the next day.

Talking It Through

The next morning we decided that instead of pressing on with the program as planned, we needed to step back and have a good old-fashioned rap session. The Japanese women needed a chance to air their grievances—their fears as well as their anger. And Carol, Heidi, and I needed an opportunity to show the Japanese activists that our focus on building a strong organization does not reflect a lack of concern for the well-being of individual women; we focus on building the organization because we believe it is the most direct pathway to securing their well-being. In that spirit, we asked the Japanese women to identify specific segments of the previous day's program that bothered them and explain what they were thinking and feeling during those segments. Although this was uncharted territory in terms of the ways we had prepared for the workshop, the process was successful in unearthing hidden points of contention and enabling us to discuss them in the clear light of day.

RECRUITING

Early in her presentation, Carol introduced two basic tenets of US-style organizing. First, instead of trying to find employees who are having troubles on the job, US organizers seek out the natural leaders in a workplace. We start by organizing the best, most popular workers, the ones who know how to get things done and are already comfortable taking the initiative, because once we get them on board others will follow. But, to the Japanese women, that strategy sounded cynical and opportunistic. Since JWUs' raison d'être was to provide emergency help to the "weak and vulnerable," an organizing strategy that focuses on the strong at best misses the point entirely. At worst, it sounds suspiciously like the logic of self-serving union leaders who are more interested in consolidating their own power than in serving the needs of working people. In fact, when Carol first suggested the strategy of organizing the strongest workers first, one of the Japanese women cried out with real emotion, "The strong don't need us!" But that's only true if the purpose of your union is to minister to the weak. Traditional labor unions do not seek to minister to the weak. They seek to improve working conditions for all workers by building strong organizations that can promote the interests of workers as a class. And the fastest way to build a strong organization is to bring on the people who are already able to stand up for themselves, who have both the courage and the workplace standing to risk taking on the boss, and whose example other, less secure workers will follow. Moreover, from a traditional union point of view, the idea that a strong individual doesn't need the union is dead wrong. Weak or strong makes no difference, without class solidarity we all stand before capital "with the feeble power of one."

The second tenet Carol introduced was the principle of proactive outreach. "We don't wait for potential members to come to us; we go out and find them," she said. On this point I thought we would be in agreement. In our previous conversations, the Japanese women told me that JWUs don't do more outreach because of resource shortages and other practical barriers. No one had ever expressed to me any philosophical objections to outreach, so I was completely blindsided when several of the women stated categorically that JWUs reject the idea of recruiting on principle. In their view, it is crucial that women take the first step toward joining the union on their own initiative. "Coming to the union on her own helps her to recover mentally and physically," Ban said. "That is the moment when she starts discovering her own power and her own courage." By reaching out to women first, the union would rob women of that empowering moment of deciding to act on their own behalf. Once again we had unearthed a significant difference in our most basic—but until now unspoken—assumptions.[6]

MOVING BEYOND OBJECTIONS

The first day had also included a discussion about how organizers might deal with prospective members' objections in order to move the conversation forward. In retrospect, I think this was the moment when the workshop began to completely unravel. When Carol talked about moving beyond objections she was making a pragmatic point that every organizer, everywhere in the world knows: when you ask someone to take action, whether it's joining a union, starting an exercise program, or running for local office, most people's first response is to list the reasons they can't do it. The reason this response is so predictable is that what they are saying is usually true: most women really are too busy; joining the union really is risky because employers routinely retaliate even though it is against the law. When organizers talk about moving beyond objections that does not mean that they think those objections are unimportant or unreal. No one knows better than Carol that the barriers women face—lack of time, lack of energy, threat of retribution—are real, but she also knows those barriers reflect the very reasons women need to join unions. Unless women organize and fight back, they will remain in the same overworked, underpaid, powerless position. "It's a question of priorities; if you want things to change, you have to find a way," Carol said.

But again we're back to the differences in mission. Carol is trying to get women to join the union, but JWU members are trying to raise consciousness. They are in the business of validating women's complaints so nothing could be more abhorrent to them than to hear a union official (apparently) brushing those issues aside. They had started their own unions precisely because they were tired of women's concerns being dismissed by male unions, and now here were US unionists sounding suspiciously like representatives of the male unions they sought to replace. Once the Japanese participants explained their reaction in those terms, we were again able to start sifting through the origins of our differences until we could again find our common ground. Carol assured them we were not dismissing the very real pressures that Japanese women face. As an organizer, her job was to help women get past that moment when all they can see are the obstacles to taking action. Perhaps this would not be the best method to use in an explicitly conflict-averse culture like Japan's; that was up to the Japanese activists to decide. But, in any case, our emphasis on moving beyond objections does not signify a lack of concern for the very real barriers to union membership that women face; instead, it is our way of addressing them.

Finally, the exercise the Japanese women had the most trouble with was the role-play in which the "organizers" were supposed to get "prospective members" to tell their own story. Those playing the organizers were not there to solve problems or even recruit the other women for the union. All they were supposed to do was use their listening and conversation skills to get the other women to open up to them, which was, after all, what they thought they'd been doing all along. Through role-play, however, the women acting as organizers discovered they had all but lost the ability to talk to other women one-on-one without trying to sell them on the union. At first they blamed Carol's method, saying it just didn't fit their circumstances. But, on reflection, some of the women realized that they had been taking shortcuts in order to keep up with their work overloads. "The ongoing negotiations wear us out," WUT member Miyako Ōga said. "We quite neglected to build trust. We have to show them that we really care." Tani agreed: "Often I am in haste to tell them what to do. But it is better to show her more options, let her talk, let her decide."

Some women realized they'd been rushing through the organizing process because of the endless time pressure they were under. Others simply hadn't been trained. One woman told us about a past attempt to organize her coworkers that had been very painful for her. After getting into a dispute with her employer, she asked her colleagues to stand up and support her but, lo and behold, she didn't get any takers. At the time she felt betrayed by her coworkers, but after opening herself up to Carol's message, she realized that it was she who neglected them. "When I had a problem I only talked about myself. I didn't ask about problems they might be having. I just asked them to help me without thinking of them." It was a startling realization for her as well as many of the other women around the table.

As we talked through the issues openly and honestly, and admitted mistakes we had made along the way, the atmosphere of defensiveness subsided. Point by point we unraveled the misunderstandings and miscommunications that had come between us. Soon we were laughing at how uptight we'd all gotten the day before. As the mood in the room lightened, a few of the women became aware of yet another source of tension.

NO "MAGIC BULLET"

In preparation for the workshop, I reminded my Japanese colleagues many times that the US educators would not—indeed, could not—provide them with ready-made, one-size-fits-all answers that they could directly import. Nor did they have some magic formula for making organizing easy.[7] Organizing is hard work for everyone, no exceptions. But what US labor educators can do is demonstrate US methods in the hope of stimulating ideas that might work in the Japanese context. We all agreed to those parameters in theory, but it didn't work out that way in practice. When faced with a technique that didn't immediately fit their circumstances, the Japanese women tended to fixate on what wouldn't work instead of asking themselves whether there was something in the underlying logic of the technique that they could use. For example, several of the techniques Carol introduced were obviously designed for large workplaces where employees can see and talk to each other throughout the day. The Japanese participants pointed out that most Japanese women work in small businesses or dispersed work settings. But instead of recognizing that they had just identified the beginning point for their own creative interventions, the women rejected her suggestions as irrelevant—and offensively so.

During the rap session, a few of the women realized that they had, not quite consciously, come to the workshop expecting easy answers, and that maybe, just maybe, some of their anger was the product of unrealistic expectations. After we probed this idea gently for a little while, Kiyomi Kurosawa, founder of Women's Union Plus in Sendai, admitted with her customary good humor that, come to think of it, she had indeed felt angry because Carol wasn't offering simple solutions. "I kept thinking she was hiding something from us, or not telling us the whole story. Surely, the Americans had some way to make this easier but they weren't sharing the final answer with us!" Kurosawa told us that she thought she had cleared her mind of any magic-bullet expectations, but once the workshop got started her hopes for quick solutions snuck up on her without her even realizing it. But the rap session helped her unpack all of that. She came to realize that the "anger" she'd been feeling was really about disappointment and avoiding the unhappy fact that there are no easy answers. "I understand now that organizing work is really diverse. There is no one single remedy or solution. Today I am convinced that this person-to-person discussion is important even if it is not the one 'pain-killer' solution."

Organizing Workshop: Take Two

We took our time with the rap session, peeling the onion layer by layer to make sure we had gotten all suspicions and bad feelings out in the open. Once we did that we decided to go back to the original lesson plan and try again.

Treading lightly, Carol introduced a lesson on using surveys as a tool for organizing. Many of the women were well versed in using surveys to collect data to document patterns of discrimination. But organizing surveys are a completely different animal. "These surveys are designed to reach out to women workers and find out what is on their minds," Carol explained. "We don't use them to uncover problems inside a workplace; we already know what the problems are. We use surveys as a way to start a conversation." A good organizing survey should be short, about ten questions, easy to understand, and include some space for women to tell their own stories. And they should be handed directly to the people you want to reach. "Ask the person to fill out the survey and let her know you will come back to collect it. Hand collecting the surveys gives you another opportunity to talk with the potential member after the person has completed a task that ties her to your organization. You could also ask each woman to take one or two surveys for her coworkers, and ask her to collect them from her coworkers and return them to you." As Carol was saying this, one of the women started to laugh. On the previous day she had told us in detail about a survey she had recently conducted in the hope of raising awareness among her coworkers. Initially, she was disappointed that the pages and pages of statistics her survey generated had so little effect on her coworkers' consciousness. But now, seeing her survey through the lens of Carol's presentation, she was laughing at her uncanny ability to violate every principle of a model she had never even heard of. Her survey was long and commodious. The questions did nothing to help women see their problems as part of a larger pattern. And she didn't ask for contact information or even talk to people when they turned in their surveys. In short, she had used her survey to collect information that was already well known to her, while at the same time missing every opportunity to use the survey to open a dialogue. "I did everything wrong according to Carol's instructions and it failed," she said. But instead of being angry, she actually seemed somewhat relieved because now she understood that she hadn't been shut out by her co-workers, she wasn't necessarily up against an impenetrable wall. She just hadn't used the most effective tactic. With a little tweaking, she could revise her survey and her survey method and try again. The contrast between that reaction and reactions we saw the day before were unmistakable. Her willingness to reflect on her past experiences and allow for the possibility that a different approach might work better made it clear that she had moved past the roadblocks of the previous day.

After that, the organizing workshop turned into a workshop like any other. We learned techniques that US unions use to develop organizing strategies for particular worksites. We discussed the importance of reaching out to young workers, building alliances with universities, and identifying places to talk to perspective members outside the workplace. We played a few rounds of our own version of "fungo," with the Japanese women tossing out typical workplace scenarios and Carol coming back with ideas for workable direct-action responses. We were even able to touch on some of the long-standing hot button issues, like whether JWUs should require members to participate in union activities in exchange for the help they are receiving. The Japanese women and I had canvassed the topic many times, but Carol hit home with her explanation of why it is important—and empowering—to ask every member to do her part: "Many people see the union as a vending machine: you put in money and if you don't get what you want, you get angry and hit it," she explained. "But a union is really more like a potluck supper where everyone knows that what you will get out of it depends on what everyone brings to the table."[8] By putting it in those terms, the women saw very clearly the difference between a union where everyone expects to push a button and get something back and the kind of union where everyone puts something of herself into it. Directly involving every member increases the union's strength, empowers the individual, and increases the individual's commitment to and understanding of the union. Also, direct involvement gives rank-and-file members the opportunity to see management in action. It's not uncommon for workers to blame their unions if they don't get the settlements or contracts they want. It's a particularly common problem for service unions where members are so far removed from the action they don't see what management gets up to in the midst of battle. But, when members are directly involved in the fight, they can see exactly who the culprit is. This was very appealing to JWU leaders who worked their hearts out for their members, only to be blamed for the company's intransigence.

(W)rapping Up

Despite the conflicts on the first day, the organizing workshop turned out to be fruitful, although not necessarily in the ways we'd intended. Because of the other matters we had to deal with, the members of this group did not get to learn and practice as many new skills as the participants in the communications and empowerment workshops did. On the other hand, they confronted crucial theoretical issues that needed to be fully examined if they were to move beyond their current impasse. They made significant strides in their ability to let down their defenses and honestly evaluate their practices and expectations in light of their actual, observable outcomes over the past decade or so. As we saw in Workshop I, the Japanese activists had already identified the gaps between their expectations and the realities of how their unions were functioning in practice, but they always pulled up short of a full, no-stone-unturned investigation of why those gaps exist—and with good reason. Their unions were born of the recognition that mainstream unions' practices left women out in the cold. Their practices were specifically designed to serve women in the ways that traditional unions could not. I always had the feeling that they resisted questioning their assumptions and practices at the most fundamental level for fear that if they let go of those founding assumptions, they'd once again end up with organizations that did not meet the particular needs of women. But the rap session helped us break through that wall. By deepening our understanding of each other, we deepened our trust, which in turn gave the Japanese women the security they needed to explore ideas beyond their comfort zone. Now that they were confident that we weren't disrespecting their organizations or dismissing the very real obstacles Japanese women face when it comes to joining and forming unions, they were able to consider asking themselves the hard questions that their own experiences were begging them to ask. That is not to say that the Japanese women came over to the US way of organizing. Not at all. On most points—such as the need for organizing, workers' power versus network power, their focus on healing individuals—the Japanese participants maintained their long-held positions. The victory was not in getting them to change their minds. It was in creating the circumstances in which they would be willing and able to consider other perspectives and make their own decisions from there.

The organizing workshop also uncovered a subtle but profound difference between our organizations that only became visible once we got down to the nitty-gritty level of developing actual practices. Awareness of our differences had certainly evolved over the course of the project, and our level of understanding was sufficient for the kinds of "big picture" discussions we had in Workshop I. But now that we were working on a more concrete level, another previously hidden difference came to the surface. When it came to mapping out organizing strategies, the JWUs' focus on healing individuals made the US emphasis on building strong organizations appear cold and opportunistic. Meanwhile, to US organizers the Japanese approach of coming to the aid of suffering victims seemed to undermine their goals of empowering women individually and collectively. We were able to overcome that tension only because we had the time and flexibility to step back from the prepared program and go into a meta-analysis of our own conversation. By unpacking the issues and understanding them in their local contexts, we were able to find common ground again and move forward with meaningful strategy discussions.

Finally, we were reminded that trust and open dialogue were the keys to our collaboration. When the conflict first emerged, emotions were running so high that the two-day session could easily have broken down and permanently damaged the project. But, by sticking to our process and drawing on the trust we had developed over time, we were eventually able to uncover and analyze the origins of previously unseen differences. We came away with a deeper understanding of how local context inflects organizations' structures, goals, and practices, and a reassurance that, despite those differences, we are ultimately seeking the same ends. This is important because as unionists—and especially as women unionists—we are used to employers, politicians, and even other social justice organizations claiming to have our interests at heart, all the while devising clever strategies to undermine our goals. Although our differences momentarily made us suspicious of each other, ultimately we were able to talk through those issues and go on to work together in ways that were more sensitive to and respectful of positions that only a few hours ago seemed hopelessly at odds.

At the end of the day, when all of the groups came together to give progress reports, the spokesperson for the organizing group did a great job of capturing the tumult they'd been through en route to new insights. A gifted storyteller, Kurosawa had everyone riveted with her dramatic retelling of the events of the first day. The tension in the room mounted as she told of the conflicts and rumblings of mutiny as the day went on. Then, just as she got to the climax of her story, the room started shaking, the windows rattling, and one faint-of-heart participant (the lone male in the room) disappeared under tabletop. It took most of us a few beats to realize that a medium-sized earthquake was shaking the foundations because the feeling of upheaval just seemed like part of Kurosawa's performance. Once we realized what was happening, we burst into laughter even though the floor was still pitching beneath our feet. "Yes, Carol shook our minds and she shook our bodies!" Kurosawa shouted over the din. "She made us think in new ways. We shall not wait in the office anymore. We shall go out and meet the people!"

Outcomes

Workshop II was a skills-development workshop. Participants in each of the three work groups learned essential skills that would help them make their unions stronger and more effective. In the communications workshop, participants worked on developing public speaking skills, building relationships with the media, using the arts both to raise awareness about women's issues in the workplace and to project positive images of women's unions and women in the workplace. They also learned techniques for identifying potential allies in their communities, such as artists, writers, and other advocacy groups, and for building coalitions with those allies for mutual support. And they developed ideas for community outreach campaigns using the arts to get their message out. Finally, the communications group learned techniques for handling conflicts inside the union and during collective bargaining.

Participants in the organizing group learned a variety of new organizing techniques and the logic behind them. They learned the steps of a successful organizing conversation, from making contact with prospective members, to getting them to tell their own stories, to helping them identify and see past their fears about joining a union, as well as other techniques such as how to use surveys and workplace mapping to organize. The Japanese participants were also introduced to US perspectives on the benefits of direct action, the importance of active recruiting, and the necessity of creating a culture of participation within the union.

Finally, the participants in the empowerment work group developed new ideas to help women to gain a voice in public policy debates, practiced recognizing discrimination in the workplace and the union and brainstormed ways to fight it, and learned techniques for enabling members to assess their strengths and weaknesses as union activists and to make plans for taking their game to the next level. Not everyone in the group understood how these skills related to women's empowerment (I discuss this problem in greater detail in the following chapters), but most of the participants understood them as useful skills for union members to have.

Workshop II was also a training-the-trainer workshop. Those in the communications and organizing groups learned adult education methods indirectly by participating in workshops that employed those techniques. Those in the empowerment group learned the principles and practices of participatory adult education directly, as that was the specific object of their study. By the end of the second day, they had explored the theory behind participatory education techniques, discussed the empowering effects of an educational approach that recognizes and respects the knowledge and experiences adult learners bring to the table, learned techniques to stimulate learning through dialogue and problem posing, and practiced designing activities to share these ideas and techniques with other activists in Japan. In that sense they had a head start on the others in terms of designing their own educational module. On the other hand, they would (theoretically) be the ones the other groups would turn to in the coming months as they sought to design communications and organizing modules.

Workshop II also provided important lessons in the fine art of transnational collaboration. On the third day of our meeting, Mabel led a session on working women's networks in Asia. Beyond introducing the participants to existing networks (their goals, strategies, jurisdictions, etc.), the session also covered basic information on how to set up and maintain effective transnational relationships in general. Within just a few months, the Japanese women would put what they learned into practice by reaching out to women's unions in South Korea to initiate what was ultimately a highly successful educational exchange.

And, of course, we learned important practical lessons about our own collaboration by reflecting on the conflicts that emerged during the organizing workshop. All of the JWUs were struggling with the same basic questions: how to attract members, how to retain members, how to get members to actively participate in the organization's mission and activities; in short, how to become stronger and more effective unions. The organizing workshop was designed to tackle these very questions, but in doing so it necessarily challenged some of their signature practices. That, in turn, led to the conflicts that all but derailed our efforts. In retrospect, I can see that we made certain decisions during the planning phase that inadvertently stacked the deck against Carol or, more to the point, whoever would have led the organizing workshop as we had conceived it.

As I said earlier, we knew the organizing workshop to be the most difficult, and the most controversial, of the three skills workshops. The Japanese women did not even agree among themselves about where they stood on organizing. Some, like Midori, thought organizing was unnecessary, in fact undoable in a Japanese context, so they preferred networking with other women's groups to trying to organize workers inside the workplace. Others, like Tani, saw it as necessary to increase their power at the bargaining table but also as a way to move beyond the stage where the union was perpetually bogged down by the steady flow of individual grievances. The women in this camp agreed that worksite organizing is not be a viable strategy in some work settings, but in other cases it could be the key to building union power well beyond what the JWUs have been able to do so far. I had been in on numerous discussions with WUT members over the years in which tempers flared over differences of opinion around organizing, so there was no question that the topic itself had the potential to set off fireworks. But there's no denying that some of the choices that we, as a group—and sometimes Heidi and I as the project coordinators—made also rendered the situation even more combustible than we imagined. The most significant of these decisions was the pedagogical style we chose to employ.

Participatory Pedagogy

During the planning phase, the Japanese participants and I decided that the workshops should both employ and present the principles and practices of a teaching style known as participatory adult education. Partly on principle and partly of necessity, we rejected traditional nondemocratic teaching methods that involve enlightened experts imparting Truth to passive recipients. Instead, we sought educators whose teaching styles generally focus on empowering adult learners to use their own creativity and experiences to discover and create knowledge for themselves. And in our case, because of the crossborder nature of the project, the discovery aspect was dramatically heightened by the fact that the US educators really didn't know what the right answers were. The Japanese women were being asked to take a look at what we do and decide for themselves whether it would work, whether it could be adapted to their circumstances, etc. This style of pedagogy requires a fair amount of letting go and seeing where the process takes you. It's liberating, unpredictable, and has great potential for fostering insights that no one, not even the instructors, could foresee. It is also the antithesis of the safe, plodding, memorization-oriented methods by which most Japanese people, particularly people over the age of 30, were educated. As teaching methods go, participatory education is a high-risk, high-wire learning adventure, which is to say it's about the most un-Japanese approach imaginable.

Left to my own devices, I probably wouldn't have chosen a teaching method that relied on unself-conscious leaps of faith. From my own (albeit limited) experiences teaching English in Japan, I knew that even now students are typically expected to absorb whatever the teacher tells them, as is and without questions. The high school students I taught had little experience with teaching methods that encouraged or even tolerated creative input. I was surprised at how reticent they were to express themselves or participate in learning activities that did not adhere to the formal structure. So, when the Japanese women said they wanted to use participatory methods, I understood their reasoning but was a little concerned about how that would work out in practice. The Japanese women assured me they *wanted* a new kind of learning experience; they *wanted* to learn teaching techniques that would nudge them beyond their comfort zone and encourage them to draw on their own experiences and creativity, because that was the kind of workshop they'd like to produce for their members back home. Also, participatory educational techniques were more in keeping with our goal of avoiding the longstanding knowledge exchange model that consisted of US experts imposing their vision on Japanese ingénues. In the end, the consensus decision was to use participatory teaching techniques, even though it constituted yet another level of unfamiliarity for the Japanese participants. And while that did prove to be a challenge for participants in all three of the skills workshops, it was especially difficult for those in the organizing workshop for several reasons.

The organizing workshop was aimed at getting to the core of their organizational problems and would therefore inevitably challenge some of their core practices. At the same time, it could not offer the immediate payoffs that the communications and empowerment workshops could. The women in Tess and Emily's workshops were learning new techniques that were not only fun but could also be put into practice fairly easily if the JWUs so chose. For example, Tess's empowerment workshop included an exercise on identifying your strengths. The exercise was easy for the women to understand, easy for them to engage in, and the outcomes were immediate, informative, and often uplifting for the participants as they discovered how their particular personality types could benefit their work as activists. By contrast, the women in the organizing workshop were being introduced to a whole different approach to organizing that would require a lot of work on their part if they wanted to adapt it for use in Japan. During the sessions, the group was introduced to US methods. But the really hard part—analyzing, evaluating, and adapting US methods and/or constructing new methods to fit their own circumstances—still lay before them. And while the Japanese women knew there could be no fast or pre-packaged answers, that didn't make it any easier to accept. Their organizations and members were in crisis and needed help now. It was frustrating for them to hear that any sort of solution was still a long way off and would require even more effort on their part. To make matters worse, we could not guarantee them success at the end of all their work. The Japanese women would need to put in a lot of time and effort to develop their own organizing techniques and no one could know what the outcome would be. That lack of certainty proved extremely uncomfortable for the Japanese women and it led to considerable frustration and anxiety about the time and money they were devoting to this part of the project.

In retrospect, though, I think what handicapped Carol most was that she had no history with the women who were participating in her workshop, and that was on me for a decision I made even before the mix-up with the AFL-CIO. During the planning phase, I could have asked someone from Workshop I to facilitate the organizing workshop but, at the time, I thought it best to bring in someone who specialized in training organizers. That was why I reached out to the Organizing Institute to begin with. Carol had it especially tough because she was a last minute pinch hitter. But even if the OI had sent the originally scheduled facilitator, who would have had more time to get up to speed on local customs, that person still would have been new to the group and, like Carol, would not have had a chance to establish a relationship with the Japanese participants. Once again I underestimated the importance of "drinking tea." Tess, Emily, and the Japanese participants had already established a foundation of trust at the Detroit meeting which enabled them to discuss sensitive issues and not feel threatened when differences emerged. But Carol did not have that advantage. She was coming in cold, with no chance to drink tea, literally or figuratively, before launching into the stickiest topics our project would address. Had they been able to meet and get to know each other beforehand, I suspect that the first day would have been less emotionally fraught. While the underlying issues would still exist (and need to be addressed), I suspect that we would have been able to discuss them more calmly if we had been starting out from a position of trust. Even so, I think in future collaborations I would ask everyone to agree in advance on a "stop the line" signal that anyone could invoke if they felt things were going awry. Once someone pulls the safety brake, the group would be asked to step back from the current discussion and go into rap session mode to ferret out any unspoken issues that were getting in the way.

And yet, despite all of these glitches, by which I mean learning opportunities, Workshop II accomplished its goals. All of the participants had been trained in one skill area. And all had been introduced to methods for training others in that same area. Now, with translated sample materials and curricula in hand, the Japanese women were ready to start thinking about ways to help their own members develop similar skills. Each of the three groups had set an action plan and meeting schedule for developing drafts of their own materials and methods for each skills-development workshop. Roughly, the plan was that we would meet again in Tokyo the following spring, and each of the work groups would conduct a workshop based on their works-in-progress. Exactly how all of that would happen was up to the Japanese activists to decide.

MADE IN JAPAN

The close of Workshop II marked the end of the educating phase and beginning of the creating phase of the US-Japan Project. For two years, activists on both sides had been preparing the Japanese women to radically reshape their educational practices in the hope of strengthening their organizations and sparking a nationwide working women's movement. Through educational exchanges with activists from the United States, Hong Kong, and Korea, the Japanese women experienced firsthand the methods women in other countries used to empower their members and build their movements. Now, in the final phase of the project, we were asking the Japanese activists to begin the hard work of creating resources for the Japanese context. At the most concrete level, we were asking them to create three educational modules covering basic communications skills, organizing skills, and techniques for empowering women. But that meant we were also implicitly asking them to create the processes and practices—and to nurture the personal and organizational connections necessary—for the geographically dispersed work groups to carry out their assigned task of developing curricula. Since the members of the work groups were spread out across the country, they would have to figure out how to work inclusively, across organizations and across distances, on a long-term, complicated task that would require significant cooperation. The hope was that, in doing so, the women's groups would be simultaneously forming the basic infrastructure for the national network of women activists they had long sought to create.

Yet, while creating new resources and a national activists' network were goals in their own right, we also had high hopes for the discoveries, insights, and innovations that would emerge through the *process* of creation. For two years we had been preparing, getting our ideas together, and laying the groundwork. Now it was time for the Japanese women to actually create something concrete, something that would be effective in the real world. Their real world. And it's at this nitty-gritty level that questions, discrepancies, and fault lines of all kinds are revealed. The process of creating their own modules would inevitably raise questions about the original materials that the Japanese women would need to discuss with each other and their US coaches. But it would also reveal differences within and across organizations, in their goals and values, and in their ideas about what their organizations can and should be. The process of creation would also inevitably reveal internal discrepancies between the values and actual practices of each organization, as well as unacknowledged hierarchies and privileges that exist within and among the groups. And all of these conflicts would need to be addressed, discussed, debated, or in some other way confronted for the process to move forward. This was definitely going to be the "breaking eggs" stage of making our omelet, but ultimately our hope was that, through this messy process of creation, the Japanese women would gain new insight into the fundamental structural problems that continued to plague the JWUs—and perhaps even begin innovating solutions.

Brass Tacks

The work groups had just shy of a year to create first drafts of their modules and have them ready to present at Workshop III. With few philosophical differences dividing them, the communications work group got off to a fast start. Workshop II ended in late July. By mid-August, they had already put together a workshop based on Emily's materials and were holding trial-run training sessions open to members of the WUT and other women's organizations that had participated in Workshop II. At this stage, their draft module was essentially a direct translation of the US materials. But with each practice session, and the feedback it generated, the communications work group pruned and revised their materials to better reflect the needs, values, experiences, and learning styles of their audience. They weeded out those portions of Emily's curriculum that didn't work well in a Japanese context, and looked to their own experiences to come up with alternative methods or techniques. For example, they figured out almost immediately that the techniques Emily introduced for dealing with an angry boss or company negotiator would not work well in a Japanese context. In Workshop II, Emily had suggested that workers can sometimes defuse a volatile situation by not responding to the boss's inappropriate outburst. The idea is that if you stay silent while another person blusters away, even the worst blowhard will eventually start to feel silly, run out of steam, or both. At that point the well-behaved person can restart the conversation, usually having won the upper hand in the bargain. That's how it often works in the United States, anyway. But in Japan, being unresponsive tends to inflame angry bosses because it is seen as aggressive and even disrespectful. The communications work group quickly spotted this problem and knew they would need to look to their own experiences to find an alternative method.

After holding a successful training session during the union's summer retreat, WUT members who were part of the communications work group decided they were ready to go public by holding their first communications skills workshop open to all interested parties. Their module was still a work in progress, but they felt it was not only time to get feedback from a wider audience, it was time to start sharing their new skills with other social justice-seeking organizations. "When we opened our workshop to the public this summer, we had fifty participants divided into four groups, each of which included members who actually experienced the module in Workshop II. Those members became the facilitators for each small group. There was a little bit of confusion and things we need to reflect on, but it was very interesting," said Midori, who was a member of the communications group. At this early stage, the communications group was already disseminating new skills to activists who were beyond the direct reach of the US-Japan Project, and they were getting valuable feedback on their modules from these new participants. Some of the out-of-town women who participated in the summer workshop further extended the cascade of learning by going back to their home organizations and conducting training sessions there. By October, the communications group had refined their materials and presentation skills well enough that they could put on a basic skills workshop that, according to Midori, was easily understandable and even let those who did not attend Emily's workshop "feel the air of it."

The process was not quite so straightforward for the other two work groups. The members of the empowerment work group had enjoyed participating in Tess's workshop back in July. They reported learning a lot about themselves and their capacities as activists. They identified which skills they already had and which they needed to develop to participate fully in their organizations. And they learned new techniques for transmitting their skills to other adult learners. But, when it came time to create their own module, the participants discovered that there were significant differences of opinion among them about whether such skills were needed and, indeed, how they related to empowerment. Perhaps not surprisingly, the participants' ideas about empowerment tended to be bound by the central missions of their home organizations.

Tess's empowerment workshop had focused on two themes: developing skills to be an effective activist, and developing skills to train others to be effective activists. Work group members who belonged to organizations that are directly involved in resolving workplace grievances (i.e., women's unions) generally recognized the importance of learning skills such as how to plan successful activities and events. And they understood how those skills related to empowerment: women who have these skills have the tools they need to stand up on their own and others' behalf. But, for members of women's organizations whose core mission was to provide resources and support, the connections were less clear. For those groups empowerment meant something closer to a process of psychological healing and discovery of self-worth that is achieved through validating, consciousness-raising activities. In fact (as the Japanese women would later learn), women's empowerment workshops in the United States typically seek to empower women both ways, as individuals and collectively. But the workshop Tess had conducted back in July was not a typical empowerment workshop. It had been custom made in response to the wish list the Japanese women created prior to Workshop II, which skewed more toward the collective empowerment skills. Later, Tess would clarify these issues in her presentation at Workshop III, but for the moment the empowerment group seemed hopelessly divided over what they want their module to achieve.[1]

Meanwhile, as late as November, members of the organizing work group had not yet agreed on whether their members even need to have organizing skills. Some work group members saw organizing as a crucial step in addressing the high turnover and low participation rates. One WUT member in particular was so excited about the idea of creating a system of member-organizers to build up the union's numbers that she kept in regular contact with Carol to develop her ideas for a Japanese organizing module. Others embraced the idea of training members in organizing skills but thought the materials and methods the Korean women's unions used were a better model for JWUs. Still others contested the need for organizing of any kind. Three members of the work group told Midori that they didn't plan to attend the Osaka meeting in December because they didn't see the point. (Fortunately, Midori was able to persuade them to come anyway, reminding them that the Osaka meeting was also an opportunity to get cross-trained in the other two skill areas.) Contentious as some of these discussions were, I took them as a sign of progress. The Japanese women were having conversations they had not had before. They were discussing new perspectives and confronting issues that had lay dormant for many years. They were questioning a priori assumptions that had escaped scrutiny in their previous analyses of their internal organizational problems. Halfway into their allotted time to create a first draft of an organizing skills module, the members of this work group were nowhere near any kind of agreement about whether such skills or such a module were necessary. But that was fine because the third goal of the US-Japan

Project was to deepen debates, discussions, and analyses around the central questions that had been hanging over the JWUs' efforts from the very beginning. All along we had been asking fundamental questions about what kind of organizations women's unions are and what kind of organizations they want to be, but for the most part those questions had remained largely at the level of abstraction. Now that we were in the nitty-gritty phase of the project, where the Japanese women were faced with choosing specific skills they wanted to transmit to their members, they were suddenly thinking about those questions in a far more concrete way. Members of each work group were asking themselves critical questions about the "fit" among their organizational models, their goals, and the resources their organizations in their current form could realistically expect to generate and then maintain over time. And those were the very questions that needed to be asked before anyone would be willing to contemplate major structural changes in the ways women's groups operated individually and as part of the larger movement.

Christmas in Osaka

On December 24, 2005, the Japanese women held a national meeting in Osaka in preparation for Workshop III. Each of the work groups hosted workshops based on the latest versions of their evolving modules. They also reported on the questions, concerns, and insights that had come up through their process of creation, and on what they needed to get out of Workshop III to move forward. The communications group had been extremely successful in adapting the materials from Emily's workshop to their needs and goals. They had little trouble understanding the purpose of the exercises and adapting them for Japanese circumstances, and they had become quite confident in facilitating small group training sessions. Since their basic communications skills module was working so well, they wanted Emily to lead follow-up workshops introducing them to more advanced communications skills. More specifically, they wanted her to facilitate workshops on community outreach and designing effective campaigns.

The empowerment group, on the other hand, was still struggling with differing opinions about the meaning of empowerment and how activist and teaching skills relate to it. They were able to reproduce the exercises they learned in Workshop II, but there was no consensus among the members about whether or not the lessons that came out of those exercises were of any value to their organizations. They suspected that there was some essential connection they weren't yet making, so they wanted Workshop III to include additional discussion sessions with Tess: one to walk through the logic of each of the activities Tess introduced in

Workshop II, and a second session to help the members of different types of women's groups clarify for themselves what they mean by empowerment and what types of skills and knowledge their members need to be active participants in their organizations.

Finally, and to no one's surprise, the organizing group had kept up its tradition of uncovering the thorniest issues during its process of creation. Although they had initially resisted the questions that Carol's workshop inevitably raised, once the group started working on their own modules they couldn't stop asking themselves those same questions: What kind of organization do we want to be? What kind of organizing do we want to engage in? Should we restructure our organizations to increase our strength or should we pare down our goals to match the limitations of the individual-membership structure? Those questions were too threatening when Carol raised them, but now that they'd had time to chew them over, the women realized that some of those issues went to the very heart of the chronic problems that women's unions faced. At the same time, they felt sure that the big industrial union model did not fit their circumstances. By this point in the project, the JWUs knew they wanted to be able to do more than provide job consultations, but what that would mean, how they could do it, and how they could do it without neglecting women who need immediate help, weighed heavily on their minds. They decided that in Workshop III they wanted to revisit these issues with a US activist who hails from an organization more like their own, namely Linda Meric from 9to5. Beyond providing feedback on their module, Linda would be asked to talk about 9to5's organizing philosophy and to give examples of actual practices on the ground.

Yet, as much as the Japanese women wanted to improve their educational materials, as much as they wanted to continue collaborating with Emily, Linda, and Tess, their primary goal for Workshop III (and the US-Japan Project as a whole) was to come away having firmly established a solid foundation for a national working women's activist network. Whether they would be ready to formally launch their national network or if there were interim steps that had to be taken was still very much up in the air, as were other specifics including its mission, goals, target constituencies, and so on. These were all issues the Japanese women wanted to discuss among themselves at Workshop III, and they wanted to leave the workshop with a firm plan of action detailing how the groups would continue to work together in the coming year to bring their network to fruition. But there was a fly in the ointment, and for once it wasn't me. In the course of developing their modules, with all the discussions and compromises that entails, the women began to notice that they don't always work and play well with others. In fact, they noticed that not only were their meetings less focused than those run by US and Korean activists, they were also considerably more contentious and less likely to produce any sort of positive outcome. In particular, they noticed that new ideas were almost always shot down with a barrage of negative responses that seemed to be more automatic than meaningful. I had to stifle a laugh when Midori confided this discovery to me. I couldn't count the number of times I'd left meetings in the early days feeling as though I'd been hit by a bus after making even the tiniest suggestion. Over time I came to realize that knee-jerk negativity was just part of the culture, of the women's groups and society at large, and it was not always insurmountable. In fact, it was almost a cherished ritual. So it was especially impressive that the women had identified the pattern in their dealings with each other, saw it as an obstacle, and decided to take action to change it. They decided that Workshop III should include a session on developing skills for facilitating and participating in positive meetings. They further decided that this session should immediately precede the final two sessions in which the Japanese activists alone would map out work plans for completing and disseminating their new educational materials, and brainstorm ways to support each other's activities over the coming year.

Although two of the three work groups had a number of philosophical issues yet to resolve—and a number of practical challenges to overcome—I was extremely encouraged by the progress the women and their organizations had made in the five months since Workshop II. The meeting in Osaka and the months leading up to it showed that, at a very practical level, their national network was coming to fruition. In preparing for the national meeting, women's groups from all over the country had worked together over time and across distances and organizational boundaries. During the meeting, they demonstrated their continued commitment to including as many voices as possible in the creation of both the educational materials and the network itself. Perhaps most important, the groups showed a growing willingness and ability to examine the ways they were interacting with each other and to seek solutions when those practices were not living up to their democratic and feminist ideals. On top of that, their modules and their ability to lead training workshops were improving with every trial run. By the end of the Osaka meeting, the Japanese women had agreed on a March 3rd start date for our final international workshop, and I for one was eager to see what new strides they would make in the intervening two months.

Showtime

In March 2006 we met in Tokyo for the last workshop of the US-Japan Project. We gathered at the same no-frills businessman's hotel with its antiseptic microrooms and faux-Starbucks café that served us so well last time. The front desk clerk was a little startled by the din we created as we greeted each other in the tiny lobby. She was more accustomed to grim-faced salarymen somberly making their way to and from the guestrooms upstairs. But we were not there on ordinary business. We were there because something we'd started years ago, something quite extraordinary, was coming to life. This was the first day of our last meeting and we had good reason to celebrate.

Work(shops) in Progress

The workshop was again held at the International Christian University, with Hwa-Mi Park, Mika Iba, and other women from progressive organizations providing translation. Each of the three work groups conducted workshops based on the latest versions of their modules. They had asked the US participants to sit in as observers and facilitate feedback sessions afterwards. Although the Japanese facilitators were generally using the same basic exercises the US educators had taught them, it was amazing to see how much more effective they were now that they had essentially been processed through a Japanese filter. The US materials we used in Workshop II had been translated at the broadest linguistic level, but these materials had now been more deeply translated into the particular culture, discourse, and practices of Japanese women workers and activists. The lessons were now in their vernacular, with situations and examples they could relate to, and they were being facilitated by people whose experiences more closely matched their own. And the results were dramatic, especially in terms of the creativity that was unleashed. Each of three modules (in their different ways) included segments that asked the participants to design activities to get their message out to the public. The women now leading these sessions had participated in similar exercises during Workshop II and they had done a good job of coming up with interesting, even plausible, ideas at the time. But the ideas that were coming out of these new, culturally translated workshops were much more engaging and Japan-flavored than any of the ideas we had seen so far. For example, one group came up with the idea of using baked goods and wordplay to increase awareness about the wage difference between regular and nonregular workers. The group planned a public awareness campaign in which union members would pass out homemade sweets to the crowd. The catch was that while some people would get a tiny sliver of something sweet, others would get significantly larger treats for no apparent reason. The idea was to make visible the difference in regular and nonregular employees' wages, while also highlighting the unfairness and arbitrariness of the distinction. The group cleverly named their hypothetical campaign the *Okashi* Project, because the word "*okashi*" means "cake" or "sweets" but it also sounds very similar to "*okashii*" which means "ridiculous."

Another idea was to hold a *senryu* poetry contest. *Senryu* is a type of Japanese poetry similar to haiku except that it focuses on human beings rather than nature, and hinges on humor rather than extolling beauty. Companies sometimes hold *senryu* contests as one of their many types of employee bonding exercises, so some of the Japanese women suggested having members compete to see who could come up with the funniest poem about their workplace. Initially the idea was that a union-based contest would give employees a safe and fun way to educate each other about their common issues, and to stimulate broader problem-solving discussions. But the technique could be used for other purposes as well. Later that year, Working Women's Voices hosted a *senryu* competition as a way of reaching out to parts of the workforce they weren't able to attract through traditional activities. Bringing in more than one hundred entries, the contest not only raised WWV's visibility, it also produced some fine new examples of working-class verse, including the crowd favorite, "My Boss is So Smelly."

Yet another idea was to use the traditions of a popular Japanese holiday, *Tanabata*, to help women talk about their problems at work. *Tanabata* is based on a legend of two lovers who were tragically kept apart in life, and after death transformed into two stars that meet only once a year (on the 7th day of the 7th month). On that date, people mark the occasion by writing secret wishes on small strips of paper and tying them to the branches of designated bamboo trees in the hope that their wishes will come true within the year. The work group suggested playfully hijacking the "secret wish" tradition to give women a safe and anonymous way to speak out about their problems on the job. Instead of writing secret wishes, women would be asked to write a short note about some problem they were having at work and tie it to the union's tree. Later, when the facilitator read the comments to the whole group, the women would quickly see that they are not alone in their work problems; many other women have the same problems they do, and there is a pattern to the problems working women have. As an added bonus, there is something empowering and deeply cathartic in being able to express forbidden sentiments they had kept buried for fear of retribution.

On a subsequent trip to Japan, when I was following up on the lasting impact of the US-Japan Project, one woman told me about using the *Tanabata* idea to help new members open up about their issues. In most cases, new members used the opportunity to voice the usual complaints: harassment, forced early retirement, gendered work assignments, and so on. But every once in a while someone would have a little fun tweaking the boss's nose, which not only adds levity to union activities, it also lets a little air out of the boss's image, making it easier for women to imagine standing up to him in the future.

Despite the light-heartedness of the activities, my sense was that they would prove to be powerful for their target audiences. I could more easily imagine

Japanese women participating in these kinds of actions than in more aggressive, confrontational actions that are more typically associated with labor unions. The proposed activities call on women to talk about themselves and their work issues, but they do so in ways that are less alienating because they are sensitive to Japanese norms and employ familiar art forms and cultural referents. And yet I was interested to see that the organizing work group had, at least at this juncture, decided to retain most of Carol's materials for their training module. They even included the role-play exercises that had unnerved them so much back in July. Some of the women later explained that over time and with practice they had begun to see the techniques Carol introduced in a new light. They were coming to see that Carol's methods were largely about learning to be a better listener, learning to draw people out, and letting them tell their own stories and come to their own conclusions about needing the help and support of a union. They were also beginning to see that overcoming objections does not mean discounting the very real problems women face in joining a union. It means trying to find practical solutions to enable women to get involved. It means overcoming fears and the natural resistance to trying something new. And it provides an opportunity for the union to gather information about what it can do to make it easier for women to participate, such as providing childcare during meetings or finding ways for women to engage in union activities from home.

I couldn't help wishing that Carol had been there to hear that discussion because it showed that, despite the initial resistance, some of the ideas she shared and the questions she raised had in fact taken root. The Japanese women had come to appreciate the value of the techniques Carol showed them, and were seriously grappling with whether and how they could be adapted for use in Japan.

Building Knowledge

Beyond providing feedback on the pilot modules, the US participants were on hand to introduce new materials and to address some of the questions that came up as the Japanese women were working on their modules. In many ways, Linda Meric's session on organizing was the most anticipated of the US presentations because the topic itself always seemed to produce so much drama. Organizing was at the center of disputes between Midori and me, between Carol and her work group, and among the Japanese women themselves, before, during, and even after the US-Japan Project had finished. It was (and still is) a contentious topic, and now the leader of an organization they deeply respected was about to weigh in.

Linda's reunion with the participants from Workshop I was a happy one. The goodwill that developed during their first meeting in Detroit was still in evidence when they greeted each other this time around. Linda has a tremendous gift for putting people at ease, which I hoped would come in handy as we once again waded into what we expected to be shark-infested waters.

She started with a brief overview of 9to5's history and mission for those who had joined the project after Workshop I. She reminded us that 9to5 is a not-for-profit association that organizes low-wage women. In the beginning, 9to5 focused on clerical workers—working women who were living at or near the poverty level but were not on most feminist groups' or unions' radar. Since then the focus has expanded to include part-time and temporary workers, and women who must supplement their income with public assistance because the jobs available to them are so low paying they can't make ends meet.

The goals of 9to5 are to: make visible the problems of low-wage women; raise the expectations of low-wage women (many of whom internalize the idea that a life of poverty is all they're worth); develop the belief that change is possible; and enable women to see they can be agents of social change. Clearly, 9to5's goals are not the goals of a labor union. It does not seek to organize workplaces to directly confront capital. Instead, its goals (such as promoting women-friendly legislation and public policy, and shaping public discourse related to low-wage women) square with the kinds of influence network-style advocacy organizations are capable of leveraging.

The parallels between 9to5 and the JWUs were easily recognizable. Like the JWUs, 9to5 has its roots in the women's movements of the 1960s and '70s. From the beginning, 9to5 has been interested in exploring the intersection of women's and labor movements. While it recognizes the benefits of workers unionizing, it also sees a need for a different type of organization, one that is better able to attract media attention and to reach out to, as Linda said, "women for whom unionizing was not an immediate option." Also, like the JWUs, 9to5 has the twin goals of empowering women individually while at the same time changing the legal and policy environments, as well as public opinion, through media appearances, public actions, testifying in government forums, and providing community education programs. Finally, JWUs and 9to5 share a focus on building alliances with other women's groups and community organizations.[2]

Where 9to5 and JWUs differ is that 9to5 actively and emphatically recruits members, believing that joining their organization empowers women individually and collectively. Linda described several of the non-workplace-based organizing techniques they use. The first was to set up information tables at places low-wage women are likely to frequent.

> When women come over to our table, 9to5 organizers engage them in conversation, asking them what they're interested in and about what kinds of issues they are experiencing. We have resource materials on the

table, including information about eligibility and registration require-
ments for low-income childcare assistance, information about how to
apply for tax credits for low-income working families, voter registration forms and voting rights information for people who have formerly
been incarcerated. Because we openly address these issues that may be
obstacles for many individuals, we build the trust of the women who
talk with us. We also gain their trust because we are there every week,
we are welcoming and we can answer or commit to finding the answers
to many questions or concerns they may have.

The resource tables are also stocked with information about 9to5 and how
women can get involved as well as fact sheets and short surveys about current
9to5 campaigns. Like Carol, Linda advocated using simple surveys as an organizing tool. "The survey gets people thinking about the issue and that they can get
involved in helping make change. It gets us their contact information, and helps
us identify people who may be directly affected by the issue and have a story to
share. We often have survey tools about several different issues, so that we can
make as many connections as possible and reach as many women as possible
through an issue they can directly relate to."

The surveys also include at least one "action step" that people can take. "It
may be as simple as signing [a] postcard supporting family-flexible policies . . . .
We get their names and contact information, they take action, it makes a deeper
connection between us and them, and it helps 9to5 build the display of support
for the policies we are advocating."

In addition, 9to5 offers various types of training sessions, usually through government and nongovernmental agencies that provide support services to low-
wage women. Over the years 9to5 has developed a variety of what they call "mini
curricula" on topics such as understanding workplace rights; dealing with workplace conflict, addressing sexual harassment, and balancing work and family.

Linda did not mince words when explaining why 9to5 offers these training
sessions:

> We always do a recruitment pitch as part of our presentation . . . . Mem-
> ber recruitment is a key part of our organizing. We recruit new members
> when we are tabling and training. We also have an annual membership
> drive, during which groups of women can join the organization at a re-
> duced dues rate. [Our] staff meet with leaders and set individual and
> chapter recruitment goals. We discuss and distribute materials with
> ideas about who to recruit and how. We provide incentives for members
> to recruit other members, such as discounts for registration and travel to
> our annual leadership conference in Washington, DC. We schedule eve-

ning and weekend times for members to come to the 9to5 office, and phone [people] we've met through tabling and training, to ask them to join 9to5. We also use phone banking to call current members and ask them to renew their membership. We provide dinner for the [callers] that we get local businesses to donate, and childcare as needed. The group atmosphere provides enthusiasm and support, so that the phoning is easier and more productive. We recognize and honor those leaders who are the most effective in recruiting new members.

Far from fearing that recruitment will somehow undermine their efforts to empower women, Linda says it is the key to developing a meaningful movement that puts real power—individual and collective—in the hands of women.

"Although we focus our recruiting energy during the membership drive, recruitment is something that we do at all events, at every opportunity. We know that we must build the size of our organization to build our strength and have the power we need to win change."

Even 9to5's job survival hotline is first and foremost a vehicle for recruiting new members. "For many women, the hotline is the way they first learn about 9to5 and how they can get involved. They call us about a job problem, looking for information, resources, referrals, and support. We provide those things, but see the hotline much more as an organizing tool. We link the caller's problem with problems being faced by other women. . . . Our goal is to change the call from being about one woman's problem to being about the need to speak out, unite together, and take collective action for change."

Empowerment and Organizing

As Linda talked about 9to5's recruiting activities, I looked around the room for signs of discomfort but everyone seemed to be listening with equanimity. Linda explained that, like Carol, she sees recruitment and empowerment going hand in hand. Indeed, 9to5 follows up its recruitment efforts with empowerment training, beginning with giving the women a chance to tell their own stories. As with the surveys, 9to5 has ready-made story forms to gather the stories of women who are willing to share them. They also train women in media and public speaking skills so they can speak for themselves. The organization also offers empowerment training in other skill areas such as organizing, facilitating meetings, working in coalitions, and serving on boards. Even their "Get Out the Vote" activities are interlaced with organizing; 9to5 organizes women to support and campaign for political leaders who advocate for low-wage workers and women, starting with providing political education. The group mobilizes women to get involved in the political process the same way it organizes women to join 9to5, i.e., by building trust, providing information, answering questions, overcoming obstacles, and encouraging participation. In that way, mobilizing women to vote simultaneously encourages them to join 9to5.

None of these ideas are fundamentally different from the techniques Carol introduced, and yet this time there was no groundswell of resistance, no expressions of outrage, no talk of walking out. Even when she touched on the most controversial topic from Carol's workshop—overcoming objections—the Japanese women didn't flinch. Part of that was because this was not the first time they were hearing these ideas. Those who had participated in the original organizing workshop had already heard them, and even those who weren't in the organizing group had been somewhat inoculated by the subsequent discussions the workshop generated.

Also, I think the women were better able to hear Linda because she talked in terms the Japanese women could relate to. Traditional union rhetoric often has a strong male vibe that can alienate Japanese women. But Linda used terms that were much closer to the way the JWUs talk about themselves and their mission. She talked a lot about providing support and assistance. Her compassion and concern for the women 9to5 reaches out to came through loud and clear. And yet, she made no apologies for asking those same women to stand up and take action. She made it very clear that for her there is no contradiction between recognizing the physical, emotional, and financial toll gender discrimination takes on women's lives and calling on (and equipping) women to be the agents of the change they seek.

Mostly, though, I think the reason the Japanese women did not feel threatened by Linda was that, like them, she was a founder of an alternative working women's organization. Early 9to5 members had the chance to structure their organization as a union but decided not to because they believed they would be better able to achieve their goals—increasing the visibility of women's issues and reaching out to nonunion women—as an alternative organization. At the same time, Linda acknowledged that that decision came at a cost. As an alternative workers' organization, 9to5 forgoes many of the legal rights and opportunities for direct organizing that unions have. And, lacking the ability to bring workers together to collectively confront their employer, 9to5 does not wield the same kind of direct and immediate power that unions can. But recognizing those limitations has not led Linda to conclude that organizations such as 9to5 are unnecessary. Instead, she argues that both types of organizations have value and can—and should—work together in complementary ways.

In the end, the session we had all worried about was an unequivocal success. Linda introduced and stimulated discussion about organizing strategies that only a few months before had provoked bitter resistance. The Japanese women were more open to her message because they did not see her as just another union bureaucrat exhorting them to toe the party line. Of course, neither was Carol, but because she represented the AFL-CIO and her curriculum was based on organizing workers in more traditional workplace situations, the Japanese women, fairly or not, associated her with the outdated enterprise unions that can't (or won't) see that their methods don't work for women. In Linda's case, there were no such associations. Like all of the Japanese women in the room, she had struggled to build and now represented a new kind of organization, so they had no fear that she was there to pressure them into forgoing their reforms.

New Beginnings

On Sunday, we came together for the last time, the Japanese women to finalize plans for launching a national network of women activists, and the US participants as witnesses to a momentous event they had helped to bring about. As her final (official) contribution to the US-Japan Project, Emily led a session on skills and guidelines for facilitating and participating in positive, productive meetings. It might seem unrealistic to think that a single 90-minute workshop could make a significant difference in long-established patterns of interaction. But there was no mistaking the change we all saw in the tenor of the discussions that followed. For the rest of the day, the Japanese participants were slated to engage in intricate, high-stakes discussions, with opinions as varied as the groups that were involved. They had tasked themselves with taking on issues that had divided them for months if not longer, and making binding decisions despite their long-standing predilection to naysay themselves into a quagmire of inaction. If they had tried to have these discussions prior to the meeting skills workshop, I would have been tempted to hide under the table. But with the introduction of just a few basic skills, such as establishing mutually agreed upon ground rules at the start of every meeting, the Japanese women were able to pick their way, not perfectly but productively, through difficult issues that had fragmented them in the past. By the end of the day they had waded into an array of complicated issues from developing work plans for completing their modules, to reassessing perspectives on organizational structure and organizing practices, to considering policy proposals and legislative campaigns the groups might want to collectively pursue in the coming year. The discussions did not always go smoothly. The usual fault lines appeared at the usual times and in the usual places: worker power versus network power; recruiting versus waiting for women to take the first step; state solutions versus direct action. Plus, a few new fissures appeared.

I was surprised by some fairly acrimonious complaints that the budding movement has so far been too Tokyo-centric, leaving the groups in other regions with not enough input and too much of the burden of traveling. These are all tough issues and many of them had, in the past, derailed important discussions among the participating women's groups. But this time the women had tools for de-escalating disagreements and seeking positive solutions that encouraged and respected multiple perspectives. Throughout the day we saw various women trying to exercise their new skills when the discussion began to veer off course or when someone began to dominate the conversation. They repeatedly got off topic but then repeatedly brought the conversation back to a more productive place. It was a truly impressive first effort at breaking old habits and, as I would later learn, the first step in a radical reshaping of the ways Japanese women's groups and other progressive organizations interact with each other.

But that outcome was still on the horizon. The most immediate effect of the workshop on positive meetings was that the women were finally able to create a pathway forward on an issue that had been fragmenting their efforts for several months. From the beginning of the project, the women's groups had told us that building a national network of Japanese women's organizations was their ultimate goal. More than increasing their organizations' memberships, more than building on international alliances, the women's groups sought to build power by "connecting the dots" as one participant had put it. And, to a large degree, they had. In the course of participating in the US-Japan Project—through planning the workshops, disseminating new information and skills, and creating their modules—the Japanese groups had established the relationships, structures, and practices that constitute the basic infrastructure of a national network. But some of the members, including Midori, felt they were not ready to function as the comprehensive women's advocacy network. Midori and others argued that, until more members were trained and available to take on leadership roles in existing women's organizations, there simply was not enough womanpower to take on the additional legislative and movement-building responsibilities that a comprehensive women's advocacy network would entail. Also, the groups needed more time to work out the philosophical, logistical, and practical issues, as well as a consensus on overall mission, before taking such a large step. However, that did not mean they weren't ready to establish a national network of any kind.

By this point, most of the participating groups agreed that their organizations, individually and as part of a larger movement, would be greatly strengthened by increasing members' education. And they agreed that educating more members was the first step toward building the broader advocacy network they'd set their sights on. So, after much discussion, they decided they would begin by establishing a national education network, whose mission would be to produce and disseminate educational materials for feminist and workers' organizations, to facilitate information and resource sharing, and to build awareness of the need for membership education in democratic organizations.

On the last day of the project, the Japanese activists voted to form the Working Women's Educational Network (WWEN), in the hope that member organizations would soon be able to train new generations of union leaders, which would in turn free up long-serving union leaders to pursue movement-building activities. Ideally, the combination of training new activists and recruiting new organizations and community leaders to join the movement would move the Japanese activists closer to their goal of creating a national advocacy network.

Once the WWEN had been named and its first year's worth of projects mapped out and approved by the Japanese participants, the US-Japan Project officially came to an end. The JWUs and other participating women's groups had developed a long-range vision for a national women's movement, created institutions and practices to support their efforts, and laid out detailed work plans for the coming year, which not only increased the chance they'd follow through on their new goals, but also structured continued collaboration among the women's groups for at least the next twelve months. The disparate smattering of lone and rudderless women's unions was no more. Each union still existed as its own entity and still retained its original flavor and purpose, but was now also part of a larger collective of working women's organizations that potentially could amplify their voices, raise their public profile, consolidate political and people power, and, by pooling resources, help each group combat the chronic problems small grassroots organizations face.

I was happy with that outcome. Thrilled, actually. Considering where we started and how isolated and stuck in place the JWUs seemed when I first met them, it was almost unfathomable how far we'd come in what suddenly seemed like a very short time. Corporate Japan, with aid of the government and the winking complicity of most enterprise unions, had told working women to pull themselves up by their own bra straps and, by god, they'd done it. But they hadn't done it alone. They'd done it with the solidarity of other women who had answered the same call. And so, while I was thrilled at the progress they had made, I was also a little sad to hear that finding a way to continue working with US women didn't figure more prominently into their future plans. They certainly weren't opposed to the idea of further US-Japan collaborations, but neither was it a top priority. Midori and others often told me that, given the rapidly deteriorating working conditions for Japanese women, they needed to focus their efforts on immediate issues at home before building up to broader coordinated efforts (such as an international part-time workers' campaign). Also, they were more interested in working with women from other Asian countries in part because they believed their circumstances were more similar. I am not sure that's true but, since we are talking about people's comfort levels, perception matters and, in any case, it's their call. They are eager to work with us again when time and money permit, but they see developing ties among themselves and with other Asian women's groups as the more immediate concern. That was not the decision I'd hoped for but it was a decision I had to accept.

Leaving the ICU campus was a little sad for those of us who had to board planes and return to the United States because we could see that a flurry of activity was about to burst forth in Japan. On the bus ride back to our salarymen's hotel, I sat in melancholy but grateful contemplation as my Japanese colleagues buzzed and laughed and planned all around me. I knew, I could feel in my bones, that they were about to go forth and do great things, and I wanted to stay and be part of that. But that is not how this game is played. I knew that I and all the other US participants had to step back and let this new movement take off in whatever direction the Japanese women saw fit. From here on out, my only role would be to track and report their progress and the long-term effects of our collaboration. But I did have something to keep my sadness at bay. In the midst of their final discussions, the Japanese women had laid out some very specific work plans for the coming year, with very specific deadlines attached. So, as melancholy as I was about leaving that day, I already knew I'd have reason to come back at the end of the year to see how close they had come to achieving those goals. And it's a good thing I did. Even with all the times my Japanese colleagues had surprised me with what they could accomplish in a relatively short time, I could not have imagined the extent of the transformation I would see on my return a year later.

A MOVEMENT TRANSFORMED

My promise to myself in taking on this project—in asking so many busy women to volunteer time that was already spoken for three times over, and in asking the Japan Foundation to commit funds that many other worthy projects were also seeking—was that, in the end, this project would make a meaningful, lasting impact on working women's fight for equality in Japan. Although I had very specific hopes, I tried not to make a priori assumptions about what that impact would or should look like, what kinds of changes would or should grow out of our collaboration. But I did promise myself and all the other participants that the project would not be simply a solidarity-building exercise aimed at raising our spirits and giving us the strength to fight another day. And it would definitely not be one of those foreign-visitor lecture series that were usually interesting and informative but had the shelf life of raw fish in July. This project came with a much higher price tag (in time, money, and expertise) than typical grassroots exchanges, so I felt obligated to ensure that the outcomes would be robust and lasting enough to justify the costs. In March 2007, one year after the project ended, I returned to Japan to find out if we had hit our mark. I had high hopes, of course. I had spent enough time with my Japanese colleagues to know that they routinely exceeded not just my expectations, but the expectations of most labor and business leaders they encountered. Even so, I could not have anticipated the profound transformation that had in fact taken place. Once isolated groups of bone-weary activists, Japanese women's organizations had taken on a new vitality and developed a new unity that was sparked by the US-Japan Project and went well beyond. The groups had gone on to develop new materials, ideas, and practices that were wholly their own. And they had dramatically extended the network ties the project had fostered. They were working together to educate each other, to share information and resources with each other, to support each other's campaigns; in short, they were working together in a host of new ways that strengthened the organizations individually and the women's movement as a whole.

Transformations at the Movement Level

No longer isolated and spinning their wheels for lack of direction, the women's organizations had built a strong coalition around the need to train women and other progressives in basic activist skills. Following Workshop III, women's groups began holding workshops to train their own members and members of other progressive organizations in their regions. Meanwhile, Mabel and Midori crisscrossed the country as itinerant trainers, conducting workshops based on materials from an array of international sources. Their mission started out small and fairly local, but as word of their workshops got out, invitations poured in from all over the country asking them to bring their new methods to other regions where progressive organizations were struggling to emerge. And not just women's organizations: labor and social justice organizations of all kinds were eager to learn the new skills everyone was buzzing about. Hundreds of new activists were trained in just the first few months. Midori told me she was simultaneously as exhausted and as energized as she'd ever been.

Working Women's Educational Network

Most of these educational activities were held under the auspices of the newly formed WWEN, which was already holding its second national conference at the time of my visit. The group had met in July 2006 (about six months after the final US-Japan workshop) to discuss possible distribution methods for the educational materials they had created or received from other sources. In March 2007 the member organizations met to report on their educational activities since the end of the US-Japan Project. Beyond training activists in the skills they had learned through the project, groups were already developing new lessons on a variety of topics. A women's organization called Equality Action 21 had already made three videos designed to raise awareness on issues such as the inequality between regular and temp employees, and to prepare women to hold positive discussions with their bosses to address those issues. The videos came with written training scripts so that women could practice talking about the value of their work and how to make a case for equality. Also in the first year, Working Women's Voices had developed a one-and-a-half-hour workshop on identifying and addressing problems in the workplace, along with accessible, step-by-step instructions that other groups could follow if they wanted to conduct the workshop on their own. Using the same process of trial and error, feedback and revision that we used during the US-Japan Project, WWV created a set of activities and materials that promoted dialogue around women's workplace issues and could be easily reproduced by facilitators from other organizations. Women's Union Plus hosted a workshop for women in the Sendai region.[1] The workshop included training in positive listening and facilitation skills which, as we had seen in other parts of the country, almost immediately increased productivity and participation in union meetings. It also included a session on mapping the workplace in preparation for bargaining. In the beginning, the participants did not understand the point of mapping, but once they participated in the process, the purpose and value of the exercise became clear. "Mapping gets people to talk about which problems each person is having," said Women's Union Plus leader Kiyomi Kurosawa. "It creates a 3-D picture of what is in the workplace and what is in others' minds. The situation becomes very concrete for us, very real. Now, when we simulate bargaining in preparation for a session, we have a visual tool to help us."

Listening to the regional reports, I couldn't help noticing how often the presenters mentioned the newcomers' inability to understand the purpose of activities until after they had participated in them. Kurosawa mentioned it with the lesson on mapping. And Kazuko Sazaki from Working Women's Voices reported that participants who had not been involved in the US-Japan Project had trouble understanding the meaning of early versions of their workshop. Participants in those early workshops often were confused and disoriented by the unfamiliar teaching methods and by the expectation that they should actively participate in the learning process rather than simply receive knowledge. They had no frame of reference for making sense of the exercises they were asked to engage in, but also no language to express what it was that they didn't understand. That led to some heated discussions, not unlike what we saw happen during the organizing session in Workshop II. But eventually, the facilitators were able to piece together the participants' feedback to figure out what the problem was: most participants needed additional information to contextualize the workshop, to clarify its meaning and methods, and to have concrete examples of the kinds of workplace problems they are seeking to address. Working Women's Voices subsequently revised their workshop to include additional information to help orient participants to the process they are about to engage in and to ensure that they have basic background information needed to participate in discussions.

Although both Women's Union Plus and WWV were able to overcome initial resistance to their cutting-edge methods, the WWEN conference participants agreed that the problem itself is not going away any time soon. Resisting the New is a well-established pattern in many aspects of Japanese culture, and what these workshops were asking people to do was so new that they consistently produced negative first reactions. We even saw it among the young people who had recently joined the WWEN. Posse, an organization for young male and female activists interested in gender equality, faced the same kind of negativity when they first offered a workshop to explore work-life issues for women. "Most of the participants had never experienced workshops, so their resistance was strong," one Posse member said. As an icebreaker activity, the facilitator asked the participants to list some of their weak points and then come up with ways to describe those qualities in positive terms. "People who were not used to this kind of activity got very intense. It was very hard for them. But we all supported each other and finally it worked well."

But obviously, not all is stodgy in a land that's famous for TV personalities dressed up in turtle suits. The fact that new women's organizations exist, and that those organizations have embraced a radically new concept in education and are now creating their own versions of it, tells us that, despite first reactions, innovation can and does happen here. We saw that time and again as organizations found ways to revise their workshops in response to participants' feedback. And there were other signs that Japanese women's groups and the movement itself was continuing to evolve. While many of the sessions focused on developing educational materials, the WWEN conference kicked off with a full-day workshop on, of all things, leadership, a topic that seemed irrevocably off-limits just one year earlier. "When we thought about leadership in the past, we thought about particular leaders we had in the past," Kurosawa said. "But through this training we got past those stereotypes and learned about a different concept of leadership, where everyone is trained and takes turns being the leader." At the time we were planning Workshop II of the US-Japan Project, I had made these exact arguments about the need for all members to be trained in leadership skills, but the term was so repugnant to the Japanese women that we had to use the term "empowerment" instead of "leadership" when referring to the skills they would learn in Tess's workshop (which in turn led to a proliferation of confusion and misunderstandings as the project went on). But again, the idea that there could be different kinds of leadership was not something they could learn simply by listening to someone else. In order for the concept to fully come to life, the women had to be ready to learn it, and they had to learn through their own process of discovery. One year earlier they were not ready, but now they had reopened the question on their own and were actively redefining the concept for themselves in a way that was commensurate with their mission, values, and needs.

Action Center for Working Women

The WWEN Conference provided clear evidence that the Japanese women's groups had finally achieved Tani's vision of a member-to-member, organization-to-organization "cascade of learning," which was successfully preparing hundreds if not thousands of women to take on more leadership responsibilities within their unions. That in turn opened the door to a second transformation within the women's movement. From our first meeting, Midori and Tani had told me they wanted and needed to step down from their positions as leaders of the WUT. Each had devoted much of her adult life to bettering women's lives. Each had a broad range of activist skills and a long list of goals she wanted to achieve for the advancement of working women. But for more than a decade, the endless demand for individual consultations kept them yoked to that single task. All other goals and aspirations for building the women's movement were put on hold, leaving the bulk of their skills and knowledge to lay fallow because so many women were in immediate need of assistance and so few were trained to provide it. And they were not alone in that feeling. I heard that lament again and again from other JWU founders who felt they had held leadership of their unions for too long. Now, with so many newly trained activists, the "old girls" cohort was finally able to move on to pursuing their dream of creating an umbrella organization that would unite women's unions and other women's organizations throughout the country. All along the founders had said that, since JWUs were not in a position to organize in the traditional way, they would have to build their power through networking across groups, but because of the steady stream of consultations and bargaining, they had never had the time or resources to devote to building such a network. But with a new wave of women stepping into leadership roles or at least taking on more leadership responsibilities, and the ties that were forged during the US-Japan Project, first-generation leaders such as Midori, Tani, Yakabi, and Ban were finally able to turn their attention to creating a national center for working women's organizations.

In January 2007 they launched the Action Center for Working Women (ACW2) to provide support, education, advocacy, political activities, and other movement-building functions that the overburdened women's unions could not handle on their own. The ACW2 acts as a clearinghouse for information on legislative initiatives, court cases, political campaigns, and ongoing labor disputes. In addition to providing job consultations, ACW2 trains members to provide job consultations to others using the participatory education methods the Japanese women learned through the US-Japan Project and other crossborder exchanges. It also seeks to build support among scholars, lawyers, politicians, teachers, journalists, and other professionals who help shape public policy and opinion, as well as other progressive labor organizations such as the Center for Transnational Labor Studies. The ACW2 also helps to build and maintain ties with activist groups in other countries, including Korean women's unions and various US feminist and labor organizations. While this new organization does provide an important link connecting working women and their organizations at the national level, as of 2016 it has not yet evolved into the national center of member organizations. So far the members are individuals not organizations. But the hope is that it will eventually become, or become the model for, the umbrella organization that leaders such as Midori and Tani continue to strive toward.

Transformations at the Organizational Level

To a woman, every union member I interviewed said that their union meetings were dramatically more positive and productive. They were getting things done faster, more efficiently, and with far less automatic negativity than had been their habit. In fact, sometime after the project ended, Mabel sat in on a WUT meeting and said she was stunned to see how much more positive and focused the meeting was. Also, members who had gone through the training reported that their ability to connect with newcomers and potential new members had improved tremendously. Improvements in their listening skills and ability to communicate made them more effective in providing help to women who reached out to the union, and made the experience of providing job consultations more rewarding. One woman told me that when she went back to answering the hotline after her training, she was shocked to discover that she had "not really been listening with [her] heart." Instead, she had simply been waiting for her turn so she could start talking about joining the union, which was exactly the opposite of what she thought she was doing and what she intended to do.

Toyomi Fujii, who replaced Midori as head of WUT, said that one of the most important changes was the significant improvement in members' communications skills, including her own. "I was very bad at speeches. I always tried to avoid having to speak. But now I realize that we must consciously make the places for us to be heard." Once a month the WUT holds Speak Outs in front of a nearby train station. "The workshop gave us more confidence. We strongly believe we need this union. We know how important our work is. Now we have more confidence to talk to others about that." The workshops have also improved members' ability to communicate with each other inside the union. "Before, in meetings I tried to be as reserved as possible because I was so vulnerable if someone speaks against me. But now I can say what I want to say."

The most important change, according to Fujii, is that more members, including young members, actively participate in the union. "We see more members raise their hands in meetings. Before, we felt that the board members always had to be in the center, leading. Now that has changed. We can be on the sidelines."

Remaining Challenges

Although it was not an explicit goal of the project, I had hoped that in the course of our discussions we would innovate an alternate structure that could help JWUs overcome problems inherent in the individual-union model but without abandoning their central mission. Unfortunately, that did not happen. As much as the Japanese women would like their organizations to have wider and deeper impact, the question of how to reorganize still takes a back seat to dealing with the immediate needs of the members. For now the JWUs, of necessity, retain their individual-membership structure, but in doing so they also retain many of the institutional ills that prompted us to develop the project in the first place. Although their new organizing skills have enabled members to talk more effectively with the women who come to them for help, the union has not fundamentally changed its approach to recruiting or organizing inside workplaces. They still rely on attracting women in crisis, which means they continue to be overwhelmed by requests for consultations. Attrition also remains a serious problem. Since individual-membership unions do not create an ongoing presence in the workplace, JWUs are not able to offer women a strong enough reason to continue their membership once their immediate crises have been resolved. Nor has the WUT been able to break down the image of the union as an outside agency that handles your problem for you. Members still think of the union as an organization that is supposed to do something for them as opposed to seeing themselves *as* the union and the source of their own solutions. But that is no surprise as that is how the JWUs present themselves in their outreach to new members, and it is indeed how they operate in practice.

Despite the many achievements of the US-Japan Project, the ur-problem, namely the JWUs' insistence on an organizational structure that produces the very conditions that are the most immediate threat to their long-term survival, remains largely unchanged. Although many of the leaders now recognize the links between individual membership and low participation and high attrition rates among members, they say they cannot scrap the individual-membership structure without viable alternatives already in place. Traditional unions are not a good fit with Japanese working women's lived reality, but the model that best fits women's life and work circumstances tends to be organizationally weak and habitually under-resourced. So what's a poor women's union to do?

In lieu of an overall transformation, one possibility is for JWUs to make even greater use of the network that was created through the US-Japan Project by establishing some sort of organizational division of labor for this stage of the movement. The JWUs try to do it all, but with an organizational structure that does not support such a broad range of goals. But perhaps JWUs would benefit from reconceiving themselves not as unions with all the dimensions that term implies, but more as grievance resolution centers that work in tandem with other women's organizations within the network that are better suited to handle other aspects of what usually falls under the union rubric. For example, they might be better off focusing entirely on providing job consultation and bargaining assistance, while leaving other activities such as organizing, providing education, and developing legislative campaigns to broader-purposed women's organizations such as the ACW2. As the newly strengthened women's movement makes gains in the legislative arena (such as winning improvements in labor law that give women more job security), conditions at the worksite might become more favorable for organizing. If that happens, JWUs might then shift their focus to organizing inside enterprises, which ultimately should cut down on the number of requests for individual bargaining.

To some extent, JWUs are already moving in this direction with the establishment of ACW2 and WWEN. These organizations now spearhead efforts that used to fall on JWUs' shoulders. Perhaps with more exposure to organizations such as 9to5 and US-style workers' centers, which take on only the tasks they are organizationally equipped to handle, Japanese activists might be more comfortable with and better able to conceptualize new ways to redistribute the tasks and services of a traditional union among different types of women's organizations. But no matter what form the JWUs take, they need to find ways to address their funding problems. By 2007, the WWEN had already secured one government grant to support its educational activities. Accepting government funds was not unprecedented; the WUT used government funds to launch and maintain a women's support and crisis intervention center known as JOMU.[2] But women's groups generally shy away from government financing because of all the strings attached, so the fact that the WWEN had reached out to the government meant the members were, for better or worse, going beyond their comfort zone. An even bigger step would be to explore the possibilities of switching from membership dues to charging fees for services rendered. A fee-for-service structure might make JWUs less financially dependent on long-term membership. The drawback is that, in order to keep services affordable to low-wage women, JWUs would still need to find additional sources of outside funding, but that seems to be true in any case. Another possibility, which could also help with the problem of workload, might be to devise a formal service-for-service commitment in which women agree up front to give back a certain amount of their time, rather than simply hoping that they catch the activist bug through their experience with the union. Most of the union leaders I spoke with were resistant to the idea because they do not want to make demands on women who come to them for help. But perhaps it is time for the leaders to revisit this position. It is possible that this talk of suffering and victimization might be offensive—or at the very least "smell of red rust"—to younger Japanese women who do not see themselves in those terms. And indeed, it is not unrealistic to think the older activists would be willing to rethink their stance. Over the course of the collaboration, their ideas and attitudes about involving younger generations evolved markedly.

In the early days of the US-Japan Project, JWU leaders talked about the importance of bringing younger women into their unions, in part because young women workers lack sufficient union representation as much as older women do, and in part because the JWUs needed to attract new people to share the workload and help build the larger movement. In actual practice, when younger women joined JWUs they were not given much voice because the older women were unwittingly reproducing the age hierarchy that exists in the society at large. Eventually, through the discussions that took place during the US-Japan Project, the older members began recognizing how undemocratic their approach to younger members actually was and they started focusing on putting more decision-making power in the hands of younger members. In part, this was a move to enhance union democracy. But it was also because core members who were desperately tired and burned out saw young women as a source of energy and new ideas. As one leader told me in the starkest terms, "They are not tired yet." Of course, they had known that all along, but after the US-Japan Project they were more trusting of the younger women and more aware of their own biases about age.

Reflections on JWUs

My own thoughts on the viability of JWUs as an alternative form of workers' organization have evolved over the course of the project. In the beginning, I could not wrap my head around the idea of an individual-membership union. The concept itself seemed like a contradiction in terms, rooted in a fundamental misunderstanding about what unions are and where their power comes from. Over time I came to realize that it wasn't a misunderstanding at all. The Japanese women understood how traditional labor unions worked and had intentionally rejected that model when they created their own organizations. Through the project I came to understand they had good reasons for choosing the individual-membership structure despite its many weaknesses. I even came to accept that, at this stage, individual-membership unions might be the best option for Japanese women. But on the question of whether individual-membership unions, and JWUs in particular, will usher in the kinds of deep structural changes that would be needed to achieve their vision of true equality for all, there I remain cautiously pessimistic.

For all their analyses of how workplace practices create and sustain gender inequality, JWUs lack an overall critique of capitalism, which limits their project and their vision in a number of ways. In particular, neither their philosophy nor their practices take account of the internal logic of capital, which exceeds moral-ity, ethics, or the free will of the individual players, and which structures, main-tains, and depends on inequality and exploitation. For example, JWUs tend to talk about discriminatory labor practices as willful corporate misconduct— something that bad companies do to make money but that good companies could choose not to do—as opposed to recognizing them as part of the very fabric of capitalism. I never heard any discussion among members about what would happen if a given company went rogue and started adopting fair workplace prac-tices. But management knows all too well: its prices would go up, its profits would go down, and the well-meaning capitalist would be put out of business by its ethically challenged competitors or, at the very least, be liable for failing in its fiduciary responsibilities to its investors. (Unless, of course, the company was "too big to fail," in which case it might get a government bailout, but that would probably come with a "restructuring" plan that would require the kind-hearted company to return to its capitalism-approved practices.) Although they never word it this way, management tells us all the time that the logic of capitalism simply does not allow individual companies to choose how they will treat their employees. It does not allow owners or management to act on their own moral and ethical principles if those actions come with a price tag that disadvantages the company relative to its competitors. Capitalists have to do what the other capitalists are doing or they'll be crushed by the higher operating costs they would incur. By asking companies on a one-by-one basis to ban discrimina-tory practices that cut labor costs, the JWUs are essentially asking companies to voluntarily commit corporate suicide. But with no serious investigation of the inner workings of capitalism, JWUs are unable to see that companies are implicated in a system whose laws they must obey or perish, which in turn limits their ability to develop strategies that are adequate for achieving their long-term goals.

For example, JWUs are entirely too sanguine about the possibilities for achieving deep and meaningful change through moral or ethical persuasion. As feminist organizations, JWUs are ambivalent about wielding power. They talk about "powering up" and becoming empowered, but "power" in those contexts seems to mean something closer to women recognizing their self-worth and having the confidence and knowledge to be able to argue their case at the bargaining table. When questioned on the subject of wielding power, most of the women told me they reject the traditional tactic of using superior strength to force an employer's hand because that would mean engaging in the kind of domination that feminists condemn. Instead, they prefer to seek change through meaningful dialogue. In negotiations they often emphasize things that are morally or ethically "right." But again, under capitalism what is right and moral can only be taken into account in so far as that is good or at least neutral for the company's bottom line.

Most companies recognize the benefits of keeping employee morale high and of maintaining a good reputation in society. But there is always a cost-benefit analysis to their good deeds. Appeals to ethics or social responsibility might persuade a company to settle an individual grievance or adopt a fairly low-cost improvement, especially if it quells cries for more onerous concessions. But appeals to ethics alone will never convince an employer to scrap even the foulest practices if those practices significantly cut costs. There can be no argument about this. We have seen companies all over the world that are willing to commit profoundly immoral acts in pursuit of profits. Toyota and GM were willing to let customers die rather than admit design flaws in some of their models. The Gap and Nike have no qualms about using healthy young bodies to sell goods made in sweatshops by young people whose bodies have been decimated by deplorable working conditions and extreme poverty. Despite profits in the billions, companies such as Wal-Mart and McDonald's do not shrink from denying frontline workers full-time employment in order to avoid providing healthcare benefits. If ethics were ever going to matter, surely we would see companies make humane decisions when actual lives and limbs are at stake. But we don't. Ethics and morality simply don't come into it because corporations don't have morality or ethics. They don't care about what's right or what's fair because, despite the hallucinatory proclamations of the US Supreme Court, corporations are not people. We lose track of that sometimes because human beings represent them at the bargaining table, but those human beings are not there as themselves. They are there as representatives of capital and, as such, are deaf to any argument short of what is most profitable for the company.

The JWUs are, of course, well aware that profitability is the magic word for getting management's attention. In fact, they often couch calls for gender equality in arguments about potential benefits to the company: equal opportunities for women employees enables the company to take advantage of untapped human resources; providing childcare helps the company retain skilled employees, thereby reducing hiring and training costs; flexible scheduling cuts down on absenteeism, and so on. But such arguments not only leave women in low-skilled positions out in the cold, they also concede capital's assertion that profitability is the only yardstick by which workplace practices should be measured. Equal treatment has no standing of its own. Principles have no place in the discussion. Profitability is all that matters, and while it might benefit the company to cater to women in elite positions, the bulk of its profits depend on access to a steady supply of cheap, disposable labor.

The lack of a critique of capital also limits these activists' ability to analyze the ways capitalism structures inequality more generally in Japanese society at large and within and among other countries.[3] Japanese activists say they want a society in which men and women are equal in their jobs and in their homes, where women can express their full potential, and where men can achieve more balanced lives that include family and leisure time, not just work. But again, this is an idealized vision with no investigation of whether or how it could play out in a capitalist context. The women do not deal with the question of how this dramatic shift would affect Japan's economy or how it would affect Japan's standing in the global economy, except to say that Japan would have to be satisfied with a somewhat smaller economy and a more modest place in the world. But of course, it is not that simple. The ramifications for the national economy would be staggering as investment capital, including foreign investment, seeks more profitable ventures, domestic unemployment rises, etc.

Another problem is that at the same time the JWUs project a vision of a scaled-back economy that would allow men and women to enjoy more balanced lives, they also seek more opportunities for women to advance within the capitalist economy. That is in itself a paradox, but, more importantly, it reveals a failure to understand how elite women's elevation to the ranks of management would affect women in less valued positions. Women who hold management positions are just as beholden to the logic of capital as their male colleagues. They too become human representatives of capital, responsible for enacting and enforcing the demands of profitability no matter the human or environmental cost. When women in lower job classifications come to them seeking relief from layoffs or wage cuts, they too will have to invoke bottom-line arguments to protect their own positions. By helping elite women move into management roles, JWUs inadvertently foster class divisions among women, fragmenting solidarity and costing low-wage women powerful allies.

Nor do JWUs account for how climbing the corporate ladder at home would affect women in developing countries. The JWUs consider women in other Asian countries their natural allies, but if they succeed in abolishing practices that drive down the cost of Japanese women's labor, companies that can do so will offshore their exploitative practices and take advantage of women in even more vulnerable positions (Kanai 1996). Similarly, if working women better their own positions by embracing capitalist values, they run the risk of alienating progressives who are concerned with environmental issues. With no critique of capital, they remain blind to the ways their successes could enable and promote environmental atrocities including clearing rain forests and fracking in pursuit of profit. The JWUs generally object to such practices in theory, but they make no connection between their aims to securing a better position within a capitalist society and the perpetuation of exactly these sorts of scorched-earth policies.

That said, JWUs remain an important innovation in Japanese women's fight for workplace equality. Despite current limitations, JWUs' promise lies in the fact that they are—not just chronologically but on principle—intentionally evolving organizations. Where established unions often seek to maintain the status quo within their organizations, JWUs invite dialogues with academics, activists, lawyers, political leaders, and members of other community and alternative organizations in pursuit of new ideas for organizational development. These unions actively engage in organizational self-analysis and theory-building, to strengthen their organizations now, but also with the goal of remaining fluid enough to respond to changes in working women's needs, circumstances, and ideas over time. The downside of that strategy is that flexibility also means uncertainty. Japanese Women's Unions look markedly different now compared to when I first encountered them in 2000, and how they will evolve in the future remains an open question, except that I can say with confidence that they will not all evolve in the same direction. But that might not be a bad thing as long as they can continue to work cooperatively and in complementary ways.

For much of the twentieth century, women's movements in Japan frequently disintegrated as organizational and philosophical differences fragmented potentially powerful alliances (Mackie 2003). Such fracturing is by no means limited to Japanese movements. Nevertheless, it has been a serious limiting factor in Japanese women's ability to push forward what is arguably the most gender-recalcitrant society among industrialized nations. What we saw over the course of the US-Japan Project was that while plenty of differences exist within and among the various types of working women's organizations, and while the actual human beings involved are as given to the foibles of leadership as the next social visionary, they are also self-consciously seeking new ways of interacting with each other—individually and as organizations—to foster and extend true democratic participation. Again and again we saw the Japanese activists come into conflict—with me, with Carol, with each other. We saw them react in the ways people tend to react when long-held ideas, assumptions, and practices are called into question: they got angry, they defended their positions, and they threw up barriers to block themselves off from engaging with the offending ideas. But then they did something extraordinary. Each time, they regrouped and started seeking a pathway forward. We saw it when they agreed to the rap session with Carol; we saw it when they asked us to teach them positive meeting skills; we saw it when they continued to participate in the project even when they were frustrated with me as the human representative of the bureaucratic roadblocks we encountered. Most of all we saw it when they implemented their new, positive meeting skills to work out an array of sticky issues they needed to confront in order to launch the ACW2. The member organizations persevered because, ultimately, what they believe in more than anything else is including all previously excluded voices. And this is where the network structure will best serve them.

To use the vernacular of the members, I don't think "network power" can ever supplant "worker power" when it comes to confronting capital. But, for an interim strategy of creating new avenues for pursuing gender equality by passing women-friendly legislation and public policy while also providing aid to individual women with immediate workplace grievances, a network of different kinds of women's organizations with different but complementary skills, strategies, and areas of expertise might be exactly what they need. The challenge of holding such a network together is daunting indeed, but so far their self-awareness of both the difficulty and the necessity of building a movement based on inclusion has enabled the women and their organizations to weather the kind of conflicts that fractured movements in the past. That, along with their growing faith in and focus on empowering young people to shape the movement going forward, represents a fundamental shift in local activist culture and a reason to hope that the gains of Midori and Tani's generation will continue and be amplified in the future.

Since the end of the US-Japan Project, Midori has become increasingly involved with providing training to young women's organizations. Her experiences with these groups, in particular with their readiness to embrace new ideas and ability to translate those ideas into meaningful action, gave her a hopefulness I had not seen before. Some two months into the nuclear disaster that followed the 2011 Tōhoku earthquake and tsunami, while drinking in a sake bar in Tokyo whose proceeds were going to families whose homes and businesses had been destroyed, Midori told me, "I am not worried about the next generation anymore. I can relax now because I know they can do it."

LESSONS FOR BUILDING CROSSBORDER COLLABORATIONS

I wrote this book primarily because I wanted to tell the story of Japanese women's unions and their ongoing efforts to create new forms of organizations that can and will represent women and other marginalized people in the workforce. But as a person who firmly believes in the necessity of a transnational labor movement, I also wanted to share some of the cultural lessons that we learned in the course of this particular collaboration, in the hope that a warts-and-all accounting of our experiences might facilitate more and better US-Japan and other crossborder solidarity work in the future.

Planning for Difference

Beyond the hard work and commitment of the participants, probably the most important factor in the success of this collaboration was that, from the beginning, we planned for difference. During the planning stage we tried to anticipate significant differences that could cause friction or misunderstanding and designed the project to make these differences an explicit part of the conversation. We dedicated the entire first workshop to getting each other up to speed on our different histories, laws, institutions, values, and current issues. We also tried to identify and build in discussions about potentially confusing terms and concepts, such as "collective bargaining" and "individual membership." And we tried to anticipate social and cultural differences that might give us trouble. For example, during the preparatory phase we talked quite a lot about differences in US and

Japanese speech norms. We tried to prepare the US participants for the Japanese style of indirect speech, which is simply the proper rendering of the Japanese language (speaking directly in Japanese is the equivalent of baby talk), but to foreigners it often comes off as cagey, secretive, or, dare I say, inscrutable. And we tried to prepare the Japanese for the directness of US speech which, to an unsuspecting Japanese person, could feel a lot like getting a bucket of cold water in the face—startling, if not outright rude in its abruptness. By discussing these issues up front, examining their origins and meaning in the local context and, conversely, how particular culturally specific behaviors appear to foreign people, we were able to neutralize some of their power to sidetrack us and the project. And yet, we still regularly found ourselves stepping in cultural quicksand because, while our cultures differ in many screamingly obvious ways, the differences that matter most are the ones that are so subtle you don't know they're there until you've stepped in them.

Inherited Tensions

Among the glitches we were able to anticipate were the historical and current inequalities between US and Japanese women. From the very beginning, we were all a little skittish about engaging in a project that bore even a surface resemblance to the long-standing pattern of westerners coming to "educate" the putatively backward Japanese. Throughout the twentieth century, westerners showed up on Japanese shores as missionaries, political, legal, scientific, and business advisers, teachers, and occupiers aiming to, in one way or another, educate the Japanese. Often but not always they were invited, often but not always they were received warmly. And in some cases, the encounters yielded at least some positive outcomes. Christian missionaries, for example, founded schools for girls and played a crucial role in establishing the practice of educating girls. The US occupation was the force behind the adoption of the Japanese Constitution, which for the first time put sovereignty in the hands of the Japanese people. Nevertheless, those advances (and certainly not all of the ideas that Westerns imported into Japan can be unequivocally deemed advances) came at high cost. Japan existed in a quasi-colonial relationship with the West in general and the United States in particular, and any encounter that smacks of that history inevitably courts feelings of resentment.

Heidi and I were very conscious, even self-conscious, about that legacy when we took on this project. We tried to develop the project in a way that would allow us to resist that dynamic as best we could given the stated goals of the Japanese women, namely that they felt in crisis and wanted help. With this conflict in mind, we sought to develop an exchange that would not assume that either side had any answers to impart to the other. We assumed that both sides had ideas to share and that it would be left to the participants to decide whether and how to use or adapt or develop ideas they encountered through the exchange. In practice, however, we were not always able to maintain an awareness of the two-directional learning arrow, particularly in Workshops II and III when the immediate concrete task involved US labor educators modeling their teaching materials and techniques. If one looked at those moments in isolation, it might appear as if we had reproduced the colonial dynamic. Looking at the project as a whole, however, both sides were always learning from the other. As the US labor educators were modeling their methods, they were also gaining knowledge about alternative workers' organizations and the rise of alternative unions in Japan. And they were engaging in dialogue with other activists who were experimenting with new forms of organization to confront many of the same problems that marginalized workers in the United States face. In other words, US educators were adding to their skill and knowledge sets as much as the Japanese "students" were, just in different ways.

Still, what the US participants were getting out of the exchange remained pretty abstract to the Japanese participants. On a day-to-day basis, despite our best intentions and efforts, the project had echoes of the traditional dynamic, and that made most of us feel a little itchy at times, although never enough to give up the benefits of the exchange.

Another preexisting source of tension was the common misperception Japanese people have about life in the United States. Many Japanese people—particularly those whose knowledge of the United States is based primarily on media images—tend to imagine working-class US citizens as more affluent than they really are; our companies, our government, and our male coworkers as fairer and more committed to democracy than they really are; and American women as uniformly empowered individuals who are neither afraid to stand up for themselves nor at risk of incurring retribution if they do so. This unrealistically rosy picture of life in the United States worked against us in developing solidarity. Based on that image, the Japanese activists often thought that we couldn't possibly understand their situation, which at times became an excuse to dismiss uncomfortable suggestions with an implied "easy for you to say."

Although the real inequality between us did, inevitably, remain a divisive presence, the US participants' presentations in Workshop I provided the reality check we needed to at least get past some of the false perceptions. Taken together, those presentations provided a far more accurate picture of American women's lived realities over the last hundred years, a better appreciation of the risks, dangers, and humiliations that US labor feminists have had to brave, and a more grounded sense of what we still needed to achieve. Most of all, they seemed to help the Japanese participants see past some of the stereotypes that have stood in the way of US and Japanese women achieving a sense of solidarity. While we were planning the US-Japan Project there were times when we wondered if we were doing the right thing devoting so much time (one-third of the project) to getting to know each other better. Looking back on it now, I have no doubts whatsoever. Although there were still a number of discoveries yet to come, the basic knowledge and perspective we gained from that original meeting laid the groundwork for everything that followed. We could not have achieved what we did without that step.

Practical Challenges
Differences in Work Styles

Nowhere did I feel the cultural distance between me and my Japanese colleagues more strongly than in our work styles. I had never thought of myself as having any particular work-style allegiances in the past. Nor did I have any particular image of a Japanese work style beyond the familiar stereotype of the diligent, obedient worker bee. But once we started planning the first workshop, I found myself leaving almost every meeting feeling—quite unexpectedly—like I wanted to pull out my hair in frustration. That had never been the case before. In the two years of discussions that led to the US-Japan Project we frequently differed over organizational and strategic issues, but those were philosophical discussions. We were exploring ideas; we didn't have to come to any sort of agreement. But once the project was officially under way, suddenly our work was directly linked. We were no longer working in parallel. We were more like clumsy contestants in a three-legged race. We had to find some way to get in synch. The problem was that we didn't know how or why we had suddenly gotten so out of step with each other. I had to sit down and really think about it for a long time. We weren't usually disagreeing about substance. In fact, we weren't necessarily disagreeing at all. Yet I consistently found myself feeling frustrated and irritable by the end of our meetings, and with no clear idea why. I finally had to mentally map the course of our conversations to figure out when, with whom, and under what circumstances tensions started to arise. As I reflected on these and similar experiences that other Americans who had worked in Japan related to me, I started to realize there was an overall pattern to the way I approached the tasks at hand, and it was consistently different from the way my Japanese colleagues did. Specifically, where I tend to approach each new task by jumping right in, kicking around ideas, and coming up with action plans, my colleagues never wanted to make even the smallest move without considering the issue from every conceivable angle, and investigating every imaginable question, before taking any definitive action or making a definite decision. Where I consistently approach a task by picking a starting point and building from there, they consistently sidle up to an issue, circle it, and examine it. They don't make any decision until they are ready to make all the decisions. It made their pace seem glacial and it made me want to scream.

Several years later, I came across an account of the differences between US and Japanese engineers' work processes in Darius Mehri's *Notes from Toyota-land* (2005). Mehri was an American engineer working in a Japanese firm that designed and manufactured auto parts. He and one of his Japanese colleagues were assigned to design a device that would reduce the aerodynamic drag of the vehicles the company produced to improve their gas mileage. Other companies already had such devices but Mehri's company did not. Mehri describes his approach:

> For inspiration, I consulted my fluid mechanics textbook. I thought about the basics physics of the design problem and worked out some equations. After a few days, I approached [the boss] with my ideas . . . . [He] looked at me askance and demanded, "How do you know this? We've never designed a drag-reducer before."
>
> Now I was confused. Hadn't he expected me to use my engineering education and experience to develop a creative design? No, he had not. The next day I discovered the approach he preferred. Suzuki walked in to the office with a large cardboard poster showing pictures of all the drag-reducing products currently used in the industry. He had gotten these pictures from the industry magazines. [The boss] got very excited and studied each one, while Suzuki looked on proudly. (Mehri, 2005, 144)

The boss was happy with Suzuki because, above all, the Japanese process emphasizes doing enormous amounts of preliminary research before anyone starts throwing ideas around. Where the US method might give wider berth for creativity to flow, the Japanese prefer a method that ensures the project would move forward with as few mistakes or setbacks as possible. The Japanese work process is a front-loaded one. Extensive, cautious study is undertaken before any action is taken, as Mehri learned when the engineers in his section were assigned to compare and analyze a European competitor's product.

> When we entered the chop shop later that day my mouth dropped. Enormous efforts had been expended in displaying how the European design compared with [our company's] and other competitor's [sic] similar products. Large excruciatingly detailed charts filled the walls, comparing efficiency, gas mileage and other indicators. All the relevant parts had been cut up and placed on a table for us to examine. Each part was compared with the corresponding parts of the competitor's products. The benchmark was so thorough that there was even a comparison of the number of bolts used to put the products together. (Mehri, 2005, 145)

Unbeknownst to me at the time, that same dynamic was at work in those early meetings with my colleagues at WUT. I thought we would start by mapping out the big-picture parameters—what we wanted the workshop to accomplish, who our target audience was, what kinds of presenters we might want to invite. I thought we would make some decisions about those broader issues at the first meeting, and then go on to fill in the details over time and in accordance with the priorities we laid out in the beginning. The Japanese women, on the other hand, came to the meeting assuming that if anyone raised a suggestion, that person had already researched and thought out every possible angle of their plan down to the smallest detail. In practice, that meant that my Japanese colleagues routinely pulled our meetings off course by asking what seemed to me to be utterly random, off-the-wall, maddeningly inconsequential questions for this stage of the process. Several months before the Detroit workshop, we held a meeting to go over the list of presenters and topics for the program. But the meeting got completely out of control as the women peppered me with questions about ridiculously minute details: What was the name of our B&B? How far was it from the conference venue? Would we take a taxi or bus? What does the meet-up spot at the Detroit airport look like? How would we find each other? These were all questions we'd eventually want to discuss, but this meeting was about something else entirely and my head was starting to spin from the range of questions they were expecting me to be able to answer months before the workshop. I was getting so agitated I thought I was about to lose my temper, but then, above the din of the disintegrated meeting, I heard one question ring out with an absurdity that eclipsed all others. At a time when we were supposed to be focused on the content of the workshop, one of the Japanese women had the nerve to shout out, "At the restaurant, will there be steak on the menu?" At that point, I just had to laugh. Either every one of my colleagues had simultaneously lost their minds or there was something going on that I didn't understand. I assumed it had to be the latter but it was several more months before I was able to recognize that it was a matter of our different expectations about how the planning process would unfold.

Differences in Meeting Styles: This Meeting is Now Called to Chaos

Those random-question barrages might have been more manageable even before I figured out their origin had there been some norms around how meetings should be conducted. Generally there are, in both the United States and Japan. But among the particular Japanese women's groups involved in our collaboration, meetings were mind-numbing free-for-alls, often bearing little resemblance to the printed agenda and rarely observing the one-person-at-a-time principle of polite conversation. The utter breakdown in orderly behavior was especially jarring to me as so much of daily life in Japan was almost suffocatingly rule oriented. Even the WUT's formal union meetings had a recognizable structure and operating procedures. But not our meetings. For some reason, possibly because they were trying to do away with the old meeting norms that reproduce rigid hierarchies but had not yet developed anything to put in its place, our meetings and the meetings among the women's groups on their own were the Wild West of public discourse.

In the early stages of planning Workshop I, I would go into meetings prepared with agenda in hand and a clear set of goals for what we needed to accomplish in the meeting. And every time, I would come out of the meeting feeling like I had been hit by a bus. Somehow, I was never able to answer all their questions and I was rarely able to keep the meeting on track. Initially, I thought I must not have prepared properly (which in a sense I hadn't; see section above), but over time I realized it wasn't just me. It happened no matter who was running the meeting because there was no shared set of expectations about how meetings should proceed. That's why I was so delighted (and secretly amused) when, in preparation for Workshop III, the women's groups discovered that there was something a little off about the way their meetings ran and asked us to include a session on how to facilitate a positive meeting.

The Japanese women's groups have come a long, long way on this issue. The strategy of setting ground rules at the start of each meeting has been particularly effective in helping to tame their unruly meeting style. They have also developed stronger norms about (and mechanisms for enforcing) staying on topic, talking one at a time, and resisting the impulse to automatically naysay. In fact, of all the skills training workshops the Japanese women have offered since the end of the US-Japan Project, their workshops on meeting skills have had the most direct, positive effect on individual organizations and the movement as a whole.

Etiquette Trumps Efficiency, Every Time

At the risk of appearing to contradict myself given the above description of the JWUs' utter lack of meeting etiquette, rules of social etiquette, where they exist, always, always come before any other consideration. I don't generally think of myself as a rude person. I don't show up to parties empty-handed and I try to get thank-you notes out in a semi-timely fashion. But when it comes to work-related interactions, I have occasionally been known to put getting the job done over other considerations. I come out of a journalism background. When we were on deadline, the usual social niceties often dropped by the wayside. People shouted, talked over each other, and ran past each other in corridors without stopping to say hello. Not that we were openly rude to each other, but a little brusqueness was understandable when someone had something urgent to attend to. But for the Japanese women, certain social rules were never expendable. They were, in fact, the key to getting things done quickly and efficiently.

For me, the most mind-bending moment of the collaboration came immediately after we learned that our grant application had been approved and we could officially get to work planning the US-Japan Project. I was on fire. I could not wait to get started. From the very first time we met, Midori and Tani had impressed upon me the urgency of the Japanese women's situation. They told me time and again that working conditions were steadily getting worse, that women were suffering, and that we had to do something NOW. And so, the minute we got the go-ahead from our funders, I thought we were ready to roll. "Let's pick a date! Let's send invitations to those other JWUs we've been dying to meet!" But when I blurted out those sentiments at the union meeting, I could feel everyone in the room seize up in alarm.

After several very uncomfortable moments of staring at each other in utter confusion, someone finally explained that they couldn't possibly invite those other women's organizations because, "We've haven't met them before." What? I thought that was the whole point—meeting up with organizations they'd never been able to meet up with before. That's *why* we got the grant to begin with! I thought my head would explode from the sheer irrationality of their position. But the reality is that, in Japan, no matter how urgent the situation might be, you just can't put standard etiquette aside. (I once saw paramedics, while racing to attend a medical emergency, stop and take their shoes off before entering the building.) Midori explained that most of these women had never formally met each other. Some might have occasionally crossed paths at political events or conferences, but they really did not know each other at all. It would seem strange to a Japanese person to get a letter out of the blue asking them to participate in some conference they had no previous (official) knowledge of. The women and the organizations in question would need to develop some connection, some rapport before we could think of inviting them, and before they could think of accepting. Metaphorically or literally, we had to find some way to drink tea together before we could move forward.

Another nicety I didn't know about in advance: once we established some connection with the groups we wanted to invite, we would need to seek unofficial assurances that they would accept an invitation before we could actually send an invitation. Weirdly enough, I actually did have some familiarity with that concept. I knew that, in other Japanese contexts such as business and government meetings, it was standard practice to hold "the meeting before the meeting." The principal parties try to come to an agreement on all agenda items before the meeting of record to make sure no one runs the risk of being contradicted in public. It turns out the same rules apply for invitations. Years later when I was back living in the United States, an American professor approached me, visibly frazzled and looking for advice. She had been invited by a Japanese organization to give a talk to a group of Japanese academics and policymakers. This was the first time she had worked directly with a Japanese organization and she was finding the process mystifying. In particular, she was alarmed because she kept getting e-mails inviting her, even though she had already—and repeatedly—accepted. She was getting agitated because she couldn't understand what part of "yes" they didn't understand. But I explained that they were still in the phase where they were having the meeting before the meeting. None of those e-mails were the official invitation. Those e-mails were simply part of the laborious process of getting all their ducks in a row, with commitments and all details absolutely, irrevocably nailed down, before any official, public action is taken. I explained that, after every detail of her trip and her talk were set in stone, she would get the "official" invitation (which did indeed arrive on exactly that schedule). It wasn't that they didn't understand her, it was just the way things are done there.

Although grassroots women's organizations tend to be less formal and far more forgiving than business or academic organizations, the WUT members could not bring themselves to send out invitations to other women's groups until we had assurances that they would accept. (Interestingly, this did not seem to extend to the invitations to the US participants. The Japanese participants wanted a say in whom we invited, but they seemed perfectly happy to let Heidi and me determine when and how we invited them. Apparently, they did not mind if Heidi and I got turned down, only if they did, even though it was all the same project. Or, more likely, perhaps they just assumed we would naturally be taking the same precautions.)

The bottom line was that anytime I tried to save time by skipping over some seemingly trivial social nicety, I ended up losing more time doing damage control than I would have by just observing local customs to begin with. That sounds easy enough to do, but when we had a job to do and not enough time to do it, I found myself again and again reverting to my previously unexamined habits of efficiency *über alles*. Until this experience, I had no idea how much of a "typical American" I am in this regard, and how hard it is to keep those habits of a lifetime in check when the pressure is on.

Beyond Words

Obviously, the main difference we planned for was the difference in language. As expected, overcoming the language barrier was the most significant and costly challenge we faced. Translation and interpretation costs far exceeded our original estimates.[1] If it hadn't been for the numerous translators and bilingual members who volunteered their services along the way, the project would have broken down. But money was not the only problem. We also discovered that hiring highly respected professional translators and interpreters was not good enough. For Workshop I, we hired highly recommended professional translators and interpreters, and paid a pretty penny for them, I might add. But they turned out to be disasters. Although they were very skilled in translating materials for business and academic audiences, they had no understanding of our issues, our terms, or our audience. The translations of our written documents came out stiff, formal, and largely incomprehensible because the translators didn't have enough background in labor and women's issues to fully capture our meaning. But the real disaster was the garbled mess served up by the simultaneous interpreters in Detroit. One interpreter was so lost he virtually shut down, even though he had received written transcripts of the presentations in advance. What we ended up hearing through our headsets was little more than confused mumblings that took on an increasingly desperate tone as the day went on. If the Japanese women in particular hadn't had written documents, such as they were, in front of them, most of the English language presentations would have been a complete waste of time.

To be fair, though, it was not, in the main, the translators' fault. Particularly for languages that are as far apart as Japanese and English, translators and interpreters are not one size fits all. We needed people who understood our issues and had a sense of who our audience was in order to fully understand the meaning and render it into language that was accessible to participants on the other side.

After the first linguistic disaster, WUT members were able to recruit professional interpreters who were also involved in the women's movement. These women were essential to the success of the project on two fronts: they were knowledgeable about our subject area so they were able to render meaningful, accessible translations, and they were willing to work for reduced rates. By the end of the project when we were running out of money, some were even willing to donate their work. It was only because of their generosity and commitment to the women's movement that we had access to enough language help to get us through the formal part of the program. But they went beyond even that. Several women (some professional interpreters, others bilingual speakers) provided pro bono interpretation between and after the formal sessions, which again proved vital to the project's success.

Although in the end our project was successful, we could have achieved even more had we been able to (or known we needed to) secure more funding than we stipulated in our original estimates, or had we been allowed to redistribute the funds we had in accordance the way our needs evolved over the course of the project. Many of the Japanese women said they would be willing to pay their own transportation and lodging costs if we could reallocate that money to go toward more translation, but the terms of the grant did not allow for that kind of flexibility. I can't help wondering what other breakthroughs we might have had if we'd been able to provide more translation for the US participants to join in the rich online discussion that took place among the Japanese organizations during the concept-development phases between the workshops. But we woefully underestimated the amount of interpretation the project would need, we failed to appreciate how specialized our topics were, and it was only because of connections within the movement that we were able to overcome these problems. We lucked out, but it could just as easily have gone the other way. I hope future projects will learn from our near disaster and be more strategic and realistic about the costs and complexities of translation. Above all else, the lesson we learned was that we were at our best when we had the sense and humility to remember that there were always some gaps between what one side said and the other side understood, and to proceed accordingly.

Institutional Barriers

One of the great ironies of this kind of project is that that which brings you together can also tear you apart. I'm referring in this case to grant money. We needed grant money to be able to get together in one place and talk to each other across languages. We needed grant money to provide lodging and meals and meeting space. Grant money quite literally made the project possible. But it also, time and time again, came between us in ways that not only caused miscommunication and occasionally mistrust, but sometimes reinforced exactly the kinds of stereotypes and divisions that have historically hampered US-Japan collaborations. It was not the grant money itself, but rather the various rules and institutions that are invoked the minute grant money comes into play.

The process of procuring a grant required that we specify in advance exactly how we were going to use the money. In our case, we were seeking funds to allow us to reach out to and communicate with the other women's groups and find out what we could learn from each other. We had to write a detailed grant proposal that stipulated what the project was going to look like, who and how many participants would be invited, what we planned to do in each workshop, what our overall goals were, and what outcomes we would work towards. The problem was that this meant a small group of us had to decide many of the specifics of the project *before* we would be able to get any money, which meant before we had the resources to involve the other women's groups and get their input. When we were writing the grant and spelling out all the specifics, we tried to signal that the proposal represented our current vision but that we wanted the project to have the flexibility to evolve over time as more groups became involved and were able to give us their input. In other words, I was thinking of the grant proposal as a rough sketch of what we intended to do but with the understanding that the project would be allowed to evolve as the participants' needs and ideas evolved over the course of the workshops. We expected the project to produce ideas and solutions that none of us had thought of before, and so, by definition, the project needed to be able to develop in ways we couldn't anticipate at the outset. That was a fundamental tenet of the project and I thought our grant proposal reflected that. But I was wrong. Where I saw the proposal as a first draft of an evolving game plan, the granting institution saw it more as tablets of stone from which no deviation was allowed.

Although I thoroughly understand the granting institution's position—it has a duty to ensure that its resources are used responsibly and for the purposes they were intended—the resulting inflexibility became a sticking point that forever haunted the project. As I mentioned in chapter 5, the first instance occurred when, partway through Workshop I, the Japanese women suggested changing the format from three international meetings to two international meetings with a few smaller meetings among the Japanese groups in between. The Japanese women felt it would better suit their needs and I supported the idea because I believed in the importance of the organic evolution of the project based on our experiences together. But it was not to be. We were told we could not change the format, but that decision was not made on the merits of the Japanese women's suggestion. It was based solely on the fact that it was a deviation from the original proposal.

Another instance of institutional inflexibility arose just a few weeks later. During our preparations for Workshop II, the Japanese women became increasingly uncomfortable about going into a workshop on creating teaching modules when they had only a vague idea of what a teaching module is. After the first round of satellite meetings, the women asked me if we could provide translated copies of a variety of teaching modules to give them a better idea of what we were talking about. Laying our hands on sample modules was no problem. Several of the US organizations from Workshop I were happy to share their materials with us. We were also able to find modules from other women's organizations on the Internet. The problem arose when we tried to get them translated prior to Workshop II. Again, the Japanese women were requesting a small change in the preconceived game plan to accommodate needs that emerged in the course of the project, and again we were thwarted by administrative constraints. Although we had been granted funds to cover three workshops, not all of the funds were available right away. Instead, the grant monies were split into two installments, the first available in 2004, and the second not available until 2005. We hoped that we could pay for sample modules to be translated from funds left over from Workshop I. If that failed, that is, if no funds were left over from what we budgeted for Workshop I, we thought we could take a look at our budget for Workshop II and see if we could reallocate some of those funds to enable us to pay for translation.

But it wasn't that easy. By early December we still did not have a final accounting from WSU (which administered the grant), so we didn't know if we had any funds remaining in our 2004 pot. Part of that was WSU's fault. The business office was spectacularly error-prone, as we would see over and over again throughout the project. But part of the problem had to do with snags in getting the right reimbursement checks to the right people. Bad addresses, transposed identification numbers, and other bureaucratic issues meant several checks had not yet been cashed and we could never get a reliable answer from the accounting office about whether the bottom-line number they were giving us included those outstanding checks or not. Our next tactic was to ask the granting institution if we could use some of the funds allocated for Workshops II and III for translation, but we were told we could not use funds from the 2005 pot to cover expenses in 2004. We would have to wait until after the New Year to begin any translation. That might not seem to be a big problem; we simply had to wait a few weeks before we could comply with the Japanese women's request. In fact, it turned into quite a dustup because the Japanese women could not understand why we were "dragging our feet." As much as we tried to explain that there was a bureaucratic problem, they continued to code the delay (in receiving an answer and in receiving the actual funds) as a personal failing on my part. In their minds, I was being controlling and undemocratic in the allotment of funds. They seemed to think we had one big pot of money that we could dip into and use however we wanted so long as it was related to the project. No amount of explanation about earmarks and bureaucratic constraints seemed to break through that image. I was never entirely sure why; bureaucracies in Japan are every bit as rigid, cumbersome, and occasionally counterproductive as any in the United States. I knew for a fact that my Japanese colleagues had experienced the frustrations of administrative red tape before. But for some reason, they did not code the absurdities of US bureaucracies as being parallel to the absurdities of Japanese bureaucracies. Instead they interpreted each incident as a lack of democracy on our part.[2]

Administrative Differences

Although Heidi and I procured the grant, we could not administer it. Nor could any of the grassroots organizations it was intended to serve. Grants of this type typically are administered through a university and the recipients must follow that university's disbursement policies in order to access the funds. But grassroots Japanese organizations and US universities are very different types of organizations, with very different rules, assumptions, and concerns, and that gap caused hardships for the Japanese in a variety of ways. For example, unlike many Japanese institutions, WSU's policy was to reimburse the participants for their expenses rather than provide the funds up front to be used at the time of the expenditure. The Japanese participants were startled by the expectation that they lay out the money for plane tickets to the United States, in part because Japanese institutions tend to provide expense money up front and in part because the practice of reimbursement after the fact is inherently class insensitive. It assumes people have extra money laying around that they can shell out and wait several months to get back. But that is not the reality for low-wage working women in our group. Wayne State's reimbursement policy created financial hardships for people and that did not help in our efforts to create goodwill.

Having to go through two levels of US administrative systems (Wayne State's and the Center for Global Partnership's) also exacerbated my Japanese colleagues' impression that I was not being democratic with the funds. They regularly called on me, in the interest of democracy, to put the grant money in one pot and let them decide how to use it. For example, in the later workshops in Tokyo, the women wanted to change the reimbursement structure. Instead of fully reimbursing ten people for travel and overnight accommodations as stipulated in the grant proposal, the Japanese activists wanted to reimburse twenty people for travel and nothing for accommodations. I would have been happy to do that, especially if it meant more people could attend. But I had no authority to change the reimbursement rules, no access to the funds except through the university, and the university said we couldn't do it. Why? Because that was the rule and Wayne State, as an institution, was responsible for enforcing the rules no matter how counterproductive they might be. But the Japanese women, most of whom were not used to dealing with university bureaucracies, could not fathom that level of counterintuitive inflexibility so they understood it instead as an excuse for the Americans to maintain control.

A second challenge was the disbursement of funds across two different countries with very different banking systems and payment norms. In particular, we had endless problems booking hotels, meeting space, and food services for the two workshops that were held in Tokyo, because Japanese businesses expect to be paid up front while Wayne State would only release funds as reimbursements. The Japanese women had to go to ridiculous lengths and endure significant financial hardships to cover basic operating costs that should never have come out of their pockets. Then, adding insult to injury, Wayne State insisted on reimbursing them with checks, an antiquated form of money transfer that is not used in Japan. (In Japan everything is done by electronic transfer but, at least for the first two workshops, Wayne State claimed there was no way they could do that.) This was no small problem. When I tried to cash my first reimbursement check, I inadvertently caused a scene in my local bank. I received my money only after insisting in a way that most Japanese people would have considered the height of rudeness. I also had to spend two hours filling out the paperwork and pay a $50 fee, all to cash a check for about $200.

Many of these problems might have been alleviated if a Japanese organization had been allowed to administer a portion of the grant funds to pay local expenses in accordance with local business practices. Further, requiring the funds to be administered through a university (as opposed to being administered by one of the participating grassroots organizations) sent a mixed message to the participants. Although the program is specifically designed to benefit and empower grassroots organizations, grant protocols usually require that recognized mainstream institutions administer grant funds. Several participants noted the irony of this practice as it seemed to treat grassroots organizations as somehow less trustworthy than established, middle-class institutions, which seemed at odds with the CGP's mission. Indeed, an enormous amount of time and money could have been saved if, for example, Women's Union Tokyo had been responsible for administering funds on the Japan side, and 9to5 on the US side.

In the end, these sorts of institutional and administrative complications reinforced some of the barriers we had hoped to break down. On the last day of the

US-Japan Project, when the Japanese participants announced their goals for the coming year, I was a little disappointed that continuing to work with US women's organizations didn't figure more prominently in their plans. They were by no means against the idea, but neither was it the priority. And I understand why. Overcoming the language barrier is prohibitively expensive for small grass-roots groups. We all knew that any chance of future collaboration hinged on getting grant money to support it. With no grant money on the immediate horizon, the Japanese women had to focus on the realistic options they had before them. Also, Midori told me that, given the rapidly deteriorating working conditions for Japanese women, Japanese activists needed to focus on immediate issues at home before building up to broader coordinated efforts. Moreover, if they are to get involved in transnational projects, they are generally more interested in working with women from other Asian countries in part because they believed their circumstances were more similar. All of that is understandable, and yet there was more to their decision. The Japanese women clearly wanted to establish ties with US activists, and there was no question that they appreciated our input, but it was equally clear that they wanted to stay in control of their own movement. Heidi and I knew going into the project that Americans have a reputation for trying to dominate and impose our vision on others. We tried very hard to maintain an environment of respectful dialogue and equality in participation and decision making. But our national image made the Japanese women particularly sensitive to any signs of overreach on our part. And while I do think we made significant progress in building trust among the women who participated directly in the project, there is no getting around the fact that the controversies related to disbursing grant monies contributed to our image as control freaks. That was frustrating because, in the end, the money we needed to bring us together to a smaller extent also pushed us apart. But that is the inevitable outcome of resource inequality. Democratic decision making is always compromised when someone else controls the purse strings.

Individualism and Collectivism Revisited

In chapter 6, I talked about our insight that one reason the Japanese participants reacted so negatively to the organizing workshop was that we had very different ideas and values around the concepts of individualism and collectivism. At the time, we understood the conflict as an expression of the differences in what each side saw as their primary mission: where the US participants, acting primarily as unionists, focused on helping Japanese women to organize and exercise their collective power as workers, the Japanese participants, acting primarily as feminists, sought first and foremost to heal, support, and empower women who were suffering under a discriminatory employment system. But in the months and years since the project ended, I began to understand that there was even more to our differences than we had been able to discover in the heat of the moment. Looking back on it now, I think that the biggest difference between us—and the one most responsible for the feelings of suspicion and mistrust that arose in Workshop II—had to do with the differences in how the ideologies of individualism and collectivism have figured in our two cultures over time. More specifically, I think that the Japanese women reacted so strongly to our emphasis on collectivism over individualism because for them the logic and language of collectivism have typically been used in ways that justify and perpetuate the oppression of women and other minorities.

Historically, US unionists have argued that in a capitalist society the discourse of individualism is to dissuade working people from uniting and working in their own class interests. For that reason, unionists in the West tend to regard individualism as a repressive, "divide and conquer" discourse aimed at keeping working people (and women and minorities) in their place. As progressives we consider it our job to expose the many ways the discourse of individualism enforces and reproduces the status quo, and to offer a collectivist vision as a pathway to true liberation and equality.

But in Japan, the situation has largely been the reverse. Collectivism, rather than individualism, has a long history of being used as a tool of repression and popular control.[3] The Japanese people were not legally recognized as *individuals* until 1946, when the new Constitution was adopted. Until then, they were *subjects*, existing to serve the emperor and for the good of the nation. But even after they gained the legal status of individual and were guaranteed (on paper) certain human rights, Japanese people were, and continue to be, expected to think of their duty to the group—whether it's the family, the company or the nation— first and themselves last. That might not be so bad if the group were a collective in the sense of a radically egalitarian society. But that has never been the case. The central collectives that make up Japanese society are rigidly hierarchical, with those on the bottom giving the most, getting the least, and having little chance to rectify that injustice because nice people don't worry about their personal situations; that would be selfish. In other words, where the collective in question is inherently unequal and exploitative, the logic and language of collectivism becomes a repressive discourse used to mute dissent among the most exploited segments of society in order to maintain the power and privileges of the elite. Under those circumstances, it is easy to see why JWUs would promote the idea of women claiming their rights as individuals as a pathway to liberation, particularly if you understand that the "individualism" the Japanese feminists are talking about is not the self-centered, looking-out-for-Number-One concept that reigns supreme in the United States. The sense of individualism that the JWUs seek to promote is about women becoming empowered to say, "I am. I exist. I count as a person as much as any other (male) person." It took me a long time to see it, but the move JWUs are making when they talk about individualism is not so different from the message that rang out during the Memphis sanitation workers' strike in 1968, when a column of African American men marched through the streets silently bearing signs that read "I AM A MAN." With those words, the sanitation workers were insisting on being recognized as human beings of equal value as their oppressors and deserving of the same human dignity. Japanese Women's Unions are saying much the same thing. I should have seen that sooner given that Kansai Women's Union told us as much during the Detroit meeting when they described the union's activities as "a means for women to establish independent 'selves'" (KWU 2004). When JWU members talk about claiming their "rights as individuals," they are asserting their personhood, which entitles them to the same dignities, opportunities, and responsibilities that men have. In that sense, individualism, as an expression of women's claims to their human rights, becomes a discourse for resisting a system built on and sustained by discrimination and inequality.

Once I understood that, I could finally appreciate why my Japanese colleagues reacted so passionately when we challenged their (at the time mystifying) insistence on foregrounding the individual. What was a discourse of liberation to us was a discourse of oppression to them. No wonder the Japanese women seized up in anger when we talked about prioritizing building the union over resolving individual grievances; we were speaking the language of their oppressors. All of a sudden we sounded to them like one more self-interested party exhorting Japanese women to ignore their own needs for the good of others. Of course, that was not the message we intended to send. In focusing on building the union first, our goal was to ensure that Japanese women had the power they needed to make their voices heard. But our terms had invoked a completely different script from the one we intended, and one that might have been predictable if we had gone into the project with a more sophisticated sense of how those crucial ideologies have played out in the two countries. This was an important lesson because it revealed radical differences in how we understood two salient concepts and, perhaps more importantly, it taught us critical skills for managing emotionally charged disputes that threaten to fracture our unity. More than any other conflict we faced, the differences in how we experience and what we mean by individualism and collectivism revealed the absolute necessity of taking local context into account. The idea that an organization calling itself a "union" could be fundamentally centered on the individual and habitually leery about the needs of the collective taught us that we should not take any concept, any principle, or any term for granted. And it taught us that, in the face of conflict, the best first step was usually to put the immediate discussion on hold, and then analyze what was happening at a deeper level. When we did that, we almost always found some historical or cultural nugget that helped us understand and work through the present dispute.

Unity in Difference

And yet for all the roadblocks we faced, our crossborder project achieved most of its stated goals and then some. I was amazed, energized, and humbled by the resilience of the bonds we were able to form despite language, cultural, and institutional barriers, logistical nightmares, and in the face of so many strong personalities with equally strong opinions. Our bonds were tested many times and we could occasionally see smoke rising up from some particularly heated point of friction. But ultimately we knew whatever extra challenges crossborder initiatives might bring, they also offer the promise of the whole being greater than the sum of its parts. We fully believed that in working together, in combining our knowledge and experiences, we might be able to achieve insights and innovations that neither side would come to working on their own. We believed that by working together our creativity had the potential to be more than cumulative; it could be exponential, taking us to new places we couldn't foresee at the start of the project. That belief held us together even on those days when the bank wouldn't cash our checks, the translators had the flu, and our funds were being held up by some capricious bureaucrat six thousand miles away who wouldn't answer his e-mail.

But crossborder work is not just about creating a rich environment for innovation. It is also important because any movement whose vision extends only as far as national boundaries is a partial movement. In the world of transnational corporations and the global economy, a victory in one jurisdiction often means that the newly outlawed practices get pushed off shore onto some less organized group of workers. The only way for working people to win and enforce humane working and living conditions is to work together to ensure that no nation, no region is a safe haven for exploitation. We know this. So, whether we should engage in crossborder collaborations is not the question. The question is how can we undertake more such efforts given that they are so time-consuming and expensive, and that the learning curve is often prohibitively steep? This book is my attempt to make some contribution to answering that question. When I first went to Japan as a tourist, I had access to countless travelers' guides that clued me in to basic social skills for getting around without offending people left and right. Transnational corporations and, of course, the military have their own literatures and, in some cases, curricula for preparing their representatives to operate in foreign lands. And while I generally try to avoid taking cues from the latter two sources, I think they do have something to teach those of us in the activist world about preparing ourselves for global action. We need our own literature for documenting, analyzing, and sharing our international experiences in ways that are meaningful and accessible to activists and workers, and that help to shorten the learning curve for future collaborations. Academics write on some of these issues but their priorities, perspectives, and concerns differ from ours, and their materials are often financially and stylistically inaccessible to people outside the ivory tower. We need our own stories told in our own voices, and in ways that will help to prepare other activists who are interested in working in the same areas. While frank and fearless accounts of our own efforts won't smooth the way entirely, sharing our stories can help cut down the getting-up-to-speed costs of the next project while also increasing its chance of success.

CHARACTERISTICS OF COMMON NONREGULAR FORMS OF EMPLOYMENT

"PART-TIME"

Approximately 20 percent of the working population is categorized as "part-time" (Gottfried 2008). The increase in female employment in Japan in recent decades is due largely to the rising number of nonregular, mostly "part-time" workers (Kawaguchi 2015). From 1986 to 1996 "part-time" employment accounted for 93 percent of growth of women's employment. However, the threshold for "part-time" is not pegged to a particular number of hours worked. Instead, it is defined as anything short of the number of hours that full-time employees in the same establishment work on average in a week. About 30 percent of "part-timers" work 35 or more hours per week, and it is not usual for them to work overtime (Cook and Hayashi 1980). This has led to the creation of an undeniably ridiculous employment category: full-time part-timers (Osawa 2001).

At the same time jobs are becoming less secure, the wage gap between regular and nonregular workers is widening. In 1990 the part-time to full-time wage ratio was 57.8 percent for male workers and 72 percent for women. By 2000 the figures had dropped to 51.2 percent for men and 66.9 percent for women (Gottfried 2008). In other words, the wage gap is widening at the same time part-time workers are becoming an indispensable category for the Japanese economy.

TEMPORARY

Temporary employees, 80 percent of whom are women, work under similar conditions as part-timers except that they are hired explicitly on short-term contracts. In Japan, the term "temporary worker" usually refers to people who are employed directly by the company they work for (as opposed to being employed through a temporary agency; see below). They do the same jobs and work the same hours as regular workers, but there is no promise of long-term employment or accrual of benefits or seniority over time. Like part-time employees, temporary workers are not covered by EEOL protections. In the same way that "part-time" does not necessarily mean fewer than 40 hours, "temporary" does not necessarily mean short-term engagement. In some cases people work for 20 or more years for the same company but are classified as "temporary employees." In essence, terms like "part-time" and "temporary" mean little more than reduced obligation and commitment on the part of the employer.

DISPATCH (TEMP AGENCY)

Dispatch workers are temporary employees hired through an outside agency. These jobs have all the downsides of other types of informal labor, plus the disadvantage of being under a "middle-man" employment contract, which disconnects the employee from the de facto employer, relieving the company of accountability for compliance with minimum labor standards.

Employing individuals through a temp agency technically was illegal before the passage of the Worker Dispatching Law in 1985. In its original form, the Dispatch Law limited dispatch agencies to 16 specific job categories for which they could supply workers. But business interests immediately began chipping away at the restrictions on use of dispatch workers as a source of cheap labor. By 1996 the list was expanded to 26 job categories. By 1999, instead of stipulating the jobs that were eligible for temping out, the law had been revised to stipulate the few that were *ineligible* (Gottfried 2008). Hiring through temp agencies was further deregulated in 2003 when the law was amended to allow temp agencies to dispatch workers for assembly line jobs (previously prohibited) and to extend the amount of time an employer can keep an employee on a temporary contract. For example, prior to the 2003 amendment employers could keep retail and sales workers on temporary contracts for up to one year. After that time the company was required either to make a longer-term commitment to the employees or let them go. But after the 2003 amendment went into effect, employers could keep them on temporary contracts for up to three years. Once the government began relaxing regulation, use of dispatch workers ballooned. According to one estimate, the number of temp agency workers more than doubled, from 575,879 in 1994 to 1,386,364 in 2000 (Gottfried 2008).

CURRICULUM WISH LISTS

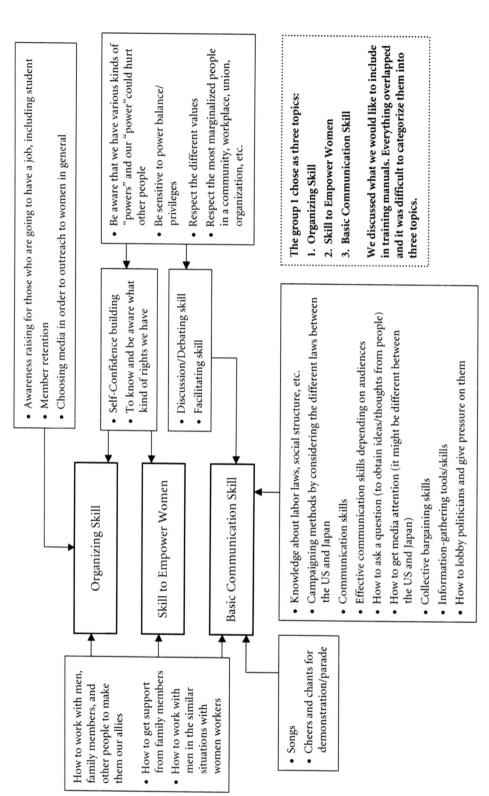

Chart 1. Group 1 Wish List for Union Skills Curricula based on March 20, 2005, brainstorming session.

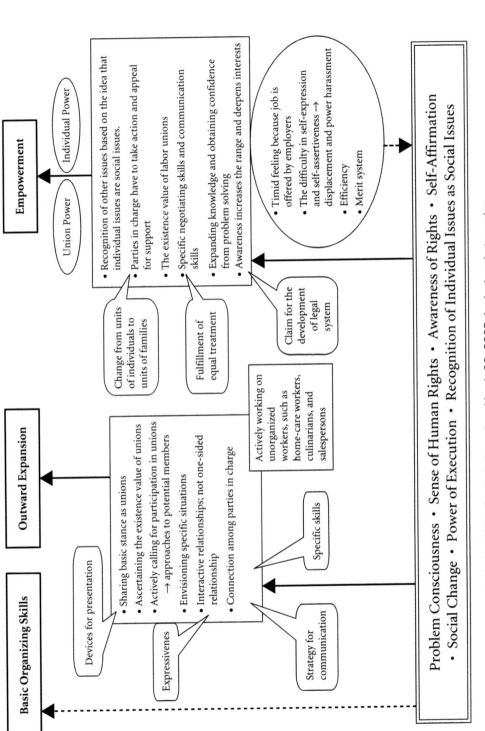

Chart 2. Group 2 Wish List for Union Skills Curricula based on March 20, 2005, brainstorming session.

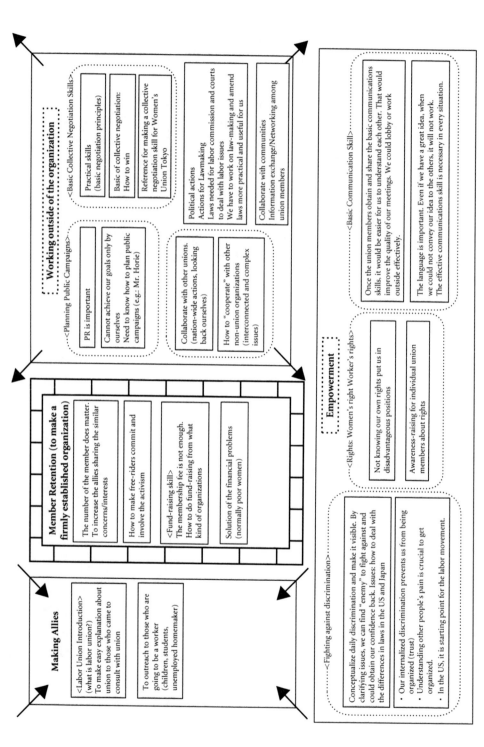

Chart 3. Group 3 Wish List for Union Skills Curricula based on March 20, 2005, brainstorming session.

Empowerment

- Learning activities for union members
- Awareness of our rights
- The lack of the spirit of volunteerism
- The positive attitude to take on collective bargaining for other union members, and the acquisition of the skills to solve issues
- The skills and education by which union members can be assured, regarding the right of collective bargaining
- The education to hand down the necessity of solidarity
- The educational manual to make women get over their aversion toward labor unions
- The challenge to create an organic relationship between union leaders, who are experienced, and union members, who are short on experience in union activities (nothing like a boss-henchperson relationship)
- How to empower union members with difficulties to express themselves, such as members who don't come to an office and who can't speak loudly
- The great difficulty for union members without knowledge regarding union activities to acquire it → The need for easier methods not dependent on a single-handed manner by an individual union member
- The reason why union activists are in an exhausted condition → The need for methods for developing core members of union activities and for building trust among the core members

Broader Cooperation of Women's Movements by Women

Present Proper External Images!

- Media created by unions
- Sending a message "Don't give up! You can change!"
- Campaign by using media → Awareness raising regarding the legitimacy of the exercise of rights at the social level
- Cooperation from professional media
- Cooperation from designers and music-related people

- Education to have women activists understand unions
- Funds for union activities → Working on media, political groups, and business enterprise
- Sending a message that funding is not cost

We are needy!
Let's raise funds!
Let's pump up the money supply from outside!

- Membership (Membership fees)
- How to raise funds from other sources besides membership fees
- Funding by the private sector
- Business promotion by women → Building up funds

Chart 4. Group 4 Wish List for Union Skills Curricula based on March 20, 2005, brainstorming session.

WHY JAPANESE WOMEN "CAN'T" ORGANIZE

The participants argued that Japanese women are not in a position to organize other workers for several reasons: because organizing involves actions that are not culturally acceptable, because it is too risky (for the organizers and anyone who gets caught listening to them), because other workers don't have time or interest in their problems, and because the women who come to women's unions are already too victimized and too vulnerable to take on any more challenges.

CULTURAL OBSTACLES

Japanese women cannot organize their coworkers because organizing involves a sort of forwardness and appearance of self-interest that are socially unacceptable in Japan. There is some truth to that. In a culture where tending to your own needs (or at least being caught doing so) is highly suspect and duty to others is highly prized, it's very hard to convince women to take the time and energy to work toward improving their own lives. Women's unions might strike a chord if they tried to frame organizing as doing one's duty to other women, but that is not in the spirit of the message the women's unions want to send. One of the goals of women's unions is challenging the notion that the proper role for women is one of obligation to others with little, if any, thought for their own hopes and dreams.

TOO RISKY

One thing the women said all the time was that they could not talk to other people at their workplace about problems they are having because the other workers would not simply clam up, they would start avoiding the would-be organizer in fear for their own job and/or relationship with management. As I mentioned in chapter 1, controlling workers through bullying and power harassment is something of an art form in Japanese companies. Employees know that sympathizing with or even talking to a disgruntled coworker could tarnish their reputation with the company, decrease their chances for raises, bonuses, and promotions, and increase their chances of an unwanted transfer.

NO SECOND CHANCES

Organizing in Japan is especially risky because of the way the labor market is structured. In the United States, where mid-career hires are not unusual, it is possible to lose your job and get another job of equal or better status in the same field. In Japan, that's not the case. A person who loses a full-time regular job will probably have to settle for a job at a smaller company, or in a part-time nonregular position, or both. Employees are well aware that if they get on the wrong side of the boss for organizing, they might well suffer the effects for the rest of their careers.

STRUCTURAL OBSTACLES

Women in nontraditional work settings and employment patterns (such as contract or temp) often have little direct contact with coworkers, work in distributed work sites, and have little or no job security. Their circumstances are therefore too precarious for them to take a chance on actions that could queer the chances of their contracts being renewed. These are indeed serious problems but working women everywhere face similar structural obstacles and work to create organizing strategies that fit their circumstances as we saw in the case of UNITE HERE Local 34.

WE'RE DIFFERENT

Many Japanese people think of themselves and their culture as being fundamentally different from the rest of the world. That belief can be a source of national pride, but it can also be used as a way to shut down dialogue if some of their practices are called into question. I have often seen the "we're different" argument used as a shield to deflect hard suggestions. In the case of gender inequality in the employment system, for example, the government cautions that change must come slowly because of the culturally specific "beautiful practices" that give Japan its special character (such as the corporate practice of having young, beautiful office flowers to pour tea for the men). In the case of the women's unions, they use the "we're different" rhetoric to shut down discussions about organizing because, by their accounting, it has not worked in the past. But, if we examine their claim that it has not worked, we see that it is only true in a very limited way. While some of the women present had been unable to organize their coworkers in their earlier attempts, Japanese women and Japanese workers have organized successfully in the past.

WOMEN ARE TOO BEATEN DOWN

"The women who come to us have already tried everything they could on their own and it didn't work, so we cannot tell [them] to go back to work and make [their] case. They come to the union for network support." Instead of training women to go back in and try to develop support among their coworkers, the union sees its job as supporting the individual woman as she confronts management as an individual grievant. "We send a letter to management to ask for negotiations, or send a letter of complaint. We see what happens and then go from there."

Carol suggested instead of sending letters to the boss to request negotiations, how about twenty workers going into the boss's office with a demand? "We can't do that," one woman said. "These women have done everything they know how to do. They are exhausted when they come to us. We can't tell them to go back to work and try to get the support of others because they have already tried to do that." Several of the non-Japanese participants argued that, in those cases, the women had tried to do that on their own, but without the training and support of the union. If the unions were able to use some of the practices Carol was introducing, or some new technique that might grow out of the discussion, isn't it possible that the outcome might be different? But the timing was not right for that question. The feeling in the group at that moment was too suspicious, too tense, to foster openness to new possibilities.

WESTERN WOMEN ARE TOO PRIVILEGED TO UNDERSTAND

The difference between the degrees of gender inequality that exist in the United States and Japan make it hard for US women to refute the claim that they simply can't appreciate the impossibility of organizing in Japan. But if the Japanese women made that statement in front of other women in the CAW network, for example, many of whom organize in the face of extreme physical danger, I suspect the Japanese women would have had a harder time getting that argument to fly. As Mabel pointed out, women in far more repressive cultures find ways to organize.

Notes

PREFACE

1. Based on interviews with, in Japan: Ben Watanabe, a longtime union activist and a former leader of *Sohyo*, the now-defunct militant labor federation; representatives from *Zenroren*, Japan's second largest labor federation, and Tokyo Managers' Union; labor lawyers and scholars, including members of the Center for Transnational Labor Studies and scholars from the Ohara Institute for Social Research at Hosei University; and rank-and-file public sector employees on the picket line in 1999 during the annual spring "wage offensive" or *Shunto*. In the United States: Robert Kingsley, UE director of organizing, and Amy Dean, founding director of *Working Partnerships USA* and 1999–2000 public policy fellow of the Japan Society.

INTRODUCTION

1. Women-only unions have existed in Japan in other periods and, at the present, other types of unions with all or majority women members (such as some part-time workers' unions because women make up the majority of part-time workers) do exist. However, the women-only unions under discussion in this volume differ from those organizations in that they are independent of the mainstream labor institutions, including enterprise unions and industrial federations. (For more information on women's unions in Japan in previous eras and on the differences between "autonomous organizing" and "separate organizing," see Briskin 1993, 1999; Broadbent 2007, 2008.)

2. According to the activists I interviewed, Kansai Women's Union (*Onna Rōdō Kumiai Kansai*) was founded in 1987. Foreign scholars, on the other hand, tend to date the union from 1990 (see Broadbent 2008). The circumstances surrounding the founding of Kansai Women's Union and other JWUs will be discussed in greater detail in chapter 4.

3. The initial version of the Equal Employment Opportunity Law (EEOL), which went into effect in 1986, was extremely weak. Employers were "forbidden" to discriminate against women, but only in the areas of retraining, welfare, retirement, and retrenchment. In recruiting, hiring, placement, and promotion, the law obliged management only to "make efforts" to achieve equal treatment (Mackie 2003). It also failed to add new provisions on wage discrimination, and included few mechanisms for oversight, enforcement, and sanctions (Gelb 2003; Mackie 2003; Osawa 2007). Worst of all, its many loopholes allowed management to create the new two career-track system, which was little more than a "wink, wink, nudge, nudge" way for companies to appear to be in compliance with the law while in fact continuing long-standing discriminatory practices.

4. Researchers differ on the question of the efficacy of the EEOL. For competing analyses of how and to what extent the EEOL has affected women's employment opportunities and gender equality on the job, see Abe (2011) and Blind and Lottanti Von Mandach (2015).

5. For characteristics of the most common forms of nonregular employment (part-time, temporary, and contract/dispatch employment), see appendix A. For a detailed study of the experience of part-time workers in Japan, see Broadbent (2003).

6. According to the JILPT (2014), the "overwhelming majority" of unions limit their membership to regular members. The overall unionization rate in Japan was 17.9 percent

in 2012, while the rate for part-time workers was only 5 percent. Also, the unionization rate for SMEs, in which women are significantly overrepresented, is very low. For example, the rate for companies with fewer than 100 employees is about 1 percent. This is particularly alarming considering about 42 percent of women work in companies with fewer than 29 employees (Broadbent 2007).

7. In the mid-1970s Japanese feminists launched a bold international campaign to compel their government to embrace international standards on human and women's rights, including legislation that would guarantee equal employment opportunities for women (Gelb 2003). That was an offshoot of the United Nations Decade for Women (1976–85). Prior to 1975, Japanese feminists had relatively little interaction with international feminist or labor organizations. But in 1975 Japanese women attended the first World Conference on Women held in Mexico City, where they learned that Japan lagged far behind most developed countries in accepting international human and women's rights standards. Armed with that knowledge, Japanese feminists worked to build international support to pressure the Japanese government into complying with international standards. By the mid-1980s, feminist activists had succeeded in forcing the government to sign the Convention on the Elimination of Discrimination Against Women, a comprehensive code on women's rights adopted by the UN in 1979. But gaining acceptance in principle was the relatively easy part. In practice, Japan's existing legal framework was not sufficient to support the new agreement. In order to ratify the Convention, the government would need to adopt new legislation that would bring Japanese labor law into compliance with the agreement. Japanese women's organizations used the opening to begin lobbying for an equal employment opportunity law as a centerpiece of the necessary legislative reforms. It was a clever strategic move and, by some accounts, the only reason Japan has an EEOL today (Gelb 2003). But, while the feminists won in the sense that the EEOL was eventually enacted, the negotiations around the specifics of the law were dominated by the more politically powerful and deeply entrenched voices of corporate Japan. Since the women's groups had maneuvered the government into signing the Convention without building any real ideological commitment to the concept of workplace equality, the law that got passed was a masterpiece of Swiss-cheese legislation. As Gelb explains, "The problem with the strategy of shaming the government into signing onto international standards to which it has little real commitment is that when it comes time to draft legislation to bring the country into 'compliance' with the agreement, the resulting legislation is only intended to be window-dressing and thus is often weak, lacking enforcement mechanisms, and unlikely to accomplish its putative goals" (Gelb 2003, 50).

8. According to the Ministry of Health, Labour, and Welfare's 2012 Basic Survey of Gender Equality in Employment Management, 72 percent of firms that include a sōgō shoku track requiring geographical transfers report that more than 80 percent of the employees they hired in that category were male. Meanwhile, 52 percent of corporations with an ippan shoku track stated that more than 80 percent of employees in that track were female (Kawaguchi 2015).

9. Japanese women's groups have challenged this interpretation through the courts. In 1995 six women filed a complaint against Kanematsu Trading Corporation with the Tokyo District Court. In 2003, although the judge admitted that the system is in violation of Article 14 of the Constitution, the court ruled that it did not violate the EEOL. In 2008, however, the Tokyo Court of Appeals ruled that Kanematsu's wage system violated Article 4 of the Labor Standards Law. "[T]he ruling maintained there was virtually no difference in the work performed by men and women. The court also noted that a woman's salary at the age of retirement does not exceed the regular salary of a 27-year-old male employee" (AWWC 2008, 3). The ruling was only a partial victory, however, because the court said it did not apply to two of the plaintiffs because one worked as a secretary when the claim

was originally filed and the other left the company after just shy of fifteen years of service. The plaintiffs and the company have appealed the case to the Supreme Court (AWWC 2008).

10. I use the term "women's issues" with some reservation throughout the text. Generally speaking that term gives me a rash because so many of the issues are "women's issues" only because they relate to tasks or concerns that have been coded female by gendered divisions of labor in the home, workplace, and society at large. And yet for that same reason such issues do in fact intrude on or complicate women's work and home lives more than men's, and they typically aren't addressed unless women address them. It is in that sense I refer to them as "women's issues" but at the same time I hope the reader will bear in mind the conflicts surrounding the term.

11. Unlike US labor law, Japanese law permits the creation of secondary or minority unions. Employees who are unsatisfied with their existing union have the right to organize alternative unions alongside and in competition with the original union. In other words, it is possible to have two or more unions providing representation to workers in the same bargaining unit. This situation becomes complicated in cases where the enterprise union has a union-shop agreement with the employer. Technically, a union-shop agreement requires the employer to dismiss an employee who is expelled from or otherwise leaves the enterprise union. However, the Supreme Court has voided dismissals that came as a result of an employee leaving the company union to join or form a second union outside the enterprise (Hanami and Komiya 2011, 159). Japanese law also allows for the creation of individual-membership unions because there is no minimum membership threshold for union recognition. Even if an organization only represents one employee, it is still a union in the eyes of the law and employers are (in theory) obligated to negotiate with it (Suzuki 2008).

12. For an analysis of individual-affiliation unions based on case studies of Women's Union Tokyo and Tokyo Managers' Union, see Kotani (2013).

13. In 1995 the Japanese Federation of Employers' Associations released a report called "Japanese-style Management in the New Age" which called for decreasing wages and increasing the use of "diversified employment formats," meaning nonregular, nonpermanent, and non–full-time employment (JILPT 2014, chap. 1, sec. 2, 3). That report marked a significant departure from the "three pillars" of the employment system that was credited with being the foundation of the "Japanese Economic Miracle." The three pillars of that system were seniority wages, enterprise unions, and lifetime employment. But by the 1990s employers were openly seeking to dismantle two of those three pillars through wage cuts and by restructuring the terms of employment. And they weren't alone. Through changes in fiscal policy and continuing deregulation of the labor market, the federal government and financial institutions sought to pull Japan out of the economic crises of the 1990s and 2000s by scaling back on what the neoliberalists were calling the "three excesses" of the Japanese economy: excessive equipment (capacity), excessive debt, and *excessive employment*. In other words, a large part of the administration's "solution" was that a whole lot of people would have to be thrown out of work. And so, in a radical reversal of the long-standing ethic of lifetime employment, the state began reshaping labor management policy to promote the use of short-term nonsecure labor (JILPT 2014, chap. 1, sec. 1, 6). By 2012 Japan's embrace of neoliberalism was so complete that the Abe administration was asserting three new pillars of the Japanese economy: bold monetary policy, flexible fiscal policy, and a growth strategy that encourages private investment (JILPT 2014, chap. 1, sec. 1, 6). Corporate Japan complied. Through layoffs, "voluntary" retirements, and the reclassification of regular full-time jobs to nonregular positions, an increasingly large number of Japanese workers found themselves unemployed or underemployed and outside the protection of mainstream enterprise unions.

14. Despite the name, women-only unions cannot legally exclude men, as that would constitute discrimination under the Trade Union Law. Most women's unions allow a small number of sympathetic men to join as supporters (Broadbent 2007; interview with WUT leaders 2000).

1. A UNION OF ONE'S OWN

1. How women want to be addressed, by their family names or by their given names, has become a political question in Japan. Rather than imposing one rule on everyone for the sake of consistency, I refer to each person the way she introduced herself to others. For example, Midori Ito was known to everyone as "Midori," while Keiko Tani always introduced herself as "Tani." One difference, however, is that in person I always use the honorific "san" when addressing or referring to any Japanese person. For the purposes of this book, however, I drop "san" as it is not something we use in English and can sound strangely "orientalizing" when used out of context. That said, I am not entirely comfortable with that decision because when I "hear" myself talking about them without the "san," the single name sounds so blunt to my ears that it does not match the more respectful and yet warmer tone I use with them (and genuinely feel) in real life. On the United States side, I have chosen to use last names when the relationship between the US and Japanese participants was fairly formal in nature, such as in the context of a formal presentation, and first names when the interpersonal vibe was more informal and egalitarian. Determining the formality level of other people's relationships might seem like a difficult hair to split to English-language speakers, but in the Japanese language that distinction is made explicit through the verb conjugation.

2. Women's Union Tokyo has the curious habit of referring to itself by a variety of different diminutives. When speaking, union members tend to refer to the organization as "Josei Union," meaning "women's union," but its newsletter and other printed materials often use "Women's Union Tokyo." I have chosen to use "Women's Union Tokyo" and "WUT" because, as English terms, they are more meaningful to the likely readers of this volume.

3. My first meeting with Midori and Tani was conducted with the help of the bilingual labor scholar who introduced us. However, my Japanese language skills and several of the core WUT members' English skills evolved over the course of the US-Japan Working Women's Networks Project. Since we rarely had funding for professional interpreters, in the early days we usually relied on relatively bilingual friends or union members to help us triangulate on meaning during interviews and to provide whisper translation for me during meetings and group presentations that were conducted in Japanese. As the project progressed, the union members and I became increasingly able to communicate directly in spoken Japanese. However, professional simultaneous interpretation and written translations were provided for the three international meetings.

4. When JWUs use the English-language term "collective bargaining," they mean something entirely different from what most unionists mean. In the JWU context, "collective bargaining" means that a group of women from the women's union accompany a particular individual to the bargaining table to discuss her particular issue. That is a crucial distinction in several ways. First, it means JWUs are typically not bargaining *for* a collective. In most of their cases, JWUs are bargaining on behalf of only one or possibly a few employees. There have been a few cases where the terms of a settlement were extended to employees beyond the initial grievant(s), but those employees cannot be considered part of a bargaining collective because they were not part of the dialogue that went into shaping what the union would bargain for or accept. They are, essentially, bystander beneficiaries. Second, JWUs do not bargain *as* a collective in the way most unionists use that term.

Typically, the grievant is likely to be the only person from her company who belongs to the women's union. Although other members of the women's union will attend the negotiations, none of them is likely to be an employee of that particular firm. Bargaining is collective in the sense that the grievant has people to sit with her at the table, but in terms of leverage against the company (i.e., the ability to restrict the supply of labor), she is still only mobilizing an army of one. Finally, "collective bargaining" in the JWU sense always occurs in the context of correcting an existing wrong, as opposed to positively having a voice in setting working terms and conditions. While there is tremendous value in having a grievance procedure to rectify problems when they do occur, the term "collective bargaining" as used in the West typically also implies the larger function of having a say in shaping positive workplace practices from the outset.

5. English renderings of the Japanese terms for regular employee and nonregular employee differ slightly across authors. I have chosen the spellings used in the WUT's written materials for the US-Japan Project workshop in Detroit in 2004.

6. Percentages do not add up to one hundred because respondents could choose more than one option.

7. Women who are employed and represented under a union-shop agreement might face resistance from the enterprise union, management, or both if they try to join an outside union but, as stated in the introduction to this volume, the Supreme Court recently ruled in favor of workers' rights to seek or create alternative representation (Hanami and Komiya 2011). See also note 11 in the Introduction.

8. If direct negotiations fail or the company refuses to negotiate, the grievant can take the case to the Tokyo Metropolitan Labor Relations Commission, which attempts to reconcile unfair labor practice claims. If no settlement is reached through the LRC, the grievant has the option to take her case to court, an arduous process that typically takes years. Even so, more and more women are taking their cases to court, not just in the hope of reaching a favorable settlement but also to bring their issue into the public spotlight and to set precedents which, while not legally binding, could discourage employers from engaging in discriminatory treatment of women in the future.

9. The employee's petition drive was successful. Within six months she had collected enough signatures to persuade the government to look into the matter. Eventually, the government conceded that her injuries were indeed work-related. This was a watershed victory because, according to the employee, it was the first time the government acknowledged a part-time employee's work-related illness (personal interview 2009).

10. In addition to all the cultural norms against making waves or defying authority, raises, promotions, and bonuses are based in part on annual performance reviews, which typically include rating employees on "loyalty to the company." Refusing to go along with the call to bully would be coded as a failure to show loyalty to the company and could cost an employee a raise or promotion if not their job.

2. A TALE OF TWO ACTIVISTS

1. I lived in this gritty, industrial neighborhood for about a month on one of my earlier visits to Japan. The area is known for paper factories where, for decades, employees transported large bundles of paper by strapping them to their backs and walking, bodies bent at 90-degree angles, to their destination. Now, much of that work is done by small delivery trucks, but every day I would see women from earlier generations whose bodies were permanently bent at that angle. It struck me as especially cruel that in a city of constant spectacle, their only vista was their own feet. It also looked horribly painful, and yet every day I would see these crumpled women walking through the neighborhood, greeting people with smiles and friendly salutations as they made their way to the grocery store

or the fish monger. I asked various Japanese friends why the women were bent like that. Some figured it was from age and poor nutrition but others told me it was a common infirmity among factory workers who spent a lifetime carrying heavy bundles on their backs. I never did find a definitive answer, but the mere fact that people were, and to some extent still are, used as human pack mules was one of the impetuses behind my desire to stick around and find out more about what was going on with Japanese workers behind the scenes.

2. *Shunto*, also known as the Spring Wage Offensive, refers to the annual wage negotiations between large firms and their unions, most of which belong to the Rengo labor federation. Smaller and non-union companies often follow the wage patterns set during *Shunto*.

3. Once a member files a lawsuit, the union no longer engages in negotiations on that case so the bargaining team as such is disbanded. However, members are encouraged to recruit a support group to assist them through the various phases of their court case.

3. WOMEN'S UNION TOKYO IN PRACTICE

1. On several occasions I was called upon to explain why the United States has failed to ratify CEDAW (the United Nations' Convention on Eliminating Discrimination Against Women). My Japanese colleagues found the US position unfathomable, especially considering that the only other member nations that have not ratified it are Iran, Somalia, Sudan, South Sudan, Palau, and Tonga. I had no answer for them as I shared their bewilderment.

2. Union activists use the term "organize" in several different ways. In this case, I am using "organize" to refer to the process by which individual actors gain union consciousness (what we used to call "class consciousness" before "class" was thrown upon the dung heap of other unmentionable "C-words") and become active union members rather than passive free riders.

3. According to a union survey, only five workplaces had more than one WUT member (WUT 2004a).

4. Four years after the merger, only three out of thirty employees of the older company remained, according to the WUT.

5. In a perfect world, we would have sought equal input from women's organizations in cities outside of Tokyo as well, but we were trapped by one of the many Catch-22s that would emerge over the course of this project. This snag and others are detailed in the concluding chapter of this volume.

4. FIRST, WE DRINK TEA

1. *Fureai* is a Japanese word that refers to building a bond among different types of people, for example, people of different ages or occupations. *ICORU* is a transliteration of the English word "equal."

2. Relatively progressive *Sohyo* was considered a counterbalance to the more conservative federation, *Domei*. Both disbanded in 1989, the same year the more conservative federation, Rengo, was formed. With about 6.8 million members, Rengo is now far and away the largest of the three remaining national federations. The other two federations are: *Zenroren* (about 750,000 members), and *Zenryoko* (about 160,000 members).

3. The training and educational programs that the KWU and other Japanese women's groups provided at this time differed significantly from the kinds of educational methods and materials we sought to introduce and develop through the US-Japan Project. The earlier educational programs typically focused on arming women with data on and analysis of gender discrimination in the workplace, pending legislation and how it would affect women, the true role women play in maintaining the Japanese economy, etc. The kinds of

educational programs the US-Japan Project would later develop focus on helping women acquire the skills they need to actively and effectively participate in their unions and in social movements in general, using participatory educational methods as opposed to more traditional methods based on the one-way transmission of information from teacher to students.

4. Some laws limit the use of short-term contracts and temporary labor (see appendix A), so it is possible to fight some contract terminations on legal grounds. My point is that the company does not actually have to break the law to be considered in the wrong in such cases, and to face public censure. On the other hand, it is very difficult to win cases when public opinion is the employee's only real bargaining chip. Such cases usually require significant community organizing, which can be very costly, especially in terms of time and energy, for small, independent unions.

5. To an American ear, the phrase "cheerleading squad" might sound tongue in cheek, but *ICORU* members and other activists use chipper, sprightly terms in all earnestness because they believe that part of their project is to energize and provide support to women who are being emotionally as well as physically depleted by the unreasonable work and family demands that are placed upon them.

6. Article 5 of the Public Peace Police Law of 1900 made it illegal for women to engage in political activities, including voting, holding or attending political meetings, and joining political parties (Mackie 2002).

5. UNDER THE MICROSCOPE

1. The WUT's report was careful to point out that lack of participation is not only a problem of solidarity. As working conditions deteriorate, the pool of women who can volunteer dwindles at the same time the number of women seeking help is on the rise. "[T]he system of longer working hours makes it difficult for union members to voluntarily work in the WUT office, for example taking phone duty at night. The volunteer schedule sheet used to be filled with the names of executive board members and other union members [volunteering to cover shifts] from 6:00 p.m. every Monday, Wednesday, and Friday, but currently there are very few names on the sheet. . . . Bargaining takes place almost every day, and full-time staff members take charge of most cases" (WUT 2004b, 7).

2. In Japan, unpaid overtime is generally referred to as "service overtime." This is in addition to the scheduled overtime that is officially required.

3. I was surprised here at the union's use of the word "advertising" as opposed to the more expected term "organizing." At first I thought it was a translation error. It was not until Workshop II that I and the other US participants discovered, with great surprise, that the Japanese women had deliberately not used the term "organizing." As readers will later see, we were even more surprised when we found out why.

4. According to Smith, the C&Ts had not always backed Local 35 in past disputes against management. Some had even crossed Local 35's picket lines.

5. Case in point: we can't even discuss the issue of status inequality without reproducing it because any term we have to refer to those in nonelite occupations sounds pejorative: ordinary, regular, everyday, etc.

6. The situation is a little murky because, at first blush, the problem seems to be US academics, because subsequent meetings that included Japanese academics did not have to meet such high middle-class standards of comfort. But that's because the particular Japanese academics who attended those meetings were also part of the grassroots women's movement. Had we invited Japanese academics who had the same relationship to our project that the first round of US academics did, we would have had to provide fancier accommodations than we did or risk offending.

7. Given the choice, the Japanese women would have said to put the US contingent in a fancy hotel and let the Japanese stay in a more modest dwelling. Despite all the tensions around inequality between the United States and Japan, the Japanese women would have preferred that to spending the extra money for them to stay in middle-class establishments that they didn't particularly value. But, of course, that is unthinkable from a conference organizer's perspective. Imagine the fall-out from intentionally designing a conference that purposely treats invited guests differently on the basis of race and nationality.

8. This issue will be discussed in greater detail in the concluding chapter.

6. CRISIS OF DIFFERENCE

1. For translated samples of the wish lists the Japanese participants created, see appendix B.

2. In the United States we would typically call these "leadership skills" but the Japanese women bristled at the word "leadership" because to them it inevitably implies hierarchy. We tried a variety of options: participation skills, executive skills, activist skills, and in the end the group decided on "empowerment skills." That decision made sense at the time and for the people who were in the room to hear the discussion. But, over the course of the project, it produced quite a lot of confusion and conflict—some productive, some not—among the Japanese women. We later learned that some of the women who signed up for the empowerment skills workshop expected something more psychological, something that would help them feel more confident or secure as a person, whereas the actual focus of the workshop was to develop skills that would enable women to plan as well as participate in union activities.

3. Mabel's real name is Au Mei Po but, like many Asian people, she uses a western name when working with activists outside of Hong Kong to make pronunciation easier. Also, I have inverted the word order to match the western convention of given name first for the sake of consistency.

4. The Japanese participants gave a number of reasons Japanese women can't organize, all of which have an element of truth to them in the sense that they do indeed make organizing difficult for Japanese women. But those same obstacles hold true for women everywhere. Although ultimately the barriers that the Japanese participants pointed to should not be used as reasons to give up on organizing, they are real enough that it might be useful for activists to study and understand them. For a brief discussion of the specific obstacles to organizing that the participants raised, see appendix C.

5. Originally we asked Mabel if she would like to facilitate the organizing workshop, considering her extensive organizing experience in Asian countries and her well-established ties with many of the Japanese participants, but she preferred to lead the session on networking among women.

6. It is possible that some of the differences in our ideas about organizing stem from the fact that, unlike US unions, Japanese unions do not have to win certification elections in order to be officially recognized bargaining agents, and therefore might have less experience with and motivation for organizing. On the other hand, such institutional differences do not explain their discomfort with the concept of organizing entirely. The Japanese activists were explicit that their primary objection was that outreach robs women of the empowering act of making the first move.

7. When the participants invoked the phrase "magic bullet" it was clear from the context they were going for the more conventional phrases "magic pill" or "silver bullet," but as there is nothing incorrect about it, I decided to go with their creative mash-up.

8. The Japanese women didn't know the expression "potluck," but they understood the concept when someone suggested the word "*yosenabe*," which is a kind of soup that calls for a wide variety of ingredients. This became their metaphor for the benefits of

everyone making a contribution. Interestingly, though, the meaning of that metaphor shifted over time. In the beginning, they understood it as a way to illustrate the need for everyone to participate, which is to say they recognized it as a tool for internal organizing. But when I interviewed the Japanese women a year later, I noticed they started using the term *yosenabe* to signify that everyone has something of value to contribute. Even women who think they don't know enough or have enough experience to take part in union activities are assured that everyone has something to add and every contribution matters. They had taken the concept and refashioned it as a tool for individual empowerment.

7. MADE IN JAPAN

1. Part of that confusion grew out of our earlier decision to use the term "empowerment skills" instead of "leadership skills" as a concession to the Japanese women's discomfort with the latter. Had we been able to refer to the skills in Tess's workshop as "leadership skills" or "activist skills," I suspect we would have avoided this specific confusion. But once we used the term "empowerment," we unwittingly invoked a term that has different meanings across the different types of Japanese women's organizations that were involved in the US-Japan Project.

2. Coalition-building by 9to5 also extends to politically active faith-based communities, which are in much shorter supply in Japan than in the United States.

8. A MOVEMENT TRANSFORMED

1. Although the Women's Union Plus workshop was based on materials from the WUT, it quickly took on its own local flavor. "[The participants] were asked to describe themselves positively," Kurosawa said. "But people who come from [the] north are shy so we used animal analogies for introductions." One woman described herself as a fish in a river, meaning she is quiet and doesn't talk much. Another woman described herself as a chicken, which everyone in the room but me knew meant that she was unique. I never tire of such cultural surprises.

2. The name JOMU is a mash-up of the Japanese words "*Josei*," meaning women, and "*Mugen*," meaning dream or vision.

3. Interestingly, many strands of postwar feminism, such as those calling on women to use their power as consumers to win advances in environmental issues and food safety (i.e., "housewife feminism"), were widely criticized as feminism that lacked an analysis of gender, whereas, with JWUs we are arguably seeing a workers' movement that lacks a class analysis.

CONCLUSION

1. Translation refers to written text; interpretation refers to spoken word.

2. The true irony was that in this case the foundation that denied our request was a Japanese institution, but as I was the messenger who brought the news that we could not use 2005 funds to cover expenses incurred in 2004, the Japanese activists coded the denial as an example of inflexibility on the part of US institutions.

3. In *Portraits of the Japanese Workplace*, Kumazawa (1996) makes a similar argument, in which he contrasts US and British unions, rooted in the development of a class consciousness as an explicit rejection of individualism, with Japanese enterprise unions, which he argues are an outgrowth of the new ideology of individualism (a product of the then-emerging bourgeois culture) and a rejection of the collectivism of the feudal past. While I don't agree with all aspects of his analysis, I do agree with his assertion that traditional notions of Japanese as group-oriented and Americans and British people as individualistic tend to paper over far more robust factors in the development of labor relations in each country.

References

Abe, Yukiko. 2011. "The Equal Employment Opportunity Law and Labor Force Behavior of Women in Japan." *Journal of the Japanese and International Economies* 25: 39–55.

AMPO-Japan Asia Quarterly Review. 1996. *Voices from the Japanese Women's Movement.* Armonk, NY: M. E. Sharpe.

Asian Women's Worker Center. 2008. "Tokyo Appeals Court Judgement—Kanematsu Trading Corp's Gender Wage Discrimination Found Unlawful." *Resource Materials on Women's Labor in Japan* 37: 1–4.

Blind, Georg D., and Stefania Lottanti Von Mandach. 2015. "Decades Not Lost, but Won: Increased Employment, Higher Wages, and More Equal Opportunities in the Japanese Labour Market." *Social Science Japan Journal* 18 (1): 63–88.

Brinton, Mary C. 1993. *Women and the Economic Miracle: Gender and Work in Post-War Japan.* Berkeley: University of California Press.

Briskin, Linda. 1993. "Union Women and Separate Organizing." In *Women Challenging Unions: Feminism, Democracy, and Militancy,* edited by Linda Briskin and Patricia McDermott, 89–108. Toronto: University of Toronto Press.

——. 1999. "Autonomy, Diversity, and Integration: Union Women's Separate Organising in North America and Western Europe in the Context of Restructuring and Globalization." *Women's Studies International Forum* 22 (5): 543–54.

Broadbent, Kaye. 2003. *Women's Employment in Japan: The Experience of Part-time Workers.* New York: Routledge.

——. 2005a. "For Women, By Women: Women-only Unions in Japan." *Japan Forum* 17 (2): 213–30.

——. 2005b. "*Pawaa Appu* Women-only unions in Japan." *Electronic Journal of Contemporary Japanese Studies.* Article 8. http://www.japanesestudies.org.uk /articles/2005/Broadbent.html.

——. 2007. "Sisters Organising: Women-only Unions in Japan and Korea." *Industrial Relations Journal* 38 (3): 229–51.

——. 2008. "Japan: Women, Labour Activism and Autonomous Organizing." In *Women and Labour Organizing in Asia: Diversity, Autonomy and Activism,* edited by Kaye Broadbent and Michele Ford, 156–71. New York: Routledge.

Cobble, Dorothy Sue. 2004. *The Other Women's Movement: Workplace Justice and Social Rights in Modern America.* Princeton, NJ: Princeton University Press.

Cook, Alice H., and Hiroko Hayashi. 1980. *Working Women in Japan: Discrimination, Resistance, and Reform.* Ithaca, NY: ILR/Cornell University Press.

Fine, Janice. 2006. *Worker Centers: Organizing Communities at the Edge of the Dream.* Ithaca, NY: ILR/Cornell University Press.

Gelb, Joyce. 2003. *Gender Politics in Japan and the United States: Comparing Women's Movements, Rights, and Politics.* New York: Palgrave Macmillan.

Gilpin, Toni, Gary Isaac, Dan Letwin, and Jack McKivigan. 1988. *On Strike for Respect: The Yale Strike of 1984–85.* Chicago: Charles H. Kerr Publishing.

Gordon, Andrew. 1998. *Wages of Affluence: Labor and Management in Postwar Japan.* Cambridge, MA: Harvard University Press.

Gottfried, Heidi. 2005. "Hard Times, New Deals: The Next Upsurge?" *Critical Sociology* 31 (3): 391–99.

——. 2008. "Pathways to Economic Security: Nonstandard Employment and Gender in Contemporary Japan." *Pathways from Casual Work to Economic Security: Canadian and International Perspectives, Special Issue of Social Indicators Research* 88 (1): 179–96.

Gottfried, Heidi, and Jacqueline O'Reilly. 2002. "Re-regulating Breadwinner Models in Socially Conservative Welfare Regimes: Comparing Germany and Japan." *Social Politics* 9 (1): 29–59.

Hanami, Tadashi, and Fumito Komiya. 2011. *Labor Law in Japan.* Alphen aan den Rijn, Netherlands: Kluwer Law International.

Japan Institute for Labour Policy and Training. 2007. "Labor Situation in Japan and Its Analysis: General Overview 2006/2007." http://www.jil.go.jp/english/lsj/general/2006-2007.html.

——. 2014. "Labor Situation in Japan and Its Analysis: General Overview 2013/2014." http://www.jil.go.jp/english/lsj/general/2013-2014.html.

Kanai, Yoshiko. 1996. "Issues for Japanese Feminism." In *Voices from the Japanese Women's Movement*, edited by AMPO-Japan Asia Quarterly Review, 3–22. Armonk, NY: M. E. Sharpe.

Kansai Women's Union. 2004. "Women's Labor Union (Kansai) Activities Report." Paper presented at the US-Japan Working Women's Networks Project Workshop I, Detroit, September 24–25.

Kawaguchi, Akira. 2015. "Japanese Women Face Tough Reality in Work and Marriage." http://www.nippon.com/en/in-depth/a04601/?utm_source=Nippon.com +Newsletter&utm_campaign=a116043fe2-Newsletter_2015_08_24&utm _medium=email&utm_term=0_e230632244-a116043fe2-249187041.

Kotani, Sachi. 1999. "Josei no Atarashii Rodoundo: Josei Yunion Tokyo." ["Women's New Labor Movement: A Case Study of Women's Union Tokyo."] *Journal of Labor Sociology.* 1: 3–25.

——. 2013. 『個人加盟ユニオンの社会学－「東京管理職ユニオン」と「女性ユニオン東京」（1993 年–2002 年）』(*Sociology of Individually-affiliated Unions: Tokyo Managers' Union and Women's Union Tokyo, 1993–2002.*). Tokyo: Ochanomizu Women's University Press.

Kumazawa, Makoto. 1996. *Portraits of the Japanese Workplace: Labor Movements, Workers, and Managers.* Edited by Andrew Gordon. Translated by Andrew Gordon and Mikiso Hane. Boulder, CO: Westview Press.

Kume, Ikuo. 1998. *Disparaged Success: Labor Politics in Postwar Japan.* Ithaca, NY: Cornell University Press.

Lam, Alice. 1995. "Equal Employment Opportunities for Japanese Women: Changing Company Practice." In *Japanese Women Working*, edited by Janet Hunter, 197–223. New York: Routledge Press.

Liddle, Joanna, and Sachiko Nakajima. 2000. *Rising Suns, Rising Daughters: Gender, Class and Power in Japan.* New York: Zed Books Ltd.

Mackie, Vera. 2002. *Creating Socialist Women in Japan: Gender, Labour and Activism, 1900–1937.* New York: Cambridge University Press.

——. 2003. *Feminism in Modern Japan: Citizenship, Embodiment and Sexuality.* New York: Cambridge University Press.

——. 2005. "Embodied Citizens: Feminism in Imperial Japan." In *Women in Japanese History*, edited by Gordon Daniels and Hiroko Tomida, 95–120. London: Global Oriental Publishers.

Mehri, Darius. 2005. *Notes from Toyota-land: An American Engineer in Japan*. Ithaca, NY: ILR/Cornell University Press.

Molony, Barbara. 1991. "Activism among Women in the Taishō Cotton Textile Industry." In *Recreating Japanese Women, 1600–1945*, edited by Gail Lee Bernstein, 217–38. Berkeley: University of California Press.

Nolte, Sharon H., and Sally Ann Hastings. 1991. "The Mejii State's Policy toward Women, 1890–1910." In *Recreating Japanese Women, 1600–1945*, edited by Gail Lee Bernstein, 151–74. Berkeley: University of California Press.

OECD. 2013. "Employment rate of women." *Employment and Labour Markets: Key Tables from OECD*, No. 5. doi:http://dx.doi.org/10.1787/emp-fe-table-2013-1-en.

Ogasawara, Yuko. 1998. *Office Ladies and Salaried Men: Power, Gender and Work in Japanese Companies*. Berkeley: University of California Press.

Osawa, Mari. 2001. "People in Irregular Modes of Employment: Are They Really Not Subject to Discrimination?" *Social Science Japan Journal* 4 (2): 183–99.

——. 2007. "Comparative Livelihood Security Systems from a Gender Perspective, with a Focus on Japan." In *Gendering the Knowledge Economy: Comparative Perspectives*, edited by Sylvia Walby, Heidi Gottfried, Karen Gottschall, and Mari Osawa, 81–108. New York: Palgrave Macmillan.

Sakai, K. "Gender Gap in the Workplace." *Women's Asia 21: Voices from Japan* 14 (Winter 2005): 16–18.

Shinotsuka, Eiko. 1994. "Women Workers in Japan: Past, Present, Future." In *Women of Japan and Korea: Continuity & Change*, edited by Joyce Gelb and Marian Lief Palley, 95–119. Philadelphia: Temple University Press.

Simpson, Diane L. 1985. "Women in Japan's Struggle for Labor Reform." In *The World of Women's Trade Unionism: Comparative Historical Essays*, edited by Norbert C. Soldon, 199–228. Westport, CT: Greenwood Press.

Suzuki, Akira. 2008. "Community Unions in Japan: Similarities and Differences of Region-based Labour Movements between Japan and Other Industrialized Countries." *Economic and Industrial Democracy* 29 (4): 492–520.

——. 2010. "The Possibilities and Limitations of Social Movement Unionism in Japan: In the Context of Industrial Relations Institutions." Paper presented at the Conference on Cross-national Comparison of Labor Movement Revitalization, Tokyo, Japan, December.

Weathers, Charles. 2010. "The Rising Voice of Japan's Community Unions." In *Civic Engagement in Contemporary Japan: Established and Emerging Repertoires*, edited by Henk Vinken, Yuko Nishimura, Bruce L. J. White, and Masayuki Deguchi, 67–83. New York: Springer.

——. 2012. "Equal Opportunity for Japanese Women—What Progress?" *The Asia-Pacific Journal: Japan Focus*. http://www.japanfocus.org/-Charles-Weathers/2012/article.html.

Women's Union Tokyo. 2004a. "The Introduction of the Organization Activities of the Women's Union Tokyo." Paper presented at the US-Japan Working Women's Networks Project Workshop I, Detroit, MI, September 24–25.

——. 2004b. "Case Study: Obstacles and Challenges to WUT's Growth and Survival." Paper presented at the US-Japan Working Women's Networks Project Workshop I, Detroit, MI, September 24–25.

Index

Action Center for Working Women, 155–56, 158, 164
activist unions, 48. *See also* alternative unions; social movement unionism
administrative differences. *See under* crossborder collaboration
alternative unions, xi, 1–2, 7, 8, 10, 26; male-centered, 34–38. *See also individual listings by type and organization name*
adult education. *See* participatory education
AFL-CIO, 66–67, 109–10, 132, 147
Akabane, Kayoko, 61, 70–71
American-style management, 1, 25, 76
Article 5 of Public Peace Police Law (1900), 203n6 (chap. 4)
Article 14 (Constitution of Japan), 198n9
attribution-based unions, 7. *See also* alternative unions
Au, Mei Po (Mabel), 204n3; on organizing, 117, 195; Workshop II and, 109, 117, 129, 204n5; WUT and, 152, 156

Ban, Kiyoko, 58–59, 61, 82, 121, 155
building trust: among union members, 159, 164; organizing and, 115, 122, 144, 146; barriers to, 92 (*see also* crossborder collaboration); US-Japan Project and, 100, 126–27, 132, 180
bullying, 26–30, 40, 51, 89–90, 194, 201n10. *See also under* harassment

capitalism, 63, 181. *See also under* Japanese Women's Unions
Central for Global Partnership (CGP), 9, 151, 178–79. *See also* Japan Foundation Center for Global Partnership
Center for Transnational Labor Studies, 156
Child Care and Family Care Leave Law, 74
clerical and technical workers (C&Ts). *See* UNITE HERE: Local 34
Coalition of Labor Union Women, 62, 65–67, 68–69, 81, 100
Cobble, Dorothy Sue, 61, 62–65, 81, 108
collective bargaining: JWUs and, 8, 43, 45, 48–50, 85–86, 165, 200n4

colonialism. *See* crossborder collaboration: historical tensions
Committee for Asian Women (CAW), 19, 71, 195
community outreach, 78, 95–96, 128, 137
Community Union Kansai Network, 71, 78
community unions, 2, 7, 34, 63, 71, 77. *See also* alternative unions
company unions. *See* enterprise unions
comparable worth. *See* pay equity
consciousness, 2, 9, 77, 79, 202n2 (chap. 3); collective bargaining and, 8, 45, 47; inability to foster, 44, 45, 50–51; individual versus collective, 122, 124, 136; internal organizing and, 51–52, 67–68. *See also* individual-membership unions; individualism and collectivism
Constitution of Japan, 166, 181, 198n9
contract employment. *See under* temporary employment
Convention on the Elimination of All Forms of Discrimination Against Women (CEDAW), 198n7, 202n1 (chap. 3)
crossborder collaboration: administrative differences and, 110, 178–80; benefits of, 183; historical tensions and, 166–67; ideological differences and (*see* individualism and collectivism); institutional barriers to, 105–6, 175–78, 183; language and, 174–75; meeting styles and, 171–72; need for, 9, 12–13, 52, 183–84; social etiquette and, 172–74; status inequality and, 59, 60, 63–64, 103–5, 167–68, 178, 180, 203n5 (chap. 5), 203n6 (chap. 5), 204n7 (chap. 5); work-styles and, 168–74

DePaul University Labor Education Center, 62, 96
direct action, 47–48, 51, 63, 79, 113–14, 125, 128, 147
direct-action unionism, 114. *See also* social movement unionism
direct organizing, 113–114. *See also* organizing
dispatch labor. *See under* temporary employment
displaced workers' unions, 7. *See also* alternative unions

diversified employment patterns. *See* nonregular employment; two career-track system
drinking parties, gender and, 24

Edelson, Carol, 110, 136; curriculum and, 112–13; JWUs and, 114–28, 138, 142, 144, 145, 146–47, 163, 164; on organizing, 113–17, 120–22, 124–26, 195; challenges for, 109–10, 129–32
empowerment: JWUs' interpretations of, 189, 190, 191; individual versus collective, 126, 136, 145, 204–5n8 (chap. 6); leadership and, 154–55, 204n2, 205n1 (chap. 7); meaning of, 12, 128, 135–36, 137–38, 154–55, 205n1 (chap. 7); organizing and, 145–46. *See also* participatory education
enterprise unions, xi, 6–7, 8, 10, 54, 205n3 (conclusion); eligibility for, 2, 7, 39, 40, 199n13; Japanese employment system and, 199n13; JWUs and, 2, 8, 21–22, 24–25, 38–39, 64–65, 70–74, 126, 158, 160; male–orientation of, 9, 32, 37–38, 40, 73, 77, 81, 92; union-shop agreements and, 199n11, 201n7; women and, 6–7, 32–34, 37–39, 77, 120, 126, 147, 149, 158
Equal Employment Opportunity Law, 2–3; efficacy of, 197n4; employers' response to, 5, 70 (*see also* nonregular employment; two career-track system); limited scope of, 34–35, 186; passage of, 198n7; revision of, 78–79; weakness of, 24, 197n3
Equality Action 21, 19, 71, 152
equal pay for similar work. *See* pay equity
Ewing, Tess, 62, 97–98, 108, 132. *See also* US empowerment workshop; Workshop III: empowerment session

facilitation skills, 138–39, 145, 171–72. *See also under* Rosenberg, Emily; Workshop III
feminist practices and principles, 8–9, 52, 139; cultural differences in, 180–82; power and, 161; WUT and, 38–39, 44–45
forced early retirement, 2, 22, 25–26, 41
foreign workers' unions, 7. *See also* alternative unions
Fitzgerald, Louise, 61
Fried, Leah, 62, 93
funding: JWUs and, 20, 52, 84, 88–89, 158–59; labor education and, 97
Fujii, Toyomi, 62, 156–57

gendered division of labor, 19, 23–24, 70, 199n10

gender harassment, 23–25
General Council of Labor Unions. See *Sohyo*
Gottfried, Heidi, 10, 53, 166, 178, 180; US organizing workshop and, 115, 117, 120, 130; Workshop I and, 58, 61, 81, 84, 88, 106
grassroots exchange project. *See* US-Japan Working Women's Networks Project

harassment, 41, 89, 141. *See also* bullying; gender harassment; power harassment; sexual harassment
humor as strategy, 29–30. See also *senryu*

Iba, Mika, 111, 140
ICORU, 61, 70, 71, 77–78, 79, 80–81, 202n1 (chap. 4), 203n5 (chap. 4)
improper dismissal, 22, 25–26, 41, 71, 72, 73, 75–76, 78, 199n11, 203n4 (chap. 4)
indirect discrimination, 71. *See also* nonregular employment; two career-track system
individual affiliation. *See* individual-membership unions
individualism and collectivism, 12, 119–20, 180–3, 205n3 (conclusion)
individual-membership unions, 7, 34; benefits of, 30, 40, 51; JWUs and, 30, 40, 119, 157–58, 159–60; legal basis for, 199n11; weaknesses of, 30, 41, 47–51, 84–93, 157. *See also* alternative unions; Japanese women's unions
industrial union model, 138. *See also* traditional unions: US
informal employment, 63, 186. *See also* nonregular employment
in-house unions. *See* enterprise unions
institutional barriers. *See under* crossborder collaboration
internal organizing, 52, 67, 90, 100, 204–5n8. *See also* organizing
International Christian University (ICU), 61, 109, 110, 111, 118, 140, 150; Gender Center, 53
International Labour Organization, 91
interpretation. *See* translation
Ishiro, Shunko, 61
Ito, Midori, 11, 20, 53, 62; ACW2 and, 155–56; early life of, 30, 31–34; on feminist structures and practices, 38–40; first meeting with, 17, 18–19, 200n3; on individual affiliation, 30, 40, 48; on inequality, 30, 37–38, 39; on national network, 101–2, 155; on need for women's unions, 34, 35–36; on organizing, 113, 129, 142; on organizing young women, 164; on sexual harassment, 23, 33, 36; after

US-Japan Project, 152, 155–56, 164, 180. *See also* individual-membership unions; Women's Union Tokyo

Japanese employment system, 3–4, 10, 70, 81, 100–101, 181, 182, 194, 199n13. *See also* nonregular employment; regular employment; two career-track system
Japanese women's unions (JWUs), xii, 1–2, 7–9, 30, 197n1 (introduction); capitalism and, 160–63, 205n3 (chap. 8); collective bargaining and, 200n4; education and (*see under* labor education); enterprise unions and (*see under* enterprise unions); funding and (*see under* funding); importance of, 163–64; individualism and, 119–22, 127 (*see also under* individualism and collectivism; individual–membership unions); 9to5 and, 69, 143, 146–47; organizing and (*see under* organizing); remaining challenges for, 157–59; young women and, 159. *See also listings for specific organizations*
Japan Foundation Center for Global Partnership, 9, 151, 178, 179
Japan Institute of Workers' Evolution, 74–76
Japan Institute of Workers' Evolution Union, 70, 74–76
job consultation. *See* job counseling
job counseling, 19, 74, 77, 78, 79, 138, 156, 158; demand for, 44, 72, 86–87, 90, 138, 155, 157; men and, 35–36; WUT and, 19, 20, 21, 44, 86–87, 90. *See also* job hotline
job hotline, 19, 20, 21, 71, 72, 78, 145, 156
Johnson, Gloria, 62, 66
Josei Union, 200n2. *See also* Women's Union Tokyo

Kanematsu Trading Corporation lawsuit, 198n9. *See also* two career-track system
Kansai Women's Dispute Collective, 71
Kansai Women's Union (KWU), 1, 61, 70–72, 76, 182, 197n2
Kinoshita, Takeo, 61, 69
Kondō, Keiko, 62, 72–74, 113
Korean women's unions, 136, 156
Kotani, Sachi, 85
Kurosawa, Kiyomi, 124, 128, 153, 154, 205n1 (chap. 8)

labor advisory services, 69, 86. *See also* job counseling
labor education, 9, 11, 44, 52, 54, 86–87, 90, 93–98, as internal organizing, 11, 51–52, 67,

100; JWUs and, 93, 97–98, 100, 152–56, 202n3 (chap. 4); membership participation and, 11, 51, 108; recruitment and, 145–46. *See also* participatory education
labor feminism and feminists, 9, 12, 60, 62–63, 65, 82, 100, 108, 168
Labor Standards Act, 75
layoffs: forced retirement and, 26; government embrace of, 199n13; of managers, 35; public attitudes on, 76
leadership. *See under* empowerment
League of Lawyers for Working Women, 20
lifetime employment system. *See* Japanese employment system

mainstream unions, 2, 6, 8, 77, 126, 197n1 (introduction). *See also* enterprise unions
male-centered unions. *See under* enterprise unions; alternative unions
managers' unions, 7, 35. *See also* alternative unions; Tokyo Managers' Union
meeting styles, 138–39. *See also under* crossborder collaboration
membership dues: fee-for-service versus, 158; 9to5 and, 144; WUT and, 20, 86, 88–89; WWV and, 79
membership education, 12, 44, 52, 54, 108, 148–49. *See also* labor education; participatory education
membership retention: education and, 53, 100, 108; individual-membership unions and, 50, 157; organizing and, 136; service unions and, 47; WUT and, 44, 46, 85–87, 89
Meric, Linda, 62, 68, 69, 82, 138, 142; on empowerment, 145–46; on organizing strategies, 143–45; as representative of alternative organization 146–47
Ministry of Health, Labour and Welfare, 4, 74–75, 198n8
minority unions, 199n11. *See also* secondary unions

Naruse, Emi, 62, 78–80
National Railway Workers Union of Japan, 70
National Union of General Workers-Tokyo (NUGWT), 34–36
Negrey, Cynthia, 61
network power versus worker power, 51, 126, 129, 147, 155, 164
network unions, 7, 10, 34, 38–39, 54, 143. *See also* alternative unions; individual-membership unions
New Left, 32–33

9to5, 62, 66, 68–69, 81, 82, 143, 158; JWUs and, 108, 138, 142–47

nonregular employment, 4–6, 25, 63, 73, 79, 140, 185–86, 199n13. *See also listings for specific types*

nonregular workers' unions, 7. *See also* alternative unions

nonstandard employment. *See* nonregular employment

Ōga, Miyako, 108, 122

Onna Rōdō Kumiai Kansai, 197n2. *See also* Kansai Women's Union

organizing: alternative forms of, xii, 7, 34, 39, 45, 51, 63, 81, 93–96; as women, 66–80; direct, 113–14; education and, 52, 67–68, 95–96, 98, 100; empowerment and, 145; JWUs and, 12, 40, 113, 117, 119–24, 129–30, 157–58, 193–95, 204n6; person-to-person, 52, 95, 113, 117; traditional, 1, 42, 51, 63, 147. *See also* individualism and collectivism; individual-membership unions; internal organizing; US organizing workshop; Workshop III: organizing session

organizing conversation. *See* structured conversation

Park, Hwa-Mi, 111, 140

participatory education, 12, 67, 97; JWUs and, 11, 12, 106, 108, 130–31, 148–49, 152–56. *See also* labor education

part-time employment, 25, 32, 34, 36, 82, 149, 185–86, 194, 197–98n6; JWUs and, 2, 36, 70–71, 72, 74–76, 77–80, 102, 197n1 (introduction); 9to5 and, 143; work-related injury and, 27–28, 201n9; WUT and, 20, 22, 26–27, 49, 87. *See also* nonregular employment

Part-time Workers Employment Law, 74–75, 78, 102

part-time workers' unions, xi, 2, 7, 10, 58–59, 61, 77, 82. *See also* alternative unions

pay equity, 3, 19, 61, 62, 66, 67, 71

Posse, 154

power harassment, 19, 26–28, 35, 48–50, 82, 194. *See also* bullying

precarious employment, 4, 51, 194. *See also* nonregular employment

process of creation, 102, 108–10, 134, 137–38. *See also under* Workshop II, Workshop III

providing support versus building power, 119, 127, 135–36, 181

rap session, 120–26, 132, 164

recruiting: JWUs and, 120–21, 147, 177; 9to5 and, 143–45

regional unions, 7. *See also* alternative unions

regular employment: enterprise unions and, 6, 197n6; gender and, 6, 73; versus nonregular employment, 3–5, 185–86, 194, 199n13.

Rengo, 80, 202n2 (chap. 2), 202n2 (chap. 4)

reproducing hierarchy: JWUs and, 159; WUT and, 44–45, 92–93

reproducing inequality: organizational structures and, 36–38. *See also* crossborder collaboration: status inequality; reproducing hierarchy

Rosenberg, Emily, 62; on facilitation skills, 147; on university-based labor education, 96, 97, 108. *See also* US communications workshop; Workshop III: communications session

sanitation workers' strike, 182

Sapporo Women's Union, 62, 70, 72–74, 76, 113

satellite meetings, 108, 177

Sazaki, Kazuko, 62, 74–76, 78, 80, 153

secondary unions, 37, 39, 199n11, 201n7

Seitō, 78

seniority wages, 199n13

Senryu, 141

Senshu Union, 77

Service Employees International Union (SEIU), 52

service overtime, 51, 89, 203n2

service unions, 47–48, 50, 58, 100, 114, 126

sexual harassment, 22–25, 26–27; enterprise unions and, 7, 37, 73; inside union movement, 34–36, 37; JWUs and, 2, 8, 19, 20, 71, 72, 73, 74, 78; US women and, 62, 66, 67, 82, 144

sexual violence, 72

Shunto, 36, 197n1 (preface), 202n2 (chap. 2)

Smith, Laura, 62, 94, 203n4 (chap. 5)

social etiquette. *See under* crossborder collaboration

social movement unionism, 2, 48, 100

Society for the Study of Working Women (SSWW), 20, 61

Sohyo, 7, 70, 197n1 (preface), 202n2 (chap. 4)

speak outs, 156

spring wage offensive. See *Shunto*

Steinberg, Ronnie: 61

structured conversation, 112, 115–16, 121–22, 128

student movement, 31

Supreme Court (of Japan), 198–99n9, 199n11, 201n7

surveys: as organizing tools, 124–25, 128, 144, 145

Swift, Karla, 62, 67

Takagi, Makiko, 62

Tanabata, 141

Tanaka, Kazuko, 53, 61

Tani, Keiko, 11, 20, 53, 62; ACW2 and, 155–56; early life of, 30, 31, 34; on education, 52, 93, 155; on feminist structures and practices, 38–40; first meeting with, 17, 18–19, 200n3; on individual affiliation, 30, 40, 48, 51; on inequality, 30, 37–38, 39; on national organization; 101–2, 155; on need for women's unions, 34–37; on organizing, 52, 113, 117, 129–30; on sexual harassment, 23; on WUT self-study, 85–93. *See also* individual-membership unions; Women's Union Tokyo; Workshop I

tax and pension system reform, 71

temporary employment: contract, 22, 25, 71, 79, 185–86, 203n4 (chap. 4); dispatch (temp agency) 79, 186. *See also* nonregular employment

temporary workers' unions, 2, 7. *See also* alternative unions

Tokyo District Court, 198n9

Tokyo Managers' Union, 197n1 (preface). *See also* managers' unions

Tokyo Metropolitan Labor Relations Commission, 201n8

Trade Union Law (Japan), 200n14

traditional gender roles, 3, 23–24. *See also* gender harassment

traditional unions: Japan (*see* enterprise unions); US, 54, 62, 69, 119, 121, 146–47, 160

training-the-trainer, 106, 129. *See also* labor education; participatory education

transfers, 5, 49, 71, 194, 198n8

translation, 60, 140, 200n3, 205n1 (conclusion); across cultures, 13, 117, 140; problems with, 69, 82, 99, 108, 111, 115, 118, 174–78, 180

two career-track system, 5–6, 70, 197n3, 198n8, 198n9

union schools. *See* union women's schools

union shop, 32, 199n11, 201n7

unionization rate (Japan), 197n6

union recognition, 199n11, 204n6

union women's schools, 97–98, 100. *See also* labor education; Women in Leadership Development

United Automobile Workers (UAW) Women's Department, 62, 66, 67, 68, 69, 81, 100

United Electrical Workers (UE), 62, 93–94, 96, 100, 108

United Nations Decade for Women, 198n7

US communications workshop, 109, 111–12, 126; outcomes, 128–29, 131. *See also* Rosenberg, Emily; Workshop II

US empowerment workshop, 109, 112, 126, 128, 131, 154. *See also* Ewing, Tess; participatory education; Workshop II

US-Japan Working Women's Networks Project, 1, 9–10, 11–13, 98–99, 101–2, 202n5; goals, 9–10, 53–54, 106–7, 133–34, 136–37, 138, 151; lessons from (*see* crossborder collaboration); origins of, 45–54; outcomes, 10, 148–50, 151–59, 164. *See also specific workshops by title*

US organizing workshop, 109, 112; Au, Mabel and, 117, 195, 204n5; conflict in, 114–24, 129–30, 204n4; content and, 112–17, 124–26; outcomes, 126–29, 147; purpose of, 112; challenges of, 109–10, 129–32. *See also* Edelson, Carol; individualism and collectivism; organizing; Workshop II

UNITE HERE, 96; Local 34 of, 62, 93, 94–96, 100, 108, 194, 203n4 (chap. 5); Local 35 of, 95, 96, 203n4 (chap. 5)

University of Massachusetts at Boston Labor Extension Program, 62, 97

Vail, Beverly, 62

Vietnam War, 31, 79

Wage gap, 3–5, 34, 71, 86, 140. *See also* nonregular employment; pay equity

Waseda University, 109, 110

Wayne State University (WSU), 53, 58, 106, 177, 178, 179

Women in Leadership Development (WILD), 62, 97–98. *See also* labor education

women in US labor history, 62–63, 66, 68, 108. *See also* Coalition of Labor Union Women; 9to5; United Automobile Workers Women's Department; UNITE HERE

women's schools. *See* union women's schools

Women's Space ON, 72

Women's Union Plus, 124, 153–54, 205n1 (chap. 8)

Women's Union Tokyo (WUT): activities, 19–20; as catalyst, 45–53; common grievances, 22–28; founders' vision for, 36–41, 96; funding for, 20, 86, 88–89; individual affiliation and, 48–51; joining, 21–22; membership of, 20–21; mission, 19–20, 41, 44; openness of, 42–43; organizational structure of, 30, 38–40, 44; in practice, 43–51; 203n1; self-study of, 84–93; as service union, 47–48; as two-tier union, 43–45. *See also* US-Japan Working Women's Networks Project

workers' centers, 63, 158

workforce gender-inequality, statistics on, 2–3

Working Women's Education Network (WWEN), 148–49, 152–55, 158

Working Women's Network (WWN), 71

working women's support organizations (Japan), 77–81

Working Women's Voices (WWV), 62, 70, 78–81, 141, 153–54

Workshop I, 57–59; challenges of (*see* crossborder collaboration); format, 61, 84–85, 168; goals, 58, 84; outcomes, 81–83, 98–102, 108–9, 167–68; participants, 61–62; purpose, 60–61. *See also listings for specific presenters and topics*

Workshop II: format, 109; goals, 106–7, 108–9; outcomes, 128–29, 132; participants, 109–10; participatory education and, 130–31; process of creation, 102, 108–10; purpose, 98; topics, 109. *See also* crossborder collaboration; *listings for specific presenters and workshops*

Workshop III: communications sessions, 134–35, 137; empowerment session, 135–36, 137–38, 205n1 (chap. 7); facilitation skills session, 138–39, 147–49; format, 135, 140; goals, 133–34, 136–39; Japanese modules, 140–42; organizing session, 138, 142–147; outcomes, 148–50; participants, 137–38; process of creation, 133–39; purpose, 98, 134, 138. *See also listings for specific presenters*

work styles, 168–71. *See under* crossborder collaboration

Yakabi, Fumiko, 61, 70, 77–78, 82, 155

Yale University, 93–96. *See also* UNITE HERE

young working women: discrimination against, 157, 159; importance to women's unions, 46, 92, 109, 125, 164; views on unions, 92, 159

Zenroren, 202n2 (chap. 4)

Zenryoko, 202n2 (chap. 4)

CPSIA information can be obtained at www.ICGtesting.com
Printed in the USA
LVOW11*1920300616

494790LV00004B/5/P